# gardening
## through the YEAR

# *gardening*
## through the YEAR

JANE COURTIER

This is a Parragon Publishing Book
This edition published in 2003

Parragon Publishing
Queen Street House
4 Queen Street
Bath BA1 1HE, UK

Created and produced for Parragon by The Bridgewater Book Company Ltd.

*Creative Director* Stephen Knowlden
*Art Director* Sarah Howerd
*Editorial Director* Fiona Biggs
*Senior Editor* Mark Truman
*Photographer and Picture Researcher* Liz Eddison
*Studio Manager* Chris Morris
*Illustrator* Coral Mula
*Designers* Terry Hirst and Alison Honey
*Indexer* Caroline Hamilton

ISBN: 0–75259–908–9

Printed in China

NOTE

For growing and harvesting, calendar information applies only to the Northern
Hemisphere (US zones 5–9).

# contents

# introduction

One of the beauties of a garden is the way it subtly alters from season to season, so slowly that sometimes you hardly notice the changes taking place. And yet the contrast between the warm and drowsy days of midsummer, with plants in full, luxuriant bloom and leaf, and the frosty midwinter, when the bare branches are rimed with ice and all plant

▼ *The pleasures of the summer garden are intensified by the gentle sound of splashing water from a garden pool.*

life seems to have frozen to a halt, could hardly be more marked. Every season in the garden has its compensations, whether it is the lusty resurgence of life in spring, the brimming bounty of summer, the brilliant colors of fall or the ethereal, sculptural beauty of plants in winter. And every season has its tasks to be performed. But while some times are far busier than others, gardening is definitely a year-round occupation if the garden is going to look good 12 months a year.

Perhaps one of the reasons gardeners find their hobby so relaxing is that plants won't be hurried—they need their time to grow. Although television has made the "instant garden" seem within everyone's grasp, the reality is not quite like that. A large part of gardening's attraction stems from watching a seed or tiny cutting slowly develop into a healthy, mature plant, or watching the small, container-grown specimen you planted years ago grow into a stately, spreading tree. While it may sometimes

◀ Freesia corms must be planted in late summer if you are to enjoy their scented blooms during the winter months.

▼ With a little forward planning, containers can provide color and interest for the patio virtually the whole year round.

be tempting to dream of a team of garden makers sweeping in to transform your plot overnight, how much more satisfying it is to be able to look around with pride and say "all my own work."

People who tend gardens are usually an optimistic, forward planning bunch—they have to be. Gardening means constantly thinking ahead. There's no point waiting until pole beans are in season before deciding it would be nice to have some of your own to pick; the seeds need sowing weeks before, in spring. And everyone knows that hyacinths make beautiful, scented houseplants for the cold days of winter, but if you want to plant your own, you have to plant them in the earliest days of the fall. The problem is, of course, that because most people lead such busy lives it is all too easy to forget such things, and that is where *Gardening Through The Year* comes to your aid—as an indispensable

memory jogger to what needs doing and when.

The gardening year divides into the four seasons of spring, summer, fall and winter, and if these are each subdivided into early, mid and late season, we have a convenient dozen "mini seasons" to equate (roughly) with the 12 months of the year. Exactly when these fall depends not on the calendar but on the climate in your area, and local climate patterns. And that is why we use these terms rather than specific dates.

The term "ornamental garden" simply refers to the decorative, non-functional aspects of the garden—attractive flowers, trees and shrubs.

I hope that *Gardening Through The Year* will remind you of all the things you want and need to do, and also encourage and inspire you to try out some new ideas, while reminding you of all that is best in the garden in the various seasons.

But most of all I hope that *Gardening Through The Year* will help you to enjoy every aspect of your garden and your gardening to the full, whatever the time of year.

# spring

Spring is a wonderful season for gardeners. Day by day we can see the garden coming to life, pushing out strong young shoots, unfolding fresh green foliage, laying down a colorful tapestry of flowers. It's also time for us to get to work because this is surely the busiest, as well as the most pleasurable, season of the year.

# early spring

*Ever-lengthening days give us more time to spend in the garden and we need it because there is plenty to be done. Although the days are still chilly, with overnight frost an ever-present danger, there will gradually be more sunshine to cheer things up, and a distinctly milder feel to the air.*

Better weather, spring sunshine, and the obvious signs of growth and flowering around the garden make everyone feel optimistic and enthusiastic, but it pays to be cautious for a little while yet. In many places reliably warm weather is still some weeks away.

Most gardeners will be hoping for several days of dry, sunny weather, preferably accompanied by a good strong breeze: ideal conditions for drying out the soil ready for seedbed preparation. The lighter the soil, the earlier this task can be done. It just involves raking the surface until the

soil is reduced to an even texture of fine crumbs, but it's essential to wait until the soil is no longer clinging and sticky.

Although the spring may seem slow to get going, it soon moves up a gear and suddenly gardeners are hard pushed to keep up. There are spring bulbs to support and deadhead, border plants to stake before they start to flop over, containers to get ready for the summer display, and sowings to make both outdoors and inside. There's also planting and pruning to be done, and dozens of seedlings jostling for space in the greenhouse. In fact sometimes it's so busy that there hardly seems time to enjoy the garden itself. So whatever else you do, make time to appreciate that delicious freshness of growth the garden offers now, for there's no other season quite like it.

◄ *As the days gradually become brighter and warmer, eagerly awaited spring flowers surge into growth.*

# EARLY SPRING TASKS

**General**

- Prepare the soil for sowing when the weather allows
- Remove weeds and apply a moisture-retaining mulch

**Ornamental garden**

- Plant container-grown trees and shrubs, and plant and divide herbaceous perennials
- Support border plants as soon as the shoots start to lengthen

- Sow hardy annuals and Lathyrus odoratus (sweet peas) outdoors
- Prune roses and shrubs such as buddleja, hydrangeas, and Cornus alba (dogwood)
- Remove winter protection from tender plants

- Fertilize spring-flowering bulbs, perennials, and shrubs if not already done
- Mulch round alpine plants with fresh gravel
- Trim back winter-flowering Calluna (heathers)

▼ *A fresh dressing of gravel around alpine plants helps to show the developing flowers off to perfection.*

**Lawns**

- Begin mowing regularly; continue to carry out repairs to turf

**Kitchen garden**

- Dig up the last of the overwintered crops and sow early crops in their place
- Plant early potatoes, rhubarb, and shallots.

- Continue harvesting rhubarb and kale
- Stake fall or early spring-sown beans and peas

- Protect early blossom on fruit trees
- Plant soft fruit bushes
- Check raspberry supports

**Greenhouse**

- Keep the glass clean for good light transmission
- Sow half-hardy annuals, herbs, and eggplant, cucumbers, sweet peppers, and tomatoes; prick off seedlings sown earlier
- Start chrysanthemums and dahlias into growth to produce cuttings if not already done.
- Take softwood cuttings of overwintered plants started into growth earlier

- Ventilate the greenhouse with care; if possible fit an automatic ventilator to allow a quick response to sudden temperature changes
- Plant tuberous begonias
- Check plants regularly for pests and diseases
- Buy growing bags for tomatoes and other greenhouse crops, and allow them to warm up in the greenhouse

- Store left-over seeds in a cool, dry place
- Repot greenhouse and houseplants as necessary
- Plant out forced bulbs in the garden when they have finished flowering

▼ *The greenhouse will soon be filling with softwood cuttings from a range of overwintered plants.*

# ornamental garden: *general tasks*

*Increasing numbers of spring bulbs are opening their flowers every day, making a wonderful display. A little care and attention now will keep them looking good and help to build them up for next year's show. Containers will need to be planted up for summer soon, so start preparing now.*

### Fertilize spring-flowering bulbs

Bulbs which stay in the ground from year to year often respond well to an application of fertilizer. It does not have any effect on the current season's flowers, but it will help to build up the bulbs and make sure of good flowering for the following year. Regular feeding is particularly important for bulbs that are growing in the restricted conditions of containers.

The time to feed is from the beginning of flowering until the leaves start to die down. It is recommended that you use a high-potash fertilizer, preferably in liquid form which is taken up readily by the plants. Follow the directions on the container regarding frequency of application.

Bulbs which are naturalized in grass are not fed very often because this tends to encourage the grass to grow strongly instead of the bulbs. A feed can be applied every few years, however, especially if the performance of the bulbs is starting to deteriorate.

◀ *An application of fertilizer while spring bulbs are flowering will help to make sure of a good performance for the following year.*

### Mulch alpines with gravel

Most alpine plants grow well in poor, rocky, free-draining soil in cold but dry conditions. In gardens they are often killed by excessive moisture which rots the roots, and if it gathers

---

#### DEADHEAD BULBS

As soon as bulb flowers fade, it pays to remove them by snapping off the stalks just below the flower head. This prevents the flowers from forming seeds, and directs the bulb's energy into next year's display. However, some flower stems do not snap cleanly, and the whole stem tends to pull out of the center of the bulb instead. When this happens use secateurs to cut off the heads. Note that deadheading can only be carried out where practical, and if there are very large numbers of bulbs it becomes too time-consuming.

## PREPARE CONTAINERS FOR SUMMER FLOWERS

Pots, tubs, window boxes, and hanging baskets have quite likely been stored away since the end of last summer. Now's the time to get them out and check them over, cleaning them thoroughly and repairing any damage or replacing them where necessary.

Garden centers offer the best choice of new containers at this time of year because later in the spring so many people are buying them that they quickly sell out.

Containers are available in plastic, glass fiber, stone, cement, wood, ceramic, and terracotta, in a wide range of styles and prices.

If you are tempted by a particularly large or heavy container, remember to allow for the extra weight of soil and plants it will hold—some containers are almost impossible to move once they are planted up.

round the neck of the plants it can rot them at ground level.

Remove all weeds from around the plants and prick over the soil lightly with a hand fork. Then top-dress the plants with gravel or stone chippings, tucking them well under the rosettes of foliage and around the necks of the plants. This improves the drainage and makes the bed look much more attractive, showing off the alpines to advantage.

Alpines do not have to be grown in rock gardens. A small raised bed or a shallow trough like an old stone sink can contain an attractive arrangement of plants and provide them with good growing conditions.

Where space is really tight, shallow pans will hold individual plants or small groups, or plants can be tucked into crevices in stone walls.

▶ *Suitable stone chippings for mulching around alpine plants can be obtained ready bagged from most garden centers.*

# ornamental garden: *sowing*

*Annual plants are among the easiest to grow, but a mixed annual border needs to be properly planned for the best results. Lathyrus odoratus (sweet pea), appreciated as much for its scent as its beauty, can be sown outside now, and herbaceous border plants will benefit from early staking.*

### Sow sweet peas outdoors

Sweet peas are often grown in rows in the vegetable garden to provide cut flowers, but they also make an attractive feature in the flower border

Dig the soil well where the sweet peas are to grow, and incorporate a dressing of general fertilizer. Tread the soil to firm it, then put the supports in place before sowing the seeds. Special stake clips are available to fix together the tops of bamboo stakes making a wigwam or an A-frame, that is then covered with plastic mesh netting to give the plants something to cling onto.

Use a sharp knife to chip the seedcoat carefully to speed germination, but be careful not to damage the lighter colored eye where the seedling will emerge. Instead of chipping, seeds can be soaked overnight in water to soften the seedcoat if preferred. Sow them about 1 in/2.5 cm deep and some 3 in/7.5 cm apart, or at the base of each cane support.

# sow an annual bed

Annuals are among the easiest of flowering plants to grow, and provide many weeks of bright color through the summer. Sowing outdoors can start now, as long as you take care to choose hardy varieties. *Alyssum*, *Calendula* (marigold), *Clarkia*, *Centaurea cyanus* (cornflower), *Limnanthes* (poached egg plant), *Nemophila* and *Nigella* are some favorites suitable for early sowing.

## SUPPORT BORDER PLANTS

Supports for border plants must be put in place early, well before the plants need them. In this way the stems can be trained up through the supports as they grow, eventually completely hiding them. There are several different types of proprietary supports, ranging from wire mesh rings on legs to hooked stakes which link together. You can also use rings of stakes encircled by garden twine, or twiggy sticks cut from the hedgerow. Whichever method is chosen, aim for a natural effect—unsympathetic staking, where whole plants are tightly trussed, each to a single stake, can ruin the whole effect of the herbaceous border.

◄ *A row of sweet peas will provide dozens of wonderfully fragrant cut flowers for the home through the summer months.*

► *Colorful annuals such as nasturtiums, easily raised from seed, will always find a place among groups of mixed summer flowers.*

Hardy annuals are sown directly where they are to grow, in well-prepared, finely-raked soil. Work out a sowing plan for the bed—put the tallest varieties to the back and aim for a good combination of colors and textures.

1 Mark out the sowing area for each variety by drawing a series of interlocking arcs on the bed, using a pointed stick or a trickle of sand (**right**). Sprinkling packets of mixed seed over the soil rarely produces a good effect.

2 Draw a series of short, parallel drills in the first patch, and sprinkle the seed thinly along the drills (**left**). Rake the soil over lightly and firm it with the head of the rake. Continue sowing the rest of the patches, running the drills in different directions to avoid a regimented appearance.

3 Weed seedlings will germinate freely along with the annuals, but the annuals will be easy to recognize as they will appear in straight rows. Remove the weeds regularly, and thin out the annual seedlings to their appropriate spacings when they are large enough.

# ornamental garden: *planting*

*Container-grown trees and shrubs can be planted all year, whenever the weather is suitable. Those planted now will give an almost instant effect because they are already bursting into leaf. Herbaceous perennials are also emerging once again, having spent the winter underground.*

## Plant trees and shrubs

Trees and shrubs are particularly valuable in the garden, providing height as well as a permanent, year-round framework. There are so many different types of trees and shrubs to choose from that there is something for every garden, even the smallest plot. Shrubs can provide a range of shapes and sizes, and can be grown for their foliage, flowers, shape, or all three. Evergreens provide year-round interest, while deciduous varieties offer the pleasure of watching the leaves change with the season— unfolding in the spring, reaching their lush pinnacle in the summer and perhaps turning to glowing shades before falling.

Flowers, too, can be had virtually all-year round, even in the depths of winter when they are especially welcome in the garden.

The choice of tree needs great care in a small garden because fast-growing varieties can cause problems with subsidence and damage to drains. However, there are many small and slow-growing trees suitable for small spaces including varieties of *Betula* (birch), conifer, *Malus* (crab apple), *Prunus* (flowering cherry) and *Acer* (maple).

◀ *Evergreens provide color and interest all year. They can be planted whenever the weather is right, but now is a particularly good time.*

## plant trees and shrubs

Depending on the weather, it may still be possible to plant bare-root trees and shrubs, but not for much longer. Once the dormant season is over and plants have started into growth, only container-grown specimens can be planted.

### PLANT HERBACEOUS BORDER PLANTS

Herbaceous perennials can be planted in the fall or spring, but remember that those planted now may need watering during the late spring and early summer. This is also a suitable time to divide existing perennials that are growing too large for their position—if you didn't manage to finish all the lifting and dividing last fall it can safely be completed now.

Check containerized plants sold at garden centers carefully at this time of year. Some may not be container grown, but the bare-root kind planted up at the end of the dormant season. The root-ball must lift intact from the pot without the soil falling away.

A good quality container-grown plant has a firm root-ball with strong, healthy roots. It can be transplanted with little check to growth at almost any time of year. Recently potted up plants, however, will be slower to establish and may not be worth the higher cost.

Container-grown plants can be planted all-year round, but spring and fall are better than midsummer when high temperatures and lack of water may put extra stress on the plant. Trees and shrubs planted now usually establish rapidly and grow away strongly.

▼ A well-chosen selection of trees and shrubs add an air of maturity and an important dimension of height to any garden.

1 Water the plant/tree well the evening before it is planted. Dig a hole deep enough for the top of the root-ball to be just covered, and break up the soil at the base of the hole (**above**).

2 Remove the plant from its pot by tapping carefully around the edge and stand the root-ball in the planting hole (**above**).

3 Fill in around the plant with soil, firming well (**above**). It is vital to keep the soil moist in the spring and summer.

# ornamental garden: *pruning*

*Pruning is one of those tasks that make many gardeners feel apprehensive because they know that it needs to be done, but they are not sure why or how. The main reasons for pruning are to keep the plant shapely, promote good flowering and fruiting, and encourage strong, healthy growth.*

### Prune roses

The first step with all types of rose is to remove all dead, dying and diseased wood. Species and old-fashioned roses (such as gallicas, bourbons, and damasks) need very little further pruning; every other year, cut two or three of the oldest stems to ground level to encourage the production of young shoots.

With large-flowered (hybrid tea) roses, all shoots should be cut back by between two-thirds and one half of their length (less vigorous varieties should be pruned hardest). Cluster-flowered (floribunda) varieties are pruned more lightly, cutting the shoots back by about one-third of their length. On both cluster-flowered and large-flowered roses, a quarter to one-third of the total stems can be cut back to the base if desired, to promote the growth of young replacement branches.

### PRUNE TREES AS NECESSARY

Ornamental trees do not need regular pruning, but, as with all plants, any dead, diseased or dying branches should be removed as soon as they are seen; large branches could be a danger if left to fall naturally. Remove branches by first undercutting them with the saw, and then cutting from the top to sever them (undercutting prevents the branch from tearing). It is not necessary to seal the cut with pruning paint.

◄ *When pruning roses of any type, use well-sharpened pruners to make a clean cut just above a healthy bud.*

# prune shrubs

The correct time and technique for pruning flowering shrubs depends mainly upon the time of year that they flower. Those that flower in late summer usually flower on new wood that has been produced that season; pruning these shrubs hard now, just as they start into growth, will promote plenty of strong new shoots and provide extra flowers.

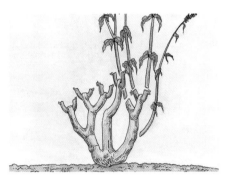

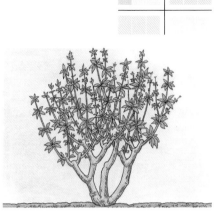

1 Shrubs such as *Buddleja davidii* benefit from being cut back severely now. Branches can be pruned to within 6–12 in/15–30 cm of soil level; long-arm pruners or loppers may be necessary to cut through some of the older stems.

2 Although such pruning may initially look very severe, strong new growth will be made almost straight away. Plants which are not pruned hard tend to become untidy and top heavy, with weak, straggly shoots.

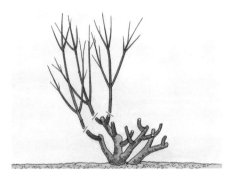

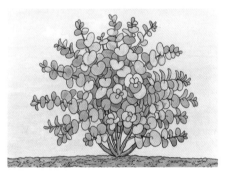

3 *Cornus alba* 'Sibirica' is grown for its brightly colored winter stems, and cutting all stems back to within 3in/7.5cm of the base insures that a good thicket of strong, bright new stems will be produced in time for next season.

4 Pruning eucalyptus back hard each spring will maintain a bushy shape and the rounded, intensely colored juvenile foliage. Cut all the previous season's stems back to within 3in/7.5cm of the main framework of branches.

5 Some shrubs that flower on older wood should not be cut down entirely in the spring, but should have about one-third of their oldest stems removed each year. This makes sure that they retain a proportion of older wood to carry the flowers while new stems are produced to replace those that are past their best. *Cotinus coggygria* (the smoke bush), *Escallonia*, *Potentilla* and *Sambucus* (elder) are among those shrubs that benefit.

◄ *Climbing plants such as clematis need regular pruning in order to promote the production of strong flowering shoots.*

# balcony and roof gardens

Where houses have limited space for a garden, it is tempting to use a balcony or flat roof for growing plants. This can be an excellent idea, but it does need some careful planning. The most important point to assess is the load-bearing capacity of the structure. The combined weight of plants, soil, and water is considerable, and many structures, particularly on older buildings, are not strong enough for the job. It is well worth employing a structural engineer to give you specific advice because the result of overloading could be disastrous.

Once you have received the go-ahead, there are other considerations to tackle. Most importantly, check that the surface is waterproof and has an efficient drainage system to channel away excess water safely. If you live on an upper floor of a block, residents below will tire of streams of water cascading off your balcony onto theirs whenever you water your plants, and damp penetrating into the fabric of a house from a roof garden could be very damaging to the structure.

Access to the garden is another important consideration. Many balconies are very small, and there may not be room to step onto the balcony itself; access

▲ *Plants are best put in containers that are filled with soilless mix because it is much lighter than soil-based mix.*

## WEATHER PROTECTION

Roof and balcony gardens in an exposed position will be made much more pleasant for both plants and people if some form of windbreak can be established on the weather side. Trelliswork clothed with climbing plants is often ideal, though if you wish to preserve a view, it may be worth having toughened glass panels professionally installed.

► *Color-themed baskets and windowboxes make this small balcony a pleasant spot to sit and add great decorative value to the house.*

may be through full length doors or only through a window. And with limited access it might make watering, repotting and tidying up, etc., quite difficult. Roofs can also have limited access, often involving awkward stairs or ladders that are fine when you are unencumbered but not much fun when you are trying to maneuver pots, watering cans, or sacks of soil mix up there. Finally, because plants will be grown in containers, remember that watering will be a daily chore in summer. Ask yourself whether it is possible to get a hosepipe to the garden, to fill a watering can nearby, or even to install an outside faucet.

## Getting down to business

Once all the questions have been resolved and you are ready to create your garden, you will need to choose furnishings and equipment. Reducing the total weight is usually the primary consideration.

If it is a roof or large balcony that you can walk around, some form of floor covering will probably be necessary. Conventional paving slabs are usually too heavy, but lighter options include timber decking, a thin layer of gravel, shredded or chipped bark, and rubber tiles or artificial turf. Plants are best grown in containers and, again, lightweight plastic or fiberglass pots and troughs are more suitable than containers of clay, pottery, or stone. Large containers can be placed on wooden pallets that will help to distribute the load more evenly. Try to position the heaviest items where the load-bearing supports are—the structural engineer will advise you.

When filling the containers, use soilless mix, based on peat or peat substitutes such as coconut fiber, because it is much lighter than soil-based mix, but it will need more frequent watering and additional feeding.

## Providing protection

By their nature, roof and balcony gardens are high up, and more exposed to the wind, which can be very damaging to plants. Because pots and soil mix are necessarily lightweight, they are also easily blown over.

A windbreak in the form of fine-mesh netting or trellis work covered with climbing plants will be a great help, but plants and their containers must be firmly secured to prevent damage in breezy conditions.

### SAFETY FIRST

Don't take risks with your balcony or roof garden. Make sure that:
• A professional confirms that the balcony or roof has adequate load-bearing properties
• It is properly surrounded by adequate railings or walls that are regularly checked and kept in good condition
• Plants, containers, and ornaments are completely secure, and there is no risk of them falling over the edge
• Water or debris does not cause a nuisance to people or their property below
• You are adequately covered by insurance

# ornamental garden: *plants in season*

Day by day, more fresh young leaves and flowers fill the garden, bringing it alive after its long dormant period. Bulbs are among the most prominent plants, but there are many shrubs, trees, and perennials now putting on a tremendous performance.

▼ *The luscious purple flowers of Aubrieta will brighten up any garden at this time of year.*

## PERENNIALS AND BEDDING PLANTS

Aubrieta
Bergenia cordifolia
Doronicum (leopard's bane)
Primula vulgaris and others (primrose)
Pulmonaria (lungwort)

### BULBS

Anemone (wind flower)
Bulbocodium vernum
Chionodoxa (glory of the snow)
Crocus
Cyclamen coum
Eranthis (winter aconite)
Erythronium (dog's-tooth violet)
Iris danfordiae, I. reticulata
Leucojum vernum (snowflake)
Muscari (grape hyacinth)
Narcissus (daffodil)
Puschkinia scilloides
Tulipa kaufmanniana, T. fosteriana,
    T. tarda and others (tulip)

▲ 'Dark Secret', an early-flowering tulip,
is a new cultivar with luscious deep colors
that will bring warmth to any garden.

## SHRUBS AND TREES

Acer pseudoplatanus 'Brilliantissimum'
    (sycamore), A. rubrum (red maple)
Calluna 'Spring Cream', C. 'Spring Torch'
    and others (heather)
Camellia japonica (common camellia)
Chaenomeles speciosa, C. japonica (japonica)
Chimonanthus praecox (wintersweet)
Clematis armandii
Cornus mas (cornelian cherry)
Corylopsis pauciflora (winter hazel)
Erica carnea varieties (winter heath)
Forsythia intermedia, F. suspensa
Magnolia stellata (star magnolia)
Prunus cerasifera pissardii (cherry plum)
Salix caprea (willow)

▶ The cheerful pink and white flowers of
Anemone blanda are happy in light shade as
well as full sun. Blue forms are also available.

# kitchen garden: *general tasks*

*Now's the time to use up some of those crops that have stayed all winter in the vegetable plot, and start preparing for the new season's harvest. With a little careful planning, it's possible to enjoy fresh produce from the kitchen garden at almost any time of the year.*

▲ *Rhubarb is easy to grow in the vegetable garden, but it is the early, tender, forced stems that have the best flavor.*

### Harvest rhubarb and kale

Rhubarb is not always considered a gourmet treat but the tender forced stems are a real delicacy at this time of year, far removed from the tough, acid, stringy stalks at the end of the season.

Kale is rich in vitamins A and C, and deserves to be more widely grown. It is usually winter-hardy, grown from seeds planted in early spring and again in late summer. For an earlier crop, start seed in a tray and transplant the seedlings.

The earliest crops of rhubarb are obtained by boxing up roots and forcing them into growth in a greenhouse, but plants can also be forced outdoors, covering the crowns in situ with purpose-made forcing pots or black plastic garbage cans to exclude all light.

Those covered up in early or midwinter will probably have shoots ready for harvesting now, depending on how mild the weather has been in the preceding weeks.

### Protect blossom on early-flowering fruit trees

Frosts are still a distinct possibility in early spring, and will kill the blossoms on some of the early-flowering fruit trees such as apricots

### USE UP OVERWINTERED CROPS
———

Parsnips will have remained in the vegetable garden all winter, ready for digging up and using as required. Now that spring has arrived, the roots will soon start into growth again, signaled by small green tufts emerging from the tops of the plants. As growth continues, the roots will become soft and flabby and not worth eating, and should be harvested now.

Leeks will also start into growth again, producing flower buds that develop in their second year. This results in a solid, rather tough flower stem in the center of the leek that spoils the taste and quality. Any leeks and parsnips remaining should be lifted now and moved to a spare piece of ground until they are used up.

▶ *A purpose-built framework to support the horticultural blanket will make it easier to protect the early blossoms of fruit trees from frost.*

and peaches, often ruining the chance of a good crop. Protect trees from night frosts by draping them with lightweight horticultural blanket or, if the trees are growing against a wall or fence, attach a roll-down screen of fine-mesh netting. Make sure that the blanket or netting does not damage the blossom as it is being lowered or removed.

When fruit trees flower early in the year, while the weather is still cold, it is worth pollinating the blossom yourself in case no pollinating insects are on the wing. Use a small, soft brush to transfer pollen gently among the flowers. A cosmetic brush is easier to use than the paintbrush that is usually recommended for the job.

## STAKE PEAS AND BEANS

The peas and beans that were sown in the fall or early spring should be provided with supports as they grow. For peas this can be plastic netting, supported by stakes at regular intervals; the plants will twine their tendrils around the netting as they grow. Alternatively a forest of twiggy brushwood sticks provides excellent support if you have a ready supply. Beans will also be happy with twiggy sticks, or you can provide them with a series of stakes along each side of the row, with string running around them to prevent the plants from flopping outward.

# kitchen garden: *planting and sowing*

*It is time for most gardeners to start sowing in earnest at last, although gardeners with heavy soils or gardens in particularly cold, exposed positions may be better advised to hang on just a little while longer. Always garden according to the prevailing conditions rather than calendar dates.*

### Prepare the soil for sowing

Soil in a seedbed should be broken down to fine, even crumbs, usually known as "a fine tilth." If the soil is left in large clods it is very difficult to get a level seedbed, and seeds will end up being buried either too deeply or too shallowly to achieve good germination.

If the vegetable garden has been left roughly dug over the winter, frosts will have got at the clods of soil, breaking them up by the action of repeated freezing and thawing.

As soon as some dry, breezy weather has dried out the soil surface sufficiently, these clods can be reduced to fine crumbs by raking. Any particularly large clods can be broken down by a smart blow with the back of the rake.

### BEGIN SOWING VEGETABLE CROPS

Some time during this month, depending on the weather, a wide range of vegetables can be sown, including beans, carrots, leeks, lettuces, parsnips, summer and fall cabbages, early summer cauliflowers, spinach, and Swiss chard. Draw straight drills using a garden line and a hoe, and sow the seeds thinly along the drill. Rake the soil carefully over the seeds, tamp it down lightly and label the row clearly.

It is too early for the more tender crops such as zucchini, marrows, and bush and pole beans to be sown outside, but they can be raised in pots in a greenhouse for planting out after the last frost.

▲ *A light touch with the rake is necessary in order to produce a fine, even surface to a seedbed. Large stones should be removed.*

## plant potatoes

If growing space is limited, plant early potatoes rather than main crops, choosing some of the more uncommon varieties that are impossible to buy from the store. The earliest crops of new potatoes have an incomparable flavor when they are freshly lifted. The foliage of potatoes is sensitive to frost, so take care about the planting time. It generally takes two or three weeks before the shoots show through the soil after planting.

1 As an alternative to immediate planting, seed potatoes can be set on a cool, light windowsill to produce shoots (**below**). The eyes that produce the shoots are clustered together at one end of the tuber (the "rose" end), and tubers should be set in egg cartons with this end uppermost.

3 Draw wide drills using a draw hoe, or use a trowel to make individual planting holes. Plant the potatoes around 5in/13cm deep. Chitted tubers should be dropped carefully into the holes with the shoots at the top; these shoots are very fragile and are easily broken. Unsprouted tubers should be planted with the rose end facing up.

4 Check the rows of potatoes regularly to see when the first shoots appear; they are dark bluish-green (**right**). Be on your guard against frost. If an unexpected frost kills the first shoots all is not lost—new shoots should replace them.

◄ *Most gardens have room for some soft fruit. Early spring is a good time to plant container-grown bushes and canes.*

2 Potatoes should be planted in well-prepared soil, in rows 18in/45cm apart, and spaced 12–18in/30–45cm apart within the row (**below**). Sprouted (or "chitted") tubers will appear through the soil more quickly after planting, but they need to be handled carefully in order to avoid knocking the shoots off.

29

# colorful ornamental vegetables

Many vegetables are now grown as much for their appearance as their table qualities, and several are more than worthy of a place amongst the ornamental plants in the flower borders. The vegetables themselves have become more exciting too, with a whole range of vibrant colors and interesting shapes and textures to liven up the kitchen. Herbs have certainly managed to bridge the gap between the ornamental and useful, with plants like

▲ *There are many decorative varieties of lettuce available. The contrast of frilly-edged against plain-leaved varieties is always effective.*

variegated thyme and purple-leaved sage happily providing color in the flower and shrub borders while still offering sprigs for use in the kitchen.

There are several vegetables that would fulfill a similar role if allowed to do so: stately globe artichokes with their dramatic spiky flower heads and divided leaves; carrots with fountains of bright green, finely divided foliage; and florence fennel, its neatly symmetrical, creamy white stem bases topped by clouds of lacy, feathery leaves. The more unusual vegetables include the asparagus pea, a rounded, spreading plant with dainty, light green leaflets, sprinkled with crimson flowers, and the deep purple, round pod bean 'Purple Queen' and 'Sequoia'. The brightly colored fruits of cherry tomatoes are also striking, particularly on varieties developed for growing in pots and hanging baskets: sweet bell peppers can be similarly attractive if prolific, small-fruiting types such as 'Jingle Bells' or 'Ace', which turns from green to red in 65–70 days, are chosen.

## Kaleidoscopic choice

A glance at any seed catalog will show what a wide range of exciting and colorful varieties of old favorites are now available. Pole snap beans have always had attractive flowers, and 'Goldmania', as its name suggests, has yellow pods and these can grow to a length of 8in/20cm. The elegant 'Trionfo' has deep plum-purple pods and looks most impressive growing on a trellis.

Bush beans also have a neat, compact habit of growth, and there are several varieties with deep purple beans. Purple-podded beans turn green when cooked, but the varieties 'Goldkist', 'Brittle Wax', and 'Gold Mine' keep their rich yellow color.

## DECORATIVE PLOTS

A decorative potager needs to be perfectly planned to achieve the best effects. Here, stately artichokes are bordered by the contrasting shapes of lettuces.

Remember that plants must be kept free of disfiguring pests and diseases—and that eating any of the components would ruin an intricate design like this!

Eggplant can be grown in the greenhouse or outside in warm, sheltered gardens. Among the most colourful varieties are 'Purple Rain', and 'Zebra', maroon streaked with white, and deep pink 'Neon.'

Lettuces are available in all varieties of colors and types. There is the red oakleaf 'Red Salad Bowl', 'Red Sails', and 'Cocarde'/'Santa Fe', 'Sweet Red' and 'Sierra' and 'Burgundy Ice' with heavily blushed burgundy outer leaves and light green inner leaves. Some varieties are extravagantly frilly edged, like 'Loma' and 'Lollo Rosso'.

You could liven up your salads even more by adding red salad onion 'Giant Red Hamburger', new Japanese cucumber 'Tasty Jade', rich brown sweet pepper 'Sweet Chocolate', pink and white beet 'Chioggia' and tomatoes such as 'Celebrity', 'Green Zebra', yellow 'Taxi', and 'Sungold' and the 'Striped German'.

## VEGETABLES IN HISTORY

Using vegetables as ornamental plants is not a new idea—the *jardin potager*, with its neat, formal rows of vegetables arranged in intricate, highly decorative patterns, is long established. The art is brought to perfection in the outstanding gardens of the Château de Villandry in the Loire Valley in France, which was recreated in the early twentieth century from sixteenth-century plans.

In the marrow family, look out for the zucchini 'Gold Rush' and the patty pan squash 'Sunburst' that has scalloped edges to its deep yellow fruit. Swiss chard 'Bright Lights' adds some of the brightest splashes of color to the garden, with pink, orange, red, or white stems, while the kale 'Red Russian' has deep crimson-veined foliage through the winter.

Carrot 'Sweet Sunshine', as its name implies, is a strong, clear yellow, while asparagus 'Purple Passion' has very striking blue-black spears. There are several purple cauliflowers, including 'Purple Head', and 'Violet Queen', and the green Romanesco type 'Tower'.

Sweet corn cobs are available in white ('Silver Queen'), mixed white and yellow ('Double Standard'), yellow and brown ('Indian Summer'), and the extraordinary multicolor 'Indian Corn' for decoration purposes, 'Fiesta'.

▲ *Swiss chard 'Bright Lights' lives up to its name with brilliantly colorful leaf stems. Both stems and foliage are also excellent to eat.*

# greenhouse: *planting and sowing*

*Increasingly, the greenhouse will be filling up with boxes and trays of cuttings, seedlings, and young plants: make sure that they all have sufficient space to develop, and keep the glass clean for good light transmission. Many houseplants will appreciate being repotted at this time of year.*

### Continue sowing

The busy sowing season in the greenhouse continues. Adjust the sowing time of greenhouse crops such as cucumbers and tomatoes to the amount of heat you can provide. There is no point in making very early sowings if you cannot supply sufficient, steady warmth to raise young plants. Crops such as bush and pole beans can also be sown indoors for planting out after the risk of frosts, but it may be a little too early for them in many places, and mid-spring is often better.

Sow some herbs now for planting out later in the spring. While many herbs are raised from cuttings, quite a number can be grown successfully from seed, including basil, coriander, dill, fennel, marjoram, parsley, rocket, and summer savory. Sow small pinches of herbs in a pot, because only a few plants will be needed.

### SOW HALF–HARDY ANNUALS

While hardy annuals can be sown outside, half-hardy varieties must be kept under cover until the risk of frost is over. They can be sown in the greenhouse now; most need temperatures of 55–70°F/13–21°C for germination.

Suitable species to sow include *Ageratum, Alyssum, Antirrhinum* (snapdragon), *Begonia, Brachycome, Clarkia, Lobelia, Nemesia, Petunia, Salvia, Impatiens* (busy lizzie), *Matthiola* (stock), *Nicotiana* (tobacco plant), *Tagetes* and *Zinnia*. Insure the trays have sufficient ventilation once the majority of the seeds have germinated, and prick the seedlings out as soon as they are large enough to handle.

◀ *Cucumbers sown now will need constant, steady warmth if they are to develop into healthy plants bearing a good crop.*

# repot houseplants

Spring is a good time to give established houseplants a new lease of life by repotting them in fresh soil mix. Some will benefit by a move up to the next size, while others can be repotted in the same size container if that is more practical.

1 Water the plants thoroughly the day before repotting them. Turn the plant upside down with your hand spread across the top of the pot and the plant's stem between your fingers (**right**). Tap the rim of the pot downward sharply on the edge of the bench or table to loosen the root-ball.

2 Slide the pot off the plant's roots (**left**). Crumble a little of the old soil away from around the top, base, and sides of the root-ball, being careful not to damage the roots.

3 Plants that have filled their pot with roots are ready for a move up to the next size. Fill the base of the new pot with fresh mix and sit the root-ball on it, adjusting the depth of soil until the top of the root-ball is just below the top of the pot.

4 Fill in round the sides of the root-ball with more mix, using your fingers or a stick to firm and push it right down to the base of the pot so that there are no air pockets (**left**). Cover the top of the root-ball with another layer of mix, and water well.

5 If a plant is already in the largest pot size that is practical, it can be returned to the same pot after step 2, with just a little fresh mix to replace that which has been crumbled away. Very large plants can be top-dressed instead of repotted; simply scrape away some of the surface soil and replace it with fresh, mixed with a little slow-release fertilizer.

◄ *Houseplants nearly always thrive best when they are displayed in groups in the home, rather than as single specimens.*

# greenhouse: *pricking off and cuttings*

*Seedlings from seeds sown earlier will need to be pricked off to pots or trays, spacing them out to give them adequate space to grow and develop. Cuttings can be taken now from overwintered roots of chrysanthemums and dahlias; these are usually quick and easy to root successfully.*

## Prick off seedlings

Seedlings are moved on to give them more room once they are large enough to be handled comfortably. It is important to handle them by their seed leaves only, and never by their stems which are extremely delicate; crushing the stem results in the death of the seedling. Water the seedlings a few hours before pricking off, and lever them carefully out of the soil using a dibble to prise them up from underneath.

Make a hole with the dibble in a tray of firmed and leveled soil mix, and then lower the seedling into it, making sure the roots reach the base of the hole. Firm in lightly. Space the seedlings so that their seed leaves are not touching. Water the pricked out seedlings so that the soil is evenly moist, then put them in a lightly shaded place for a day or two to recover.

### POT UP TOMATO SEEDLINGS

Tomato seedlings are usually pricked off from the seedtray straight into individual pots. They should be handled, like any other seedling, by their seed leaves only. Tomato seedlings need to be buried more deeply than most seedlings to encourage adventitious roots on the stem that help produce a strong plant. Lower the seedling into the hole so that the seed leaves are just resting on the soil surface, then firm and water the plants.

▶ *Never tug seedlings out of the soil or the young roots will be severely damaged. Use a dibble to prise them out gently.*

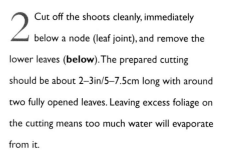

## take softwood cuttings

Plants that have spent the winter in the greenhouse are now producing strong new growth. The young shoots make ideal cuttings that root quickly to provide a plentiful supply of sturdy young plants. Most softwood cuttings are quick and easy to root in the greenhouse. Plants such as dahlias, chrysanthemums, fuchsias, and pelargoniums can be increased quite easily by this method, providing strong specimens for planting out later on.

1 It is important to use only healthy, vigorous shoots. You can either snap them off the parent plant or cut them off with a very sharp knife or single-edged razor blade (**below**). Since softwood cuttings tend to wilt easily, this job is best done in the morning while the plants are fresh.

2 Cut off the shoots cleanly, immediately below a node (leaf joint), and remove the lower leaves (**below**). The prepared cutting should be about 2–3in/5–7.5cm long with around two fully opened leaves. Leaving excess foliage on the cutting means too much water will evaporate from it.

3 Insert the cuttings into flats or pots of special seed and cuttings soil mix topped with a layer of sharp sand (**left**). The sand insures good drainage around the base of the stem and improves rooting. Firm the cuttings in with your fingers and water them well, using a fine rose on the can.

4 Place a plastic propagator top over the pot or flat, and then shade it from strong sun for a day or two with an upturned flat or piece of newspaper. This flat or newspaper can be removed once the cuttings have recovered and are not found to be wilting.

◀ *Early spring is the time to start dahlias into growth for cuttings. You will need to divide the tubers before planting in late spring.*

# mid-spring

*The garden really is looking good now, with the trees clothed in fresh young leaves, lawns becoming a richer green and spring flowers at their peak. A little warm, sunny weather brings out a real enthusiasm for gardening and there's certainly plenty to keep the keenest gardener occupied.*

▲ *Tulips and forget-me-nots make a classic combination in the spring garden. Next year's spring bedding will need to be sown soon.*

Gardeners are not the only ones who are enjoying the spring weather, and pests and weeds are now thriving. Weeding is a job that needs to be done for a large proportion of the year, but weeds are probably growing most rapidly in mid-spring. It's especially important to keep them under control while garden plants are small because they can easily be smothered by weed growth.

Pests, too, are on the increase, attracted by the tender young growth the plants are making. Slugs and snails are often a particular problem, and aphids (greenfly) can be found clustered on shoot tips, especially on greenhouse plants. Early action helps to prevent an outbreak turning into an epidemic.

There may be some slightly tender plants that appear to have been killed by the winter cold, but don't consign them to the compost pile. It is sometimes well into the summer before they show signs of recovery and start to put out buds. Check by

gently scraping a little patch of bark from the main stem—if the wood underneath is green and moist, the plant is still alive.

Spring bulbs continue to make a stunning show; wherever possible they should be deadheaded as they fade, before they have a chance to set seed. Spring bedding plants are also putting on a good performance; make a note to obtain more seeds of plants such as *Erysimum* (wallflowers), *Bellis perennis*, (daisies), *Myosotis*, (forget-me-nots) and so on, so they are not overlooked when they need to be sown in early summer. Buy them when you buy summer bedding plants from the garden center.

There's plenty to do in the kitchen garden, too, with weeding, sowing, and planting out, plus thinning out of crops that have been sown earlier. In the greenhouse shading becomes necessary soon, and ventilation and watering should be increased as the weather grows warmer and sunnier.

## MID – SPRING TASKS

**General**
- Control weeds, slugs, snails and other pests as they appear
- Check plants that appear to have been killed by frosts

**Ornamental garden**
- Plant summer-flowering bulbs and deadhead spring bulbs. Buy bedding plants from garden centers
- Continue to sow hardy annuals
- Take cuttings of border plants
- Plant Galanthus (snowdrops) "in the green" (while in leaf)
- Check for reverted shoots on variegated shrubs
- Check for rose diseases and treat as necessary
- Plant alpines and evergreens
- Prune spring-flowering shrubs such as forsythia after flowering

▼ Neatly trimmed edges set off a freshly mown lawn.

**Lawns**
- Apply a "weed and feed" combined herbicide and fertilizer
- Mow and edge lawns as necessary
- Deal with worm casts and moss
- Make new lawns from seed

**Water garden**
- Begin excavation work for a new pond

**Kitchen garden**
- Continue sowing successional crops. Prepare the trench for pole beans
- Sow winter brassicas outdoors
- Hoe off weeds regularly
- Plant out leeks and onion sets
- Earth up potatoes and plant second early and maincrop varieties
- Spray fruit with fungicide if mildew has been a problem in previous years
- Avoid spraying fruit trees with insecticides while pollinating insects are active
- Prune plums

▼ Seedlings and young plants continue to need potting up and pricking off in the greenhouse.

**Greenhouse**
- Apply shading and increase ventilation and watering
- Check heaters are still working
- Begin hardening off bedding plants
- Continue pricking off and potting up as necessary
- Plant out tomatoes in the greenhouse border
- Sow pole and bush beans, and melons

# ornamental garden: *planting and sowing*

*Alpines establish rapidly in mid-spring. If possible, grow them in a raised area so that their small but often exquisite flowers can be appreciated more easily. Galanthus (snowdrops) are best planted now before the leaves die down, and there are many summer-flowering bulbs to plant, too.*

### Plant snowdrops

Unlike many other bulbs, snowdrops are best planted while they are still in leafy growth; the dormant bulbs do not establish so well and can be disappointing. Many mail-order nurseries specializing in small bulbs advertise snowdrops "in the green," and this is the best way of obtaining some of the more unusual and expensive species and varieties.

If you already have clumps of snowdrops in the garden which you would like to increase, this is a good time to split them up and replant them in new positions. Lift the clumps carefully with a hand fork and tease them apart gently into two or three smaller groups. Replant them straight away, so that they do not dry out. Do not set the small bulbs too deep—aim for 3in/7.5cm. Heavy soils should have a little sharp sand or grit, and well-rotted compost worked in before planting.

### PLANT ALPINES

Alpine plants come into their own next month, and this is a good time to plant new specimens. Container-grown plants from garden centers can be bought and planted when they are coming into flower, making choosing attractive varieties easier.

Prepare the soil well, remembering that alpines need free-draining conditions. Plant with a trowel and firm in well. Dress around the plants with a little grit to insure good drainage round the necks and help avoid the risk of rotting.

▶ *The double snowdrop* Galanthus *'Flore Plento' is a popular variety, with delicate blooms like frilly petticoats.*

# plant summer-flowering bulbs

Although spring is the first season that comes to mind when anybody mentions flowering bulbs, there are lots of species and varieties that make a great show in the summer. They are not difficult to grow, and it's well worth planting some now.

**1** Most summer-flowering bulbs like a warm, sheltered position in full sun. The soil must be free-draining to avoid the bulbs rotting; on soils that tend to be heavy, add coarse sand or grit to the planting site and fork it in well (**below**).

**2** Bulbs should be planted as soon as they are available from garden centers. Always choose those which are large, firm and unblemished (**below**); avoid small and shriveled bulbs because they will not give good results.

**3** Dig a planting hole with a trowel, sprinkle a little sand in the base and put in the bulb (**left**). The ideal planting depth will vary from species to species and depends on the size of the bulb. In general plant the bulb at a depth twice that of its height.

**4** Cover the bulb with soil and firm it in position lightly. Once planting is completed, it is a good idea to label the planting areas clearly. This should help you to avoid accidentally disturbing the bulbs before they start to show through the soil.

◄ *Sunny yellow lilies are perfect for brightening up the flower borders in summer and can be planted now.*

# ornamental garden: *planting and protection*

*Every garden should have its full complement of evergreen plants. For many species this is a good time to plant, and there is a fine selection of flowering and foliage shrubs and trees to choose from. Apart from their ornamental value, they are excellent for providing shelter in a garden.*

## EVERGREENS AS WINDBREAKS

A hedge usually makes a much better windbreak than a solid screen such as a wall or panel fence because it is permeable, and it filters the wind rather than forcing it over and down in a potentially damaging blast. Evergreen hedges provide good wind protection all year round. The hedge can be formal, requiring more frequent clipping, or informal, as suits the garden style. Suitable evergreens include:

### Formal hedges
*Ilex* (holly): many varieties, some brightly variegated and bearing berries
*Ligustrum ovalifolium* (privet): very common; the golden variety is more colorful
*Prunus laurocerasus* (cherry laurel): large, glossy, deep-green leaves

### Informal hedges
*Berberis stenophylla* (barberry): smothered in arching sprays of deep-yellow flowers in spring
*Escallonia macarantha* and hybrids: small, glossy leaves and pink or red, tubular flowers in early summer; rather tender
*Pyracantha rogersiana* (firethorn); light-green leaves, a froth of white flowers in spring followed by colorful berries.

## Make the most of evergreens

Evergreens are important plants in any garden, giving it form and structure which persists throughout the year. They are especially valuable in winter when other plants are bare and leafless, but they also have a rôle to play in the spring and summer, forming a perfect backdrop for brightly colored flowers.

Many evergreens such as *Escallonia*, *Choisya* (Mexican orange blossom), *Osmanthus* and *Ceanothus* are a little on the tender side and are generally prone to damage from cold and wind, making mid-spring a better time for planting than the dormant season. Choose a free-draining soil and a reasonably sheltered site.

▲ *Evergreen hedges are both decorative and functional, especially when neatly and attractively trimmed.*

▶ *A mixed planting of evergreen and deciduous subjects will make sure the garden retains structure and interest throughout the year.*

# plant evergreens

Bare-root deciduous shrubs should be planted in the dormant season, but mid-spring is the best time to plant evergreens. As the weather is often dry at this time of year, special care must be taken not to let the plants dry out in the weeks following planting.

1 Prepare the planting site by digging it over deeply and adding some well-rotted organic matter such as garden compost or manure, or working in a proprietary planting mix.

2 Dig the planting hole, making sure it is deep enough for the top of the root-ball to be just level with the soil surface. Break up the soil at the base of the planting hole.

3 Evergreens are sometimes supplied as root-balled specimens, with the roots wrapped in netting or burlap. Place the complete root-ball in the planting hole before untying and removing the wrapping material, then fill in with soil and firm in the plant as usual (**left**).

4 Evergreens are particularly prone to wind damage because they have their full complement of leaves at planting time. Wind strips moisture from the leaves, leading to scorching and leaf drop. Protect plants in exposed conditions by erecting a temporary windbreak (**above**).

5 Water the newly-planted shrub thoroughly (**above**). Further watering will be necessary throughout the spring and summer after planting unless the weather is particularly wet; it is important that the soil does not dry out before the plant has a chance to get properly established.

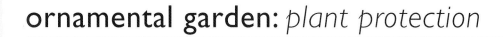

# ornamental garden: *plant protection*

*Much of a gardener's time is spent protecting plants from various pests and diseases, particularly in spring. Slugs are a major problem, but there are various environmentally friendly methods to deal with them. Roses need regular treatment against diseases, and the battle against weeds goes on.*

### Take safe action against slugs

Slugs and snails are voracious feeders on plant growth, and can do an enormous amount of damage. The chemicals in proprietary slug pellets are an effective but indiscriminate poison that is also toxic to wild animals and household pets. Conseqently, many gardeners have reservations about using them.

One alternative is trapping. Set shallow dishes containing beer or another bait into the soil to attract and drown slugs (though the rims must be high enough to prevent beneficial beetles from suffering the same fate), or place empty grapefruit or orange halves cut-side down on the soil to attract slugs that must be disposed of the following morning. Aluminum sulfate is also sometimes effective.

Biological control is a relatively new technique that is very promising; it uses a nematode with the tongue-twisting name of *Phasmarhabditis hermaphrodita*. The soil must be reasonably warm for it to work, but it can be used from now on through the summer.

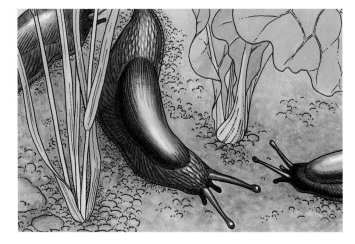

◀ *Slugs usually feed under cover of darkness, and can reduce lush foliage to a skeleton of veins overnight, especially in damp weather.*

## CHECK ROSES FOR DISEASE

Roses are subject to a common trio of diseases—blackspot, mildew, and rust. Blackspot is easily recognized because black spots or blotches with an irregular outline cover the foliage, which falls early. Mildew leaves a white powder on young leaves, stunting growth, distorting flowers and spoiling the plant's appearance. Rust is not so obvious at first; small, orange, spore-filled pustules form on the undersides of the leaves, with a pale yellow patch on the top surface. Leaves fall prematurely and the disease can severely weaken the plant.

Check the leaves regularly, including the undersides, for signs of disease. At the first sign, or even before if you have had disease problems previously, begin a regular spraying program. Several appropriate fungicides are on the market, and their use should be alternated for the best results.

# keep weeds under control

At this time of year everything in the garden is growing strongly, especially the weeds. Controlling them is important, not only because they make the garden look untidy but because weeds deprive cultivated plants of moisture, nutrients, and light.

1 Weeds are best dealt with while they are still small, when hoeing is very effective (**left**). Choose a dry, blowy day so that the weeds wilt and die quickly. Run the well-sharpened blade of the hoe flat along the soil surface, slicing the seedling weeds off from their roots rather than digging them up.

2 Hoeing is not practical where weeds are growing close to or among cultivated plants because there is too much risk of damage. Hand weeding is often the only option, using a hand fork to remove deep-rooted weeds.

3 Chemical weedkillers are often very effective (**left**). Contact herbicides (such as paraquat) kill the top-growth onto which they are sprayed, but not the roots. They are suitable for young annual weeds but are not so effective on deep-rooted weeds that will regrow.

4 Translocated herbicides (such as glyphosate) are carried to all parts of the plant including the roots, and are best for difficult weeds such as bindweed and couch grass. Great care must be taken to keep accidental splashes of these weedkillers off cultivated plants.

5 Once the soil surface is clear, apply a thick mulch of shredded bark or a similar material (**above**). This helps keep the ground weed free by preventing the germination of any weed seeds present in the top layer of soil. Any weeds that do appear in the mulch are easy to pull out of the loose material.

◀ *A hand fork is useful to help prise deep rooted weeds out of the soil. Regrowth often occurs from portions of root left behind.*

43

# ornamental garden: *plants in season*

Many shrubs and trees join the throng of flowering plants this month, and increasing numbers of border plants are producing their blooms now, too. The earliest of the spring bulbs are over, but there are still plenty providing a good show of color.

▼ *Most Euphorbias brighten spring with their lime-green flowerheads, but the steely blue leaves often persist right through the winter, too.*

## TREES AND SHRUBS

*Acer pseudoplatanus* 'Brilliantissimum' (sycamore),  *A. rubrum* (red maple)

*Amelanchier lamarckii* (juneberry)

*Berberis darwinii, B. stenophylla* (barberry)

*Ceanothus* (California lilac)

*Clematis alpina, C. armandii*

*Cytisus praecox* (broom)

*Daphne burkwoodii, D. cneorum*

*Forsythia*

*Kerria japonica*

*Magnolia soulangiana, M. stellata* (star magnolia)

*Malus* (apple, crab apple)

*Osmanthus burkwoodii, O. delavayii*

*Pieris*

*Prunus* in variety (ornamental cherry)

*Rhododendron*

*Ribes sanguineum* (flowering currant)

*Rosmarinus officinalis* (rosemary)

*Spiraea arguta* (bridal wreath)

*Ulex europaeus* (furze)

*Vinca major* (greater periwinkle), *V. minor* (lesser periwinkle)

▲ *The stately chalices of* Magnolia × soulangiana *blooms are often spoiled by late frosts in exposed positions.*

▼ *The flowering currant,* Ribes sanguineum, *is an easily pleased shrub with attractive rosy flowers and a pungent aroma to the foliage.*

## PERENNIALS AND BEDDING PLANTS

*Aurinia saxatilis*

*Aubrieta*

*Bellis perennis* (common daisy)

*Bergenia*

*Erysimum cheirii* (wallflower)

*Doronicum* (leopard's bane)

*Epimedium* (barrenwort)

*Euphorbia characias, E. polychroma*

*Helleborus orientalis* (lenten rose)

*Iberis sempervirens* (candytuft)

*Myosotis* (forget-me-not)

*Primula*  (primrose)

## BULBS

*Anemone*

*Bulbocodium vernum*

*Chionodoxa* (glory of the snow)

*Convallaria majalis* (lily-of-the-valley)

*Eythronium revolutum* (Western trout lily)

*Fritillaria imperialis* (crown imperials),  *F. meleagris* (snake's head fritillary)

*Leucojum vernum* (spring snowflake)

*Muscari* (grape hyacinth)

*Narcissus* (daffodil)

*Tulipa* (tulip)

# lawns

*The lawn is an integral part of the garden, providing a restful green backdrop against which to admire the vibrant colors of the flowers. Lawns that may have looked tired and thin after the stress of the winter should now be growing more strongly, and it's time to help them reach perfection.*

### Apply lawn fertilizer

In spring, a fertilizer containing high levels of nitrogen will boost growth and help the grass to develop a rich green colour. The phosphates and potash also included in lawn fertilizers stimulate root growth and improve resistance to disease and adverse weather conditions.

▼ *Mid-spring is an ideal time to make a new lawn from seed. Sow in soil that has been carefully prepared to create a fine tilth.*

Fertilizers are available as powders, granules, or liquids. Liquid fertilizers can be applied with a hose-end dilutor; they are fast acting and give a rapid response, but they can be expensive for large lawns. Dry fertilizers can be applied by hand but it is very difficult to achieve an even distribution, and the result can be patchy. The best method is to use a fertilizer distributor, a small hopper on wheels that applies the fertilizer at a given rate when pushed up and

down the lawn. Take care to cover all the grass evenly, and do not overlap strips or leave a gap between them because this will show up as differently colored growth later on.

## CONTROL LAWN WEEDS

—

Where there are only a few, isolated weeds in the lawn they can be treated individually, either by digging them out with a narrow-bladed trowel or special lawn-  weeding tool, or by giving them individual doses of weedkiller. "Spot" weedkillers come in the form of wax sticks, impregnated sponges, aerosols, and ready-to-use sprays.

If weeds are more widespread over the lawn surface, an overall application of selective weedkiller is necessary. This should be applied shortly after fertilizing, or you can use a proprietary "weed and feed" product that applies the two together. Be very careful not to allow lawn weedkillers to drift on to cultivated plants or neighboring gardens. Tiny amounts carried on the breeze are enough to do a great deal of damage to other plants.

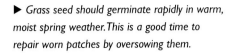
► *Grass seed should germinate rapidly in warm, moist spring weather. This is a good time to repair worn patches by oversowing them.*

## mow and edge lawns

A perfect, velvet-textured, emerald-green lawn is the envy of all who see it, but many gardeners seem to find it impossible to achieve. Understanding and employing the correct mowing technique is one simple way to greatly improve the quality of the turf.

1 Now the grass has started to grow rapidly it will need cutting more frequently—once a week at least, and twice a week as spring moves into summer. Before mowing, clear stones, fir cones, sticks, and other debris from the lawn. If you can, wait until the dew has dried.

2 Set the blades at the right height (**right**); scalping is a very common mistake. At this time of year the grass should be left between ¾ in/18mm and 1¼ in/30mm high, reducing to a minimum of ½ in/12mm high in summer (¾ in/18mm is better for most lawns).

3 Mow the grass in parallel strips up and down the lawn (**above**). If the mower has a rear roller it will produce the light and dark stripes favored by many people; in this case it is important to keep the mowing strips as straight and even as possible for the best effect.

4 Next time the lawn is mown, work at right angles to the last direction of cut—across the lawn rather than up and down. Alternating the direction at each cut makes sure that the surface of the lawn remains even, and helps control lawn weeds and weed grasses.

5 Once the mowing is finished, trim the edges to give the lawn a neat appearance (**above**). Use long-handled edging shears or, to save time, a powered edger. If the edges are ragged after the winter, recut them in spring with a half-moon edging iron, using a plank as a straight edge.

# kitchen garden: *planting and sowing*

*Time vegetable sowings so that you have a steady harvest through the summer, without a glut of crops maturing simultaneously. Be particularly careful with vegetables that have a short period of use before they spoil, such as lettuces, which run to seed, and peas, which become tough.*

### Continue sowing vegetables

As the weather becomes warmer, more and more vegetable crops can be sown. Among those that can be sown outdoors directly where they are to grow are beets, Swiss chard, various beans, carrot, kohlrabi, lettuce, pea, radish, scallion, salsify, scorzonera, spinach, and turnip. When you sow the crops, pacings can be varied according to the size of plant that is required.

Some vegetables are sown now in a seedbed and transplanted to their cropping positions later. They include broccoli, Brussels sprouts, calabrese, cauliflowers, summer, fall, and winter cabbages, kale, and leeks.

### SOW CROPS FOR SUCCESSION

"Little and often" is a good idea when it comes to sowing many vegetables for home use. This insures that crops can be picked and used when they are young and tender, and there will be a further supply following from a later sowing. Crops that can be grown in succession include beets, cabbage, carrot, cauliflower, lettuce, pea, radish, spinach, and turnip.

Sow short rows of the crops in question at two to four week intervals, or select a range of different varieties to mature at different times throughout the season.

◄ *Try to keep the vegetable garden weed-free. Supply supports to plants that need them at an early stage of growth for the best results.*

## plant onion sets

Onions are easy to grow from sets (small, immature bulbs). It is best to buy heat-treated sets because they are less likely to run to flower prematurely than those that are untreated.

1 Onions need an open position in fertile, well-worked soil which has been broken down to fine crumbs (**right**). Work a little general fertilizer into the soil immediately before planting.

2 The sets can be planted in drills made deep enough for the tops of the bulbs to be just showing above soil level when planted. Space them 2–4in/5–10cm apart in rows 10in/25cm apart: the wider spacing will produce larger bulbs.

3 In fine, very light soil, drills are not necessary—the sets can simply be pushed into the ground at the correct spacing (**left**). On heavier soil, however, this compresses the soil at the base of the set, making it difficult for the roots to penetrate; the onion sets then push themselves out of the ground as the roots start to grow.

4 Birds are often a nuisance, tugging the freshly-planted sets out of the ground. One way to avoid this is to trim away the dead, brown leaves at the tip of the set with scissors or secateurs before planting (**below**): these dead leaves form a convenient "handle" by which birds can tweak the sets out of the soil.

5 Water the sets shortly after planting if the weather turns dry, and keep them free of competition from weeds. Heat-treated sets are often a little slower than untreated sets to start into growth, but they soon catch up.

◄ *It is possible to obtain a satisfying crop of perfect, golden-skinned onions from sets planted in the vegetable garden in mid-spring.*

# pollination

Plants reproduce sexually by means of seed. The seed needs to be dispersed as widely as possible, but the plant is at a disadvantage because it is in one spot. Animals and birds, however, can move about freely; one of the main ways plants disperse seed is by encouraging an animal or bird to carry it away. Embedding the seed within a sweet, juicy, edible fruit will certainly attract a range of creatures to help distribute the seed far and wide.

The process of bearing fruit is therefore usually inextricably linked with sexual reproduction and the formation of seed. In order to form seed, pollen grains from the male part of a flower must be transferred to the stigma that is attached to the ovary, the female part of a flower, a process known as pollination.

Pollination is followed by fertilization when the male and female cells fuse to produce an embryo, or seed, which swells to form a fruit. If pollination and fertilization do not occur, the fruit generally (though not always) fails to form. When we grow fruit trees and bushes in our gardens, therefore, we need to make sure that pollination and fertilization of the flowers can take place.

## Cross-pollination and self-pollination

Many flowers achieve pollination very easily, without the need for any outside help. Although there can be separate male and female flowers (sometimes on the same plant or sometimes on separate plants), the majority of species bear flowers containing both male and female sexual organs. Sometimes pollen can fertilize the female cells of the same flower (self-pollination), but often the flowers are "self-incompatible." This means that the pollen needs to come from a different flower, or different plant or variety of the same species (cross-pollination).

Many tree fruits such as apples and pears need to be cross-pollinated to bear a good crop of fruit. Some varieties are partially self-fertile so that a small crop will be carried even if no other fruit trees are nearby, but the crop will be greatly increased by cross-pollination. As insects are responsible for pollination, trees must be within insect-flying distance of suitable partners.

▲ *Apple blossom must be pollinated before a crop can be carried. It is usually necessary to grow at least two compatible varieties.*

## Pollinating partners

The two varieties of tree grown as partners must be compatible, and must flower at the same time. There are a few incompatible varieties; for example, 'Cox's Orange Pippin' will not pollinate, or be pollinated by, 'Kidd's Orange Red' or 'Jupiter'. Fruit catalogs give details and also have information on flowering times, dividing them into early, mid-season and late, usually indicating this by numbers 1, 2 and 3. Choose two varieties from the same pollinating group—for instance, 'William's Pride' and 'Cheholis', or 'Golden Sentinal' and 'North Pole'. Varieties from adjoining groups usually have sufficient overlap to be successful, but a variety from Group 1 will not pollinate a variety from Group 3.

Some varieties of apple and pear have an extra set of chromosomes and are known as triploids: they will not pollinate other varieties and need to be pollinated by two varieties themselves. 'Jonagold', 'Crispin' and

▼ *Pear blossom: pear trees need to be cross-pollinated in order to produce a decent-sized crop of fruit.*

### HAND POLLINATION

In some cases, fruit tree blossoms need to be pollinated by hand. This is normally either because they are in flower very early in the year when there are few flying insects about, or because they are being grown in a greenhouse or conservatory where insect access is difficult. Peaches, apricots, and nectarines are the usual candidates: they are self-fertile, and can be pollinated by blossom from the same tree. Wait until several flowers are open and the pollen can be seen on the anthers. Use a small, soft brush such as a makeup brush to lightly dust each flower, transferring the pollen from one flower to the other.

'Bramley's Seedling' are triploid apples, while 'Merton Pride' and 'Jargonelle' are triploid pears.

## Looking after insect pollinators

Bees and other insects are very efficient pollinators of tree fruit. Make sure that you never spray the trees with insecticides during fruit-flowering time.

# greenhouse: *general tasks*

*Before greenhouse-raised plants can be set outside when the risk of frost is over, they must be hardened off so that the move to cooler conditions is not too much of a shock. Some young plants will be ready for a move to larger pots. With increasing sunlight, greenhouse shading becomes necessary.*

### Harden off young plants

The move from the warm, sheltered conditions of a greenhouse to the rougher, colder world outdoors can

◄ *Make sure bedding plants are thoroughly hardened off before moving them to their permanent positions in the open garden.*

result in a serious check to plant growth. Plants that are moved straight from the greenhouse to their growing positions in the garden frequently seem to "stand still" for a while until they adjust, often losing almost all the advantage they had gained from an early start indoors.

Plants should be gradually accustomed to outdoor conditions over a week or two, a process known as hardening off. A cold frame is ideal for this. Transfer plants from the heated greenhouse to an unheated frame, at first with the roof closed, then gradually increasing the ventilation until the roof is left off altogether. If a frame is not available, plants to be hardened off can be moved from the greenhouse to a sheltered position outside during the warmest part of the day, moving them back inside when conditions

get cooler. Gradually increase the length of time they are outdoors before moving them to their permanent planting positions.

### CHECK GREENHOUSE TEMPERATURES

Although the weather is now warmer, it is still too early to turn off greenhouse heaters at night. Continue to check the maximum/minimum thermometer regularly to insure that frost-free conditions are maintained. As long as an efficient thermostat is fitted there is no need to worry about wasting fuel; the heater will not start up unless triggered by low temperatures. On sunny days excessively high temperatures will be a problem though, unless the greenhouse is well ventilated. By now the weather should be reasonably mild, so if you are going to be away during the day, open the vents before you leave (unless you have automatic vent openers to do the job for you).

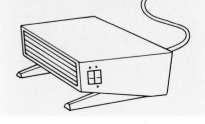

# pot up seedlings and young plants

Warmer weather and longer daylight hours mean plants in the greenhouse are growing fast. Move developing seedlings and young plants into larger pots as soon as they are ready—delaying the move will mean a check to their growth. Take care to disturb the roots as little as possible during the transplanting process.

## APPLY GREENHOUSE SHADING

Direct sun through the greenhouse glass is sufficiently strong to scorch the foliage of many plants, and shading of at least part of the greenhouse is usually necessary now. Start by shading the roof, then add shading down the side of the greenhouse if necessary as the season progresses. There are various forms of shading, including external or internal blinds, rolls of netting, and paint-on preparations. The paint-on shading usually becomes translucent when wet, automatically allowing extra light to penetrate on dull, rainy days.

1 The size of pot required depends on the size of the plants, but 3½ in/8 cm pots are usually the most practical first pot. Plants already in individual pots can be moved up to the next size container; do not be tempted to move them to a larger pot than this.

2 Seedlings should be handled by their seed leaves; the young stems are easily damaged. Fill a pot loosely with potting mix and make a hole in the soil with a dibble (**above**). Lower the seedling into it, making sure the roots are at the base of the hole. Firm the soil very gently.

3 Plants are ready for potting on when their roots become visible through the drainage holes of the pot (**above**). Water them well a few hours beforehand, then turn the pot upside down and tap the rim on the edge of the staging to remove the plant.

4 Place a little soil mix in the base of the larger pot and stand the root-ball on it. Fill in round the sides with fresh mix and firm it down; water well. Place newly-potted plants in a partially shaded place for a few days to recover from the disturbance of transplanting.

# greenhouse: *planting and sowing*

*The season is now sufficiently advanced to start sowing those more tender crops, such as melons and pole beans. Pole beans are planted out in the vegetable garden once the risk of frost is over, but in many areas melons will give the best crop if grown to maturity in the greenhouse.*

◀ *Sow melons now for a very welcome crop later on in the summer. Select varieties suitable for the conditions you can provide.*

### Sow melons

Although they like warm conditions, melons are not difficult to grow in a greenhouse, and several varieties are suitable for growing in a cold frame or outdoors even in relatively cool climates. The fruits are sweet and aromatic, making a very enjoyable summer crop. Sow two seeds per 3½ in/8cm pot of soilless potting mix. The seeds are smaller than those of cucumber, but should be sown on their sides in the same way to reduce the risk of rotting. A temperature of 64–75°F/18–24°C is suitable for germination. The plants are grown on in much the same way as greenhouse cucumbers, but the flowers will need pollinating to make sure good fruit is set. 'Sweet Granite' is one of the hardiest varieties, and 'Ambrosia Hybrid', 'Crème de la Crème Hybrid',

'Honey Pearl', and 'Supersun Hybrid' are also good for outdoor culture (under cloches or in a frame in cold regions). Seek advice from your local garden center which melons really need greenhouse cultivation.

### SOW BUSH AND POLE BEANS IN POTS

Although both bush and pole beans can be sown directly where they are to grow once the weather is suitable, raising the plants indoors will enable you to pick much earlier crops. Bush beans have small seeds and can be sown in a seed tray, spacing the seeds to give about 18 plants per tray. Pole beans do best when sown individually in 3½ in/8cm pots. Fill the tray or pots with sowing mix, firm it down, and sow the seeds by pushing them below the surface. Cover with clear plastic propagator tops.

▶ *Tomatoes can be planted in the greenhouse in mid-spring. Pests and diseases must be dealt with to guarantee a good crop.*

## plant tomatoes in the greenhouse border

Tomatoes are the most popular food crop for growing in the greenhouse, and can give high yields of fruit in the summer. Young plants are ready for setting out in their cropping positions once the first flower buds start to appear.

1 The greenhouse border is a good place to grow tomatoes because they will be less likely to suffer water shortages than if they are grown in containers. Good quality soil is necessary, preferably enriched with plenty of well-rotted compost or manure.

2 Turn the plants out of their pots by tapping the base of the upturned pot sharply. Dig a hole in the border with a trowel and plant the tomatoes, firming them in well (**right**). Water thoroughly after planting.

3 Greenhouse tomatoes are usually grown as single-stem cordons that need to be supported to enable the crop to develop properly. One method of support is to provide each plant with a tall bamboo cane, tying the stem to the cane at intervals as it grows (**left**). Take care not to damage the stem by tying it too tightly.

4 Another popular method is to train the plants up twine (**below**). Anchor a length of garden twine in the soil near the plant with a hook, or tie it loosely around the tomato stem below the bottom leaf. Take the other end of the twine up to a wire running level with the eaves. Twist the plant's stem round the twine as it grows.

5 Growing bags are a popular alternative to planting in the greenhouse border. Set two or three tomato plants per bag, cutting a cross in the plastic and folding it back to make a planting hole. Frequent watering is essential.

# late spring

*The weather is mild and there's often a good deal of sunshine. Spring blossom mingles with the early blooms of summer, and foliage still has a wonderful freshness. Gardeners should enjoy the last weeks of spring while they prepare for summer in what is always one of the year's busiest times.*

In most areas the risk of damaging night frosts will be over toward the end of the month but in the early days, and in colder regions, you will need to remain on your guard. If your garden happens to be in a frost pocket, you may need to be much more cautious than neighbors only a short distance away who are in a more favored position.

This is a good time to plant up hanging baskets, window boxes, and tubs which are very valuable for injecting concentrated splashes of color in the garden and around the house. They are increasingly popular, with a wide range of new and unusual "patio plants" available at garden centers. Keep them under cover or in a sheltered position for a few days after planting in the early part of the month. Spring bedding plants are past their best now, and

need to be cleared out to make way for the summer bedding—but don't forget to sow spring-bedding plants for next year's display.

Plants are growing strongly now but need to be regularly fed and weeded; pests must be controlled promptly. In the vegetable garden, tender crops such as pole beans, bush beans, and zucchini can be sown safely out of doors.

Finally, a pond is a great addition to any garden, adding a special sort of tranquillity with its shimmering water and colorful plants.

The gentle splash of a fountain or waterfall is an extra delight. This is the best time of year to build a garden pool, and you can rest assured that you are creating a feature that is bound to be enjoyed for many years to come.

▶ *Well-planted containers are particularly useful for adding color to the patio. Wait until frosts are over before putting them outside.*

## LATE SPRING TASKS

**General**

:: *Check for pests on plants and treat promptly*
:: *Feed strong growing plants*
:: *Treat perennial weeds with herbicide*

**Ornamental garden**

:: *Plant up hanging baskets, window boxes, and tubs*
:: *Continue staking border plants*
:: *Weed annual seedlings and thin them as necessary*
:: *Remove spring-bedding plants; plant out summer bedding*

:: *Plant dahlias*
:: *Deadhead Narcissus (daffodils). Leave the foliage in place until six weeks after the last flowers fade*
:: *Sow winter-flowering Viola (pansies), and biennials such as Erysimum (wallflowers), Dianthus*

barbatus *(sweet williams )* and Myosotis *(forget-me-nots)*
:: *Water recently-planted trees and shrubs if the weather is dry*
:: *Trim evergreen hedges as necessary*

▲ *Plant up containers with a range of summer bedding plants for a pleasing display.*

**Lawns**

:: *Lower the height of the mower blades to give a closer cut. Tackle weeds with a spot weedkiller*

**Water garden**

:: *Construct and plant up new ponds. Introduce fish once the plants are established*
:: *In existing ponds, divide deep-water aquatics and plant new varieties*
:: *Feed fish, but be careful not to overfeed*
:: *Watch for aphids on water lily leaves, and submerge affected leaves to allow fish to eat them*

▼ *Strawing around strawberry plants helps protect the fruit from slug damage and soil splashes.*

**Kitchen garden**

:: *Water as necessary, timing the watering carefully for maximum crops*
:: *Continue to make successional sowings for continuity of supply*
:: *Plant out hardened-off pole and bush beans once the risk of frost is over. Sow pole beans and bush beans outdoors*

:: *Thin out seedlings in the rows. Thin carrots late in the evening to avoid attracting carrot root fly. Stake peas*
:: *Plant vegetables in pots and growing bags*
:: *Check plums for silver leaf disease*
:: *Reduce codling moth damage with pheromone traps*

:: *Straw around strawberries and net the plants against birds*

**Greenhouse**

:: *Ventilate the greenhouse more freely, and water more frequently as the weather gets warmer*
:: *Train and support cucumbers, melons, and tomatoes*

:: *Continue pricking out seedlings and potting up rooted cuttings as necessary*

:: *"Stop" pelargoniums and fuchsias by pinching out the growing points to make them bushier*

# ornamental garden: *general tasks*

*Hardy annuals sown earlier will now be making good headway, and perennial border plants need some attention to keep them in good shape. If you want to propagate garden shrubs, layering is often successful where other methods fail. Pests continue to increase in numbers this month.*

### Check plants for pests

Garden pests of all sorts continue to thrive in the warmer weather, and plants need to be checked regularly and pest infestations treated

promptly. One of the most troublesome pests is vine weevil. Greenhouse plants are most at risk, but the adult weevils spread outside as the weather becomes warmer. Outdoor weevil activity starts now, and peaks between early summer and mid-fall. You may see leaves that have had characteristic notches bitten out of their margins by the adult weevils

◄ *Grubs of the vine weevil eat away at a plant's root system until it can no longer support the top growth and the whole plant collapses.*

but it is the damage done by the grubs that is more serious: they feed on the roots and can completely destroy the root system.

Suspect vine weevil grubs where plants suddenly wilt and die for no apparent reason, especially plants in containers.

A biological control containing nematodes can be applied now, provided there is a reasonably warm spell of weather. This will be effective against larvae that emerged from eggs laid last fall.

## STAKING BORDER PLANTS

Continue to provide supports for border plants from an early stage (see page 16). As the shoots grow, train them gently to the support; tie in where necessary with soft twine, plastic-covered twist ties or raffia. Where twiggy sticks are used, the border plants should be making sufficient growth to cover them almost completely.

Do not allow stems to flop before putting supports in, or they will stay kinked.

This type of support can be raised as the plant grows, but great care is necessary to avoid snapping the stems.

Stakes that link together can be arranged in patterns to provide support for almost any size and shape of plant.

Taller plants such as Delphiniums are likely to need individual stakes for the flowering stems.

# *increase shrubs by layering*

This is a simple way of propagating shrubs with low branches. Many shrubs are suitable for propagation by layering, including magnolias and rhododendrons, that are otherwise difficult to increase. Select a suitable low-growing branch that can be bent down to soil level. It should be a healthy, strong-growing shoot of the previous season's growth.

1 Bend the shoot down to the ground and mark the position where the stem touches the soil, about 9–12in/23–30cm behind the tip of the shoot (**right**). Dig this area over well with a trowel, then dig a hole about 4in/10cm deep with a straight, flat side furthest from the plant.

2 Bend the shoot down again to check the position of the hole. When the stem is lying at the base of the hole, the top 9in/23cm of the shoot should stick out of the ground, held upright by the straight side. Strip the leaves and leaf stalks from the length of stem to be buried.

3 Where the stem must be bent to pull it down into the hole, make a small cut on its underside with a sharp knife (**left**). This injury to the plant will encourage growth.

▼ *Give hardy annual seedlings room to develop by thinning them out. Select the strongest seedlings to remain at the appropriate spacing.*

4 Peg the stem into the hole with a piece of bent wire (**below**), return the soil to bury the stem completely. Tread the soil gently but firmly to firm it back down.

5 Tie the protruding tip of the shoot to a stake in order to keep it upright and then water the soil regularly to keep it moist. Roots will form on the buried portion of stem over the summer, and once the layer is well rooted it can be dug up and separated from the parent.

# alpine gardens

Alpine plants contain some of the loveliest species there are. Their growth is neat and compact, and in late spring the plants are often smothered with masses of flowers in brilliant, jewel-bright shades. They need special conditions in which to grow but these are not hard to provide, and alpine plants should be included in every garden. Alpines, as their name suggests, originate from mountainous regions. True alpines come from areas above the tree line, but the term is often more loosely applied to include plants from lower altitudes that should more correctly be called rock garden plants.

Alpines have a range of features that help them cope with the inhospitable conditions in which they have to grow. They have adapted to low temperatures in strong, direct sun, chilling winds, and poor or almost non-existent soil. Their growth is low, often ground hugging to avoid being battered by the wind; their low, spreading habit also helps them withstand the weight of heavy winter snow without being crushed. Since wind causes high moisture loss from the leaves as the constantly moving air whips it away, alpine plants often have leaves that cut water loss to a minimum—they may be very narrow, or have a waxy or hairy coating that also protects them from the intense, remorseless sunshine of high altitudes. Soil on the high mountainsides is poor and shallow, and plants often grow tucked into the crevices of rocks where they receive some shelter. They need to manage on very little water because the rainfall is low, and water soon drains away in the rocky ground.

Such plants might seem to be ideal for gardens—able to cope with almost any adverse conditions. Of course, this is not really the case. While they are perfectly adapted to life on the mountain tops, they may not adjust so well to some of the features of life at lower altitudes. The main problem is excess rainfall, particularly in the winter. Alpine plants must have free-draining conditions, otherwise they will rot away.

◀ *Alpine rock gardens contain plants that can deal with a range of unfriendly climatic conditions and are extremely tough.*

## Rock gardens

To grow well, most alpines need an area to themselves where they can be provided with the correct conditions. This often takes the form of a rock garden—a sloping site studded with rocks to simulate the mountainside. Care should be taken with the construction in order to make a rock garden an attractive feature; the rocks should be laid as natural-looking outcrops, not dotted randomly over the surface. Since about one-third of each rock will be covered by soil, fairly large pieces are necessary to make an impact, and they can be expensive.

▲ *True alpine plants are found in mountainous regions above the tree line, but the term is often used to describe plants from lower altitudes.*

In order to insure free-draining conditions, place a layer of rubble at the base of the site chosen for the rock garden, then top it with good quality, light topsoil. Set the rocks in position with care, making sure that the horizontal strata lines are running in the same direction. Plant the alpines in appropriate positions, using special alpine plant soil mix to fill in around them. When the whole rock garden is completed, finish it off by topdressing the surface with gravel or stone chippings, tucking it around the necks of the plants.

## Raised beds

A raised bed for alpines is an option where there is insufficient room for a full-scale rock garden, and has the advantage of bringing the plants nearer eye-level where their miniature charms can be appreciated more easily. Place rubble in the base, and fill the bed with gritty topsoil; a number of attractive, carefully positioned rocks on the soil surface will improve the bed's appearance. Plant the alpines as before, finishing off with a top-dressing of gravel.

### ALPINES IN WALLS

Dry stone walls provide an ideal place to set a few alpine plants. They can be planted in the top of the wall if there is a suitable gap that can be filled with some gritty topsoil, and they can also be tucked into the crevices on the face of the wall. Use a very narrow trowel or a spoon handle to push a little soil mix into the crevice and then carefully insert the roots of the plant, firming it in with more soil. *Lewisias, Campanulas, Gentians, Dianthus, Sedums, Saxifrages* and many others will thrive in these conditions, and enhance the wall with their flowers and foliage.

# ornamental garden: *planting and sowing*

*Most gardeners aim for a good display of flowers for as many months as possible, and now that spring bedding is past its best it's time to set out the summer-flowering plants and containers for the patio. Think a little further ahead to providing color for the fall and winter, too.*

### Replace spring plants with summer bedding

In most areas spring-bedding plants will have passed their best. Toward the end of the month the weather should be warm enough to plant out summer bedding to replace them, but make sure the plants have been hardened off sufficiently.

Fork over the soil, removing weeds along with the old plants, and work a sprinkling of general fertilizer into the surface. Turn the new plants out of their flats and disentangle the roots: bedding plants grown in individual cells establish more quickly because the amount of root damage is reduced. Plant with a trowel, firming in well, and water in the plants as each section of the bed is completed.

### PLANNING AHEAD

Dahlias provide wonderfully colorful blooms in late summer and early fall, and now is the time to plant the overwintered tubers, or cuttings rooted from them earlier in the spring. Since cuttings should be hardened off properly, and must not be planted out until all risk of frost is over, in some particularly cold areas it will be necessary to wait a little while longer.

Flowers are at a premium in the winter and early spring, but winter-flowering viola (pansies) can be relied upon to put up a good show. Sow them now, preferably in a cold frame, for planting out in the fall. Flowers will be produced in mild spells throughout the winter, with a bigger flush in early spring.

▲ *The cheerful yellow glow of marigolds will add life and color to your display of summer bedding plants.*

▶ *Once the display of spring flowers is past its best, containers can be planted up with subjects to provide summer interest.*

## plant up containers

Colorful tubs, windowboxes, and hanging baskets are immensely popular, and make very striking, long-lasting displays. Now that the risk of frosts is virtually over it should be safe to plant them and set them outside.

1 Garden centers usually have a good selection of suitable plants at this time of year. Select a variety of upright and trailing subjects, in a range of complementary colors; don't forget to include foliage plants as well as flowering ones.

2 Make sure that your containers have sufficient drainage holes, and enlarge them if necessary. Cover the drainage holes with a layer of coarse material such as large stones or crocks from broken clay pots which makes sure that excess water can freely drain away (**right**).

3 Two-thirds fill the container with potting mix, and mix in some slow-release fertilizer and water-retaining granules (**left**). These absorb moisture and "hold" it in the mix; they considerably cut down the frequency of watering.

4 Arrange the plants, still in their pots, on the surface of the soil until the design is to your liking. Aim to balance tall, upright plants with trailing ones, and to achieve a harmonious combination of colors and foliage textures.

5 Use a trowel to plant up the container, filling in with more soil mix as necessary. Firm the plants well (**above**) and water them well. If possible, leave the planted containers in a sheltered, partially shaded place for a day or two before moving them to their final positions.

# texture and color

Most people like a bright and cheerful scene, but color needs to be used with care if it is not to lose its effect. An unplanned "riot of colour" can be very effective in a small area—a hanging basket or tub, for example—but if repeated over the whole garden it has a restless, unsatisfying effect, making the onlooker tired and uneasy.

The color wheel is often used by garden planners as a useful reference tool. A simple color wheel takes colors in the order that they appear in the rainbow—red, orange, yellow, green, blue, and violet—and arranges them in a circle, with each color occupying an equal-sized segment. Colors that are adjacent in the circle

▼ *A cool, relaxing retreat on a hot summer's day: a garden carefully planned in shades of blue, white, and green.*

harmonize, while those that are opposite contrast. More complex color wheels use a much wider range of shades and hues, but the principle is the same.

Different colors have different effects on the onlooker. The hot colors—red, orange, and strong yellow—are vibrant and exciting, while the cool colors—blue, green and white—are restful and relaxing. Color can therefore be used to create the right sort of atmosphere in different parts of the garden.

Intense colors are more effective if they are given a contrasting background; brilliant scarlet flowers will stand out better against a plain green hedge, for example, than they would in a bed filled with other brightly-colored flowers. Use the color wheel to find the greatest contrast to a particular shade (it will appear directly opposite it).

▶ *Yellow flowers are given emphasis when in the vicinity of violet flowers, as the two colors are opposite each other on the color wheel.*

Pastel shades, where the pure hues have been mixed with white, are good for toning down strong colors and helping them integrate more successfully into the garden. Pink, salmon, pale yellow, and cream, for instance, have a cooling, calming effect on intense red, orange and yellow, while pale blue, pale green, and gray help to lighten an otherwise rather dark selection of hues.

When planning a color layout, it is usually better to place the strongest, brightest colors to the front, with paler shades (particularly misty greens, blues, and grays) farthest away. This also helps to make a small area appear larger. You may prefer to use brightly-colored plants as accents, drawing the eye to certain features, perhaps foreshortening a long, narrow border. Whatever the effect you wish to create, the result will be far more successful if it is planned rather than planted at random.

## *Textures*

Careful use of textures can give a whole new dimension to plant associations, both visually and to the touch.

Many different textures are exhibited by flowers and foliage: bold, spiky, lacy, dainty, hazy, feathery, soft, furry, rough, sculptured, and veined, for instance. Groups of plants with contrasting textures can be very effective. Large, bold leaves of a hosta or bergenia make a perfect foil for the feathery flowers of gypsophila or astilbe, for example. Remember that plants can be stroked, as well as seen; the soft velvet of *Stachys byzantina* (lamb's ears) or *Verbascum* (mullein) is intensely tactile.

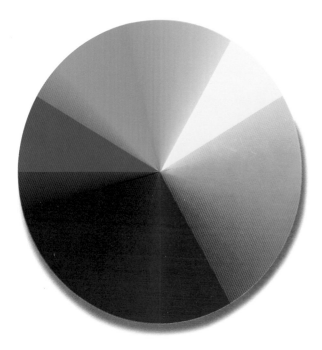

◀ *The color wheel: primary colors, red, yellow, and blue are opposite the secondary colors, green, violet, and orange.*

### CHOOSING COLORS

Many more plants in seed catalogs are now available in single colors as well as mixtures, which always used to be more popular. This makes it much easier to plan beds and borders effectively. In fact, mail-order catalogs are more likely to carry single colors than garden centers or shops, and it is sometimes necessary to go to the larger seed merchants for the best selection of varieties.

# plants in season

*Alpine and rock garden plants will be producing a bright display at this time of year. Wisteria and laburnum are draped with long racemes of colorful flowers, but rhododendrons and azaleas are perhaps the most striking plants this month.*

▼ *The fragrant flowers of wisteria are often among the most spectacular blooms in the garden in the late spring.*

▲ The glossy, aromatic leaves of Choisya ternata *(Mexican orange blossom)* are a bright lime-green in the variety 'Sundance'.

▼ Ceanothus *'Concha'*: dense clusters of brilliant, sky-blue flowers make this a popular plant for a sheltered spot.

## TREES AND SHRUBS

*Aesculus hippocastanum* (horse chestnut)
*Berberis* (barberry)
*Buddleja globosa*
*Ceanothus* (California lilac)
*Cercis siliquastrum* (Judas tree)
*Choisya ternata* (Mexican orange blossom)
*Clematis montana* and large-flowered hybrids
*Crataegus* (hawthorn)
*Crinodendron hookerianum* (lantern tree)
*Davidia involucrata* (handkerchief tree)
*Deutzia gracilis, D. rosea*
*Genista hispanica* (Spanish gorse)
*Kerria japonica*
*Kolkwitzia amabilis* (beauty bush)
*Laburnum*
*Magnolia soulangiana*
*Malus* (apple, crab apple)
*Paeonia* (peony)
*Pieris*
*Potentilla fruticosa* (cinquefoil)
*Prunus* (ornamental cherry)
*Rhododendron* (including azaleas)
*Robinia hispida, R. margaretta*
*Rosmarinus officinalis* (rosemary)
*Sambucus racemosa plumosa* 'Aurea'
    (red-berried elder)
*Sorbus aria* (whitebeam), *S. aucuparia*
    (mountain ash)
*Spiraea arguta* (bridal wreath)
*Syringa* (lilac)
*Viburnum opulus* (guelder rose),
    *V. plicatum* (Japanese snowball bush)
*Weigela*
*Wisteria*

## PERENNIALS AND BEDDING PLANTS

*Ajuga reptans*
*Aurinia saxatilis (Alyssum saxatile)*
    (gold dust)
*Aquilegia* (columbine)
*Armeria* (sea pink)
*Aubrieta*
*Dicentra spectabilis* (bleeding heart)
*Euphorbia* (spurge)
*Geranium*
*Helianthemum* (rock rose)
*Iberis* (candytuft)
*Lithodora diffusa*
*Primula* (primrose)
*Saxifraga umbrosa*

## BULBS

—

*Allium*
*Anemone* (windflower)
*Hyacinthoides non-scripta* (English bluebell)
*Convallaria majalis* (lily-of-the-valley)
*Fritillaria imperialis* (crown imperial)
*Hyacinthus* (hyacinth)
*Leucojum aestivum* (summer snowflake)
*Tulipa* (tulip)

# water garden: *ponds*

*There is a water feature to suit every garden, no matter how small, and it is well worth taking the trouble to build one. Apart from the enjoyment you will gain from the sparkling water, the fish, and the colorful pond plants, all sorts of beneficial wildlife will be attracted to your garden pool, as well.*

### Add moving water to ponds

A garden pool is always attractive, even when the reflective surface of the water is completely still—but it is even more enjoyable when the water moves. It sparkles and throws off light, making a pleasant splashing sound and helping to keep oxygen levels high for healthy fish and plants.

Movement can be provided by fountains or waterfalls, and large pools can incorporate both. A submersible pump is the easiest way to power them. Fountain kits with a variety of heads for different effects are extremely easy to install once a power supply is made available (use a professional electrician for this). Waterfalls require a little more work. Natural-looking cascades can be tricky to build; avoid preformed fiberglass waterfall sections, and construct a water course lined with butyl, concealed by flat slabs of natural stone to provide the drops.

▼ *The splash of moving water, whether from a waterfall or a fountain, helps to bring a garden pool to life.*

### WILDLIFE AND THE POND

A surprising variety of wildlife will find its way to your garden once a pool is established, and much of it will be helpful in your fight against garden pests. Frogs, toads, and newts eat large numbers of  insects, and their feeding area extends much farther than the immediate environs of the pond. Birds, who are also valuable pest controllers, will visit the pond in order to drink and bathe, and slug-munching predators will quench their thirst here, too. The spectacular dragonflies that can be seen darting over the surface are not only colorful and attractive but fearsome insect predators. A small "beach" and shallow area of the pond fringed by marginal plants will encourage a range of creatures to visit, and insure that mammals can reach the water safely.

## how to make a garden pond

Late spring is the perfect time of year to construct and stock a garden pool. It's an easier process than many people think, and a pond enhances any style of garden. Always site a pool in an open, sunny position, away from overhanging trees.

1 Select the type of pond base you require. Molded fiberglass ponds are popular (**below**), but there is a restricted choice of shapes and sizes. A flexible liner can be used for any shape of pool and is easy to transport home. Butyl rubber has the longest life, but laminated PVC is cheaper.

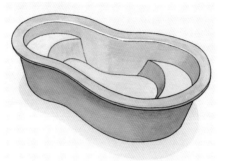

2 Mark out the shape of the pool with rope or a trickle of sand (**below**); simple, flowing shapes are best. Excavate the soil to the correct depth, sloping the sides slightly and creating a shelf for marginal plants some 10in/25cm wide and 8in/20cm below water level. Check that the top of the pond is absolutely level.

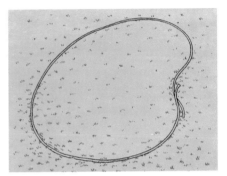

3 You should then remove sharp stones or any other objects that may puncture the liner and cover the base and shelves of the excavation with a smooth layer of sand (**left**). Stretch the liner across the hole; however, it is important not to try to drape the liner into it. You should then weight down the liner edges with bricks.

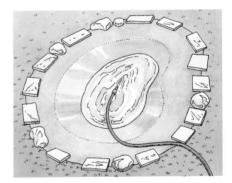

4 Lay a hose in the center of the liner and turn the water on (**above**). The weight of water will gradually stretch the liner and pull it into the hole, moulding it to fit the excavation perfectly. Once the pond is full, trim away surplus liner to leave a 6in/15cm margin all around that can be concealed with a stone edging to the pool.

◀ *Ponds will look after themselves as long as you get the right balance between plants, the wildlife, and water. Make a pool as large as you can, with a minimum depth of 2ft/60cm: very small ponds are the most difficult to keep in good condition.*

# water garden: *ponds*

*Fish are not essential in a garden pond, but they add a great deal of interest to it and will prevent mosquitoes becoming a problem. Aquatic plants such as* Nymphaea *(water lilies) are often the crowning glories of a pool; this is the perfect time to plant them, or to divide existing plants.*

### Introduce fish to garden pools

Any area of still water is likely to be visited by mosquitoes for the purpose of laying eggs, and once the eggs hatch swarms of insects can make life in the garden very unpleasant. Adding fish to the pond provides the perfect answer; they will eat the larvae as soon as they hatch and prevent them reaching adulthood. They are also very attractive, and add life and movement to the water.

Goldfish are the most common type of fish for ponds. They are cheap and easy to buy, and usually problem free. Golden Orfe are also popular with their long, slender shapes and attractive, light gold color.

Shubunkins are a type of goldfish which have mottled shades of silver, blue, red, brown, and black, while Fantails have attractive double tails.

The recommended stocking rate for fish to keep their environment healthy is three to five fish per square yard/meter of surface area of water.

▲ *When stocking fish ponds, it is important to bear in mind the recommended stocking rate of three to five fish per square yard/meter.*

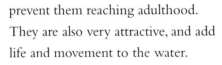

## DIVIDE DEEP-WATER AQUATICS

Aquatic plants such as *Nymphaea* (water lilies) and *Aponogeton distachyos* (water hawthorn) eventually grow too large for their planting baskets, and this has a detrimental effect on their growth and flowering. They can be divided at this time of year, giving you extra plants while improving the existing ones.

Lift the basket out of the water (it may take two people) and remove the plant; very overgrown plants may need to have the basket cut away. Divide the plant into smaller sections, each with a healthy growing point. You may need a sharp spade or knife to cut the rootstock. Replant the sections in new baskets of good loam topped with grit. Return them to the pool.

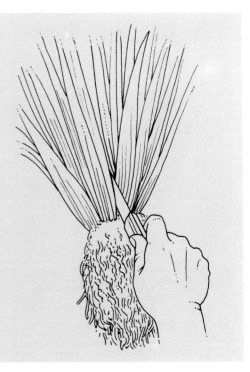

## plant aquatics in ponds

The right mix of plants is vital to keep water gardens healthy. Oxygenating plants such as *Elodea canadensis* (Canadian pondweed) are essential to keep the water clear, but aquatics with floating leaves, such as water lilies and water hawthorn, also have an important part to play.

1 Line a perforated plastic planting basket with a piece of ordinary sacking (**below**) and then fill it with good quality, fertile, loamy soil.

2 Plant the aquatic in the soil, firm in, and water thoroughly. Cover the exposed surface soil with gravel or pebbles to prevent it from being washed out of the basket (**below**).

3 Gently lower the basket into the pool until it is resting on the bottom or marginal shelf, as appropriate (**left**). Using planting baskets is better than planting direct into a layer of soil at the base of the pool as you can remove and trim plants more easily to control their growth.

4 Oxygenating plants are often sold as bunches of unrooted stems, and attaching a small piece of lead weight helps prevent them from floating to the surface. They root quickly though if the bases of the bunches are firmed into wet soil in the planting baskets (**right**).

5 Varieties of *Nymphaea* (water lily) vary in the optimum depth of water they require. Those that require shallow conditions can be planted in deeper areas by setting the planting basket on bricks or blocks to raise its height.

◄ *Feed pond fish with specially formulated food through spring and summer, but remove any food that remains uneaten after 10 minutes.*

# kitchen garden: *planting and sowing*

*Crops in the kitchen garden are growing apace. If the weather is dry, some are likely to need watering to keep them growing strongly, but it's important to know when to water. It should now be safe to sow pole beans in the open: by the time the seedlings appear, frosts should be a thing of the past.*

### Sow pole and bush beans outdoors

The soil should now be warm enough for bean seeds to germinate

◄ *Flowers on climbing bean plants sometimes fall without setting pods. This is generally due to dry soil conditions; watering will cure the problem.*

quickly, and by the end of the month, the seedlings should be safe from frosts.

Bush beans are sown in single rows, spaced some 3in/7.5cm apart. Climbing beans and pole beans need supports, and they are generally put in place before sowing; a double row of bamboo stakes, crossing at the top, works well. High yields have also been obtained from rows of stakes spaced 2ft/60cm apart, with stakes 12in/30cm apart in the row, sowing two seeds at the base of each stake.

There are many varieties of bush and pole beans available. With dwarf bush beans, look for varieties that hold their pods well clear of the ground because this avoids beans being eaten by slugs or spoiled by soil splashes. Purple- or gold-podded varieties are easy to pick because the beans are more visible. Stringless

varieties of pole bean are popular because the pods are usually more tender, and they stay in good condition longer.

### WATER VEGETABLES AS REQUIRED

A dry spell at this time of year can result in a check to the growth of young plants, and watering may be necessary. Leafy vegetables such as cabbage and spinach respond well, giving an increased yield at harvest time if they have received a steady water supply throughout the growing season. All transplanted vegetables should be watered after planting until they are well established. Other vegetables, however, should not be watered too soon because watering stimulates leafy growth that may be at the expense of flowering and crop production. Beans and peas should not normally be watered until they have started to flower (unless the plants are actually wilting), but once flowering begins, regular watering will help the flowers to set and promote the formation of a good supply of tender beans.

## plant vegetables in containers

Not everyone has room for a vegetable plot, but almost every garden has sufficient space for a few vegetables in pots and growing bags on the patio. If the right varieties are chosen, the harvest can be surprisingly good. When using pots and tubs, insure they have sufficient drainage holes and place a layer of crocks or other coarse drainage material at the base before filling with compost.

1 Prepare tubs and large pots in the normal way. Make sure there are sufficient drainage holes and place a layer of crocks or other coarse drainage material over the base before adding soil mix (**below**). The mix can be soilless or loam-based, as you prefer.

3 Growing bags can also be used for vegetables other than tomatoes (**below**). A bush-type zucchini plant (one plant per bag—it will grow quite large) will give a good crop, and try climbing beans in growing bags placed at the base of fences or walls for the plants to climb up. Both crops need frequent watering.

▼ *Zucchini make excellent subjects for a growing bag, but they will need frequent and careful watering.*

2 Tomatoes, eggplants (**below**), and sweet bell peppers are among the most commonly grown vegetables in tubs, and young plants that have been hardened off can be planted out now. Add water-retaining granules to the soil mix to cut down the amount of watering required.

4 Other vegetables that can be tried in tubs or growing bags include potatoes, beets, kohlrabi, carrots, bush beans (**below**), lettuce, and radish. Choose fast-maturing, compact-growing varieties—there are several that have been bred specifically for growing in containers on patios or balconies.

# kitchen garden: *pests and diseases*

*Birds are normally welcome garden visitors, helping to keep a wide variety of insect pests under control. Unfortunately, they also have less social habits, and can be a real nuisance in the kitchen garden when they start eating the crops. Particularly susceptible crops should be protected now.*

### Protect crops from birds

Much as we like to see wild birds visiting the garden, they become distinctly unpopular when they start wreaking havoc among developing food crops. The soft fruit season will soon be at its peak, and many birds—particularly blue jays—are just as fond of the juicy fruits as we are, demolishing raspberries and strawberries with amazing speed. Peas are also at risk: colorful, noisy jays are often also the main culprits in eating these.

Where possible, protect susceptible crops with netting, ideally in the form of a fruit cage to allow easy access. Strawberries can be protected with low polyethylene or netting tunnels. Where these are not practical, bird scarers can be tried, as shown on page 193.

### PROTECT FRUIT FROM MAGGOTS

Most people will have had the experience of biting into an apparently perfect apple only to find extensive maggot damage. The usual culprit is the larva of the codling moth, and the adults are on the wing any time now. Chemical control of the moth is difficult, but damage reduction can usually be achieved biologically with pheromone traps. They are hung in the trees and lure the male moths to the trap by the use of female pheromones; sticky paper inside the trap insures that the males cannot escape and breed. Such traps were originally used by commercial growers to indicate the best times to use insecticide sprays, but in the garden they can be used as an effective control.

▲ *The soft fruit season is probably the favorite for birds. You will need to protect your garden to prevent them feasting on your crops.*

# protect strawberries

Strawberries are a favourite delicacy for many gardeners but without some timely precautions birds, slugs, or disease are likely to devour them before we get the chance. Now is the time to take action to protect the crop, well before the fruits start to ripen.

1 Strawberries are carried very close to the ground, making them vulnerable to damp conditions, soil splashes, and attack by a range of soil-based pests such as slugs and woodlice. This is a good time to surround the plants with clean straw (**right**), tucking it well under the crowns to keep the developing fruit dry and clear of the soil.

2 Where straw is not easy to obtain, fiber or polyethylene mulching mats or sheets can be used instead (**below, left**). They prevent soil splashes and suppress weed growth, but are not so good at keeping slugs and other pests at bay.

3 Many garden birds are extremely partial to strawberries and will be drawn like a magnet when the fruit starts to redden. The only reliable way to protect the plants is by netting (**left**), but as strawberries are so low growing this is not too difficult or expensive.

4 There is no point in simply throwing netting over the plants because the fruit will still be accessible to birds. Strawberry cages are available, or you can make a framework of stakes or plastic poles to support the netting over the plants. Arrange the netting so that it will be quick and easy to remove and replace at picking time.

5 Where birds cause a lot of damage it might be worth investing in a walk-in fruit cage in which all kinds of soft fruit, such as currants, strawberries, raspberries, and blueberries, can be grown safely. Initially expensive, but such a cage is definitely worth it for large crops.

◄ *Silver leaf is a common disease of plums. Badly affected branches should be pruned back until they no longer show a brown stain in the wood.*

# greenhouse: *general tasks*

*As temperatures and the amount and intensity of sunlight increase, more and more attention will need to be paid to watering and ventilating the greenhouse. This can be difficult if you are usually out during the day, but automatic systems can do the job for you.*

## Automatic systems

Greenhouses often have to be left unattended during the working day, and this can cause real problems. The weather can be very changeable at

▼ *Trickle watering systems deliver water from a reservoir or the mains through a series of small bore tubes to individual pots or plants.*

this time of year, making it very difficult to judge the amount of ventilation or watering that will be needed while you are out. Automated watering and ventilation systems help to overcome these problems. Automatic ventilators are temperature controlled, and when fitted to at least one roof vent

(preferably more) will help to prevent overheating. Watering systems can be bought in kit form. Trickle systems are most popular for small greenhouses; overhead sprinklers can also be used but are more expensive. Other options are timed watering, using a computer fitted to the supply faucet, or capillary matting.

### CONTINUE PRICKING OUT SEEDLINGS

It is important to prick out seedlings before they become overcrowded in the flats. If they are left for too long, the roots become entangled, leading to root damage when they are eventually separated. Overcrowded seedlings are also more prone to fungus diseases, and water and nutrient shortages. When sowing flats of plants, try to sow the seeds as thinly and evenly as possible. This means the seedlings can be left that much longer in their flats without coming to harm, and will take some of the pressure off you during the busy spring period.

# pot up
# rooted cuttings

Softwood cuttings taken in early spring are usually quick to root, and should be potted up individually as soon as they have developed a good root system.

1 It is not too difficult to tell when cuttings have rooted successfully. The growing tips take on a fresh, green, lively appearance and the whole cutting looks strong and vigorous (**right**). New growth will begin, and it is sometimes possible to see root tips through the drainage holes at the base of the pot.

2 Once the cuttings have reached this stage it is time to pot them up. Gently use a dibble or pencil to prise up a cutting at the edge of the tray, levering it carefully from below to avoid tearing off any delicate new roots (**left**). If the root development is not as advanced as expected, leave the cuttings undisturbed for a while longer.

3 If there is plenty of fresh root growth, move the cuttings to individual 3½in/8cm pots (**right**). Unnecessary delay means the roots will become increasingly entangled, leading to unavoidable damage when the cuttings eventually have to be separated for potting up.

## PINCH OUT
## YOUNG PLANTS

Plants such as fuchsias and pelargoniums that have been raised from seed or softwood cuttings need to be encouraged to branch out to produce bushy specimens. This is done by "stopping" them—pinching out the growing tip when the plants are around 4in/10cm high. This will result in strong young growths being produced from the leaf axils down the stem.

# fruit and vegetables

The greenhouse provides the opportunity to grow crops that just wouldn't thrive in our climate outdoors. Tomatoes must be the best known of all greenhouse crops, but there are several others that are worth growing.

## Tomatoes

Most greenhouse tomatoes are grown as a single stem (cordon) because bush varieties require too much space. They can be supported by stakes, but it is more usual to grow them up twine that is secured to the greenhouse roof, twisting the stems carefully around the twine as they grow. Side-shoots should be removed from the leaf joints as soon as they are visible; it is easier to do this in

the morning when the plants are full of moisture. Pinch out the growing tip once it reaches the greenhouse roof.

Plants may need watering several times a day; mix water-retaining granules in the soil in pots and growing bags. Supplying sufficient water is particularly important once flowering and fruit-setting starts, as one incidence of wilting now can cause blossom end rot on a whole batch of fruits. Once the first flowers appear, give plants a fine spray of water every day to help the fruit to set, and begin feeding with a high-potash liquid fertilizer.

## Sweet Bell Peppers

Sweet bell peppers do not require side-shooting—they are grown as a bush and are generally provided with a stake as support. Tie the plant's main stem to the stake as it develops. Requirements for watering, feeding, and misting are the same as for tomatoes.

For high yields, pick sweet peppers while they are still green because allowing them to ripen on the plants reduces the total number of peppers produced. If picked as soon as they start to show a tinge of color they will usually continue to ripen over the next few days.

## Eggplant

They prefer slightly higher temperatures than tomatoes and peppers, but are otherwise grown in the same way. Like peppers, they are bushy plants, usually supported by a stake. Normally only four or five fruits are obtained from a plant. They should be cut when they are fully colored—normally deep purple, though different colored

◀ *Eggplants like to be in warmer conditions than some other greenhouse crops such as sweet bell peppers and tomatoes.*

▲ *Tomatoes, the most common greenhouse crop, may need to be watered several times a day.*

◄ *Melons: flowers will generally need to be pollinated by hand—you can use a small brush to achieve this.*

varieties are also available. Eggplants are prone to the usual greenhouse pests, but whitefly are often especially troublesome.

### Cucumbers

These climbing plants like warmth and high humidity. They are best trained up twine in the same way as tomatoes. All side-shoots produced should have their growing points pinched out at two leaves beyond the flower. Male flowers must be removed because pollinated fruits are misshapen and bitter; the male and female flowers can be distinguished by the miniature cucumber which is present right from the start on the females. Even "all-female" varieties do occasionally produce the odd male flower, so check them regularly.

Water the plants frequently and feed with a high-potash liquid fertilizer. Harvest cucumbers as soon as they are large enough; they are best cut in the morning, when they are firmest.

### Melons

Train the stems up twine and pinch out the tip when it reaches the top. Side-shoots should have their growing points pinched out when they have made five leaves. The sublaterals that develop will bear the fruit, and should be pinched out at two leaves beyond the flower.

Pollinate the flowers by hand. Keep the plants well watered and regularly fed with high-potash liquid fertilizer. Harvest the fruit as soon as they are ripe.

### BIOLOGICAL CONTROL

Greenhouse crops are particularly prone to two major pests, red spider mite and whitefly. Biological controls have proved an effective way of minimizing damage from them. Red spider mite is controlled by a predatory mite, *Phytosieulius persimilis*, while whitefly is parasitized by a small wasp, *Encarsia formosa*. Controls are available by mail order and from most garden centers. They are not intended to wipe out the pest infestation but to keep it to an acceptable level.

# summer

*Summer seems like the culmination of the gardener's year—the season that bears the fruit of all our efforts. The days are long, the weather is warm and sunny, and what better place to be than in the garden, enjoying the color and fragrance of the flowers, and the rewarding harvest of home-grown fruit and vegetables?*

# early summer

*The garden retains the freshness of spring while the floral bounty of summer starts to unfold. While there's still plenty to do, the hectic spring rush is calming down, and we can enjoy the garden at a more leisurely pace, especially as the daylight hours stretch out into the evening now.*

### The weather and watering

While everyone longs for a good spell of settled, warm sunny weather, we also need enough rain to keep the plants growing strongly but droughts do seem to be becoming more common every year. Early summer is often a time of mixed weather with heavy storms depositing gallons of water on the garden within a few minutes, but gardeners need to be prepared to get out the hose or watering can if the weather remains dry for more than a few days. It pays to conserve water by adding organic matter to the soil to increase its water-holding capacity, and by mulching to prevent evaporation from the soil surface.

### Plants and produce

At least, though, it's safe to stop worrying about damaging night frosts, and all those tender plants can now go outside, but do take care to harden them off properly first. Conditions should be near perfect for plant growth, and fast-growing plants now need regular care to keep them tied into their supports.

◄ *Flower borders are bursting with color in early summer. Opposites on the color wheel, yellow and purple provide a striking contrast.*

The early spring-flowering shrubs such as forsythia have had their moment of glory, and once the flowers are over it's time to think about pruning the plants. Roses will soon be in full bloom, but all too often the display is spoiled by pests and diseases. The latter can be prevented by regular fungicide sprays, and plants must be checked regularly for pests and treated with the appropriate controls as soon as any are spotted.

The perfect foil for burgeoning flower borders is an emerald-green lawn. Keep the lawn watered, fed, and regularly mown (not too short) for the best results. And note that the vegetable garden should now be producing an increasing number of crops to harvest; this is the time of year when they really taste their best. Toward the end of the summer the strawberries will be ready for picking, with the promise of raspberries and the rest of the soft fruit crop soon to follow.

## EARLY SUMMER TASKS

**Ornamental garden**

- *Plant out tender bedding and sow biennials and perennials*
- *Prune spring-flowering shrubs and trim hedges*
- *Trim alpines after flowering*
- *Tie climbers to their supports; increase them by layering*
- *Tie-in border plants and apply a liquid feed; deadhead as appropriate*
- *Cut down euphorbias that are past their best*
- *Treat pests as they appear*
- *Divide and replant flag irises and Primulas (primroses) after flowering*
- *Take cuttings of Dianthus (pinks)*
- *Feed and water plants in containers*
- *Spray roses against pests and diseases as necessary. Remove suckers*
- *Lift and divide Narcissus (daffodils)*
- *Mulch borders to keep down weeds*

▲ *It's now safe to set even the more tender bedding plants outdoors.*

**Lawns**

- *Continue regular mowing and watering, weeding, and feeding lawns as necessary*
- *Mow areas of naturalized bulbs*
- *Deal with moles as molehills appear*

**Kitchen garden**

- *Continue weeding and watering as necessary*
- *Earth-up potatoes and lift early varieties*
- *Sow late crops such as radishes, summer spinach, lettuces, and turnips*
- *Continue planting out beans, leeks, and winter brassicas*
- *Pinch out beans and harvest early peas*
- *Plant out outdoor tomatoes and peppers*
- *Check vegetables for caterpillars*
- *Remove runners from strawberries*
- *Thin young tree fruits*
- *Summer prune red and white currants, gooseberries*

▲ *Sweet bell peppers will grow well outdoors in mild areas.*

**Greenhouse**

- *Damp down and ventilate regularly*
- *Feed developing food crops (tomatoes, cucumbers, sweet bell peppers, eggplant)*
- *Remove male flowers from cucumbers and side-shoots from tomatoes*
- *Control pests such as whitefly and red spider mite*
- *Sow cinerarias*
- *Move pot plants such as azaleas and winter cherry outside for the summer*

# useful insects

There is a tendency to regard all insect life in the garden as potentially harmful to plants but not all insects are bad news—some are real allies in the fight against pests. It's important to be able to recognize who are your friends, because most insecticides are not so discriminating, and spraying and killing any natural predators will make the problem worse.

## Beetles

Although some beetles are pests, there are many useful species. These include ground beetles, which live on the soil surface, hunting out insects, slugs, and worms during the hours of darkness; rove beetles such as the scorpion-like devil's coach horse; and the familiar ladybugs (see opposite).

## Capsids

Yes, some capsids are well-known pests but there are other species which are definitely helpful to gardeners. The best known is the predatory black-kneed capsid that helps control aphids and red spider mites on fruit trees. Similar in appearance to capsids are anthocorid bugs, another useful ally, especially on fruit.

## Centipedes

Golden brown centipedes scurry over the soil in search of prey—insects, their eggs and larvae, along with small slugs and worms. They are often confused with millipedes (a pest) but millipedes are darker, have more legs that form a thick fringe down the sides, and roll up into a ball rather than running for cover when disturbed.

▲ *Slugs and worms may be dealt with by some useful kinds of beetles, although others are themselves garden pests.*

◀ *Hoverflies like to eat aphids and other soft-bodied insect pests and so are very helpful to the gardener.*

◄ *The familiar ladybug has a voracious appetite, consuming huge numbers of aphids and other pests in its lifetime.*

Both adults and, more particularly, larvae feed on large numbers of insect pests, especially aphids. A single larva can consume up to 500 aphids in its three-week life. Before emerging as an adult ladybugs the larva pupates, and the yellow pupa may be mistaken for a Colorado beetle, which it superficially resembles. Ladybugs are most commonly red with either two or seven black spots, but they may also be black with red spots, yellow with black spots and black with yellow spots.

## Hoverflies

Hoverflies could easily be mistaken for bees at first glance, though their method of flight is quite different—they hover almost stationary in the air, then make short, sharp darts forward. When they are at rest it's evident that they only have one pair of wings, unlike bees and wasps that have two. The larvae of the various species of hoverfly are very small, but most are efficient predators of aphids and other soft-bodied insect pests.

## Lacewings

Lacewings are very delicate insects with pale green, almost translucent bodies, large, lacy wings and very long, constantly moving antennae. Both the adult lacewings and their larvae eat aphids; the larvae are rather insignificant, long-bodied creatures that are pale brown. Lacewings are found all round the garden, and are often attracted by lighting into houses at night.

## Ladybugs

Nearly everyone can recognize ladybugs, but perhaps not so many could identify their larvae. While the adults are almost universally regarded as harmless, their small, armadillo-like, blue and orange larvae are likely to be treated with more suspicion, and are often destroyed "to be on the safe side."

## Wasps

Wasps, as everyone knows, sting, and at the end of the summer they are a real nuisance, feasting on ripe fruit, and ruining picnics and outdoor meals. Leaving aside this antisocial behavior, for the rest of the year they are a definite asset to gardeners because they collect all manner of soft-bodied grubs and insects to feed to the young wasp larvae in the nest. Other, less highly visible wasps are also extremely useful—several species are parasitic, laying eggs in the bodies of insect pests that hatch out and slowly consume their hosts. Ichneumon wasps are some of the best known, though rarely recognized in the garden. They have long, slender bodies and are not brightly coloured like the common wasp.

---

### ENCOURAGING BENEFICIAL INSECTS

One of the best ways to help beneficial insects is to avoid using insecticide sprays if you possibly can, or to use only those that are specific to pest species and harmless to other insects. Leaving a rough area of the garden with piles of dead leaves and logs, and the hollow stems of dead plants, will also encourage a wide variety of insects. Specific crops can also be grown for them—hoverflies, for instance, will be attracted from far and wide by a patch of buckwheat in flower.

# ornamental garden: *general tasks*

*Herbaceous flower borders reach their peak later this month and into midsummer, but there is work to be done now to make sure they look their best. Stake or tie-in those plants that need it, and keep weeds in the borders under control. Climbing plants also need care and attention.*

▲ *Garden pinks (Dianthus) can be propagated easily from cuttings known as "pipings," which are inserted in a sandy, free-draining soil mix.*

### Take cuttings from pinks

Pinks are very popular garden plants. They make neat, low cushions of growth with attractive silver-gray leaves; the flowers are freely produced in a wide range of red, pink, and cream shades, and many varieties are strongly fragrant. The plants are ideal for the front of the border, pots and containers, and rock gardens.

Pinks are also very easy to propagate. They are increased from cuttings that are known as "pipings." The stem has a swollen joint where each pair of leaves clasp it; if the stem is held just below one of these joints and the top part of the stem is tugged gently, it will pull out cleanly at the leaf joint to form a ready-made cutting. Make the pipings 3–4in/7.5–10cm long; they need no more trimming and can be inserted straight into pots of moist seed and cuttings mix, and firmed in well. The ideal place to root them is in a lightly shaded cold frame where they can remain over the winter.

### TIE IN BORDER PLANTS

This is a job that needs to be done frequently—if the shoots are allowed to get too long it is impossible to tie them back into the supports without giving the plant a misshapen appearance. Provide several stakes if necessary for spreading plants, and tie individual stems to them. It is often necessary to use long pieces of twine in order to achieve a natural-looking shape: keep these as low on the stems as possible, where they will be less noticeable. Plant breeders are increasingly producing lower growing, stocky varieties of border plants, but even these will usually be improved by a little judicious support to keep them in shape.

# train and support climbers

Climbing plants add an extra dimension to a garden. They make use of vertical surfaces such as walls and fences, making them more attractive features; the surfaces also increase the overall amount of growing space, particularly valuable in small gardens. Proper support and training are essential.

## MULCH BORDERS

Clear all weed growth from borders and insure the soil is thoroughly moist before applying a thick mulch of bark, cocoa shell, or mushroom compost, etc to prevent further weed growth and retain soil moisture through the summer.

1 A wooden trellis is a popular choice for supporting a climber on a wall; it should be treated with a plant-safe wood preservative. Attach wooden battens to the wall and then screw the trellis panel onto the battens (**below**), or attach it with hooks and eyes. This enables the trellis and climber to be removed carefully when wall maintenance is necessary.

2 An alternative support is horizontal, plastic-covered wires stretched taut between screw eyes screwed into the vertical surface. Space the screw eyes every 6ft/1.8m along the wall in rows 18in/45cm above each other and screw them in firmly. Loop the wire through the eyes, twisting it at each end to secure it. Tension the wire by turning the vine eye with pliers (**below**).

3 Train the shoots of the plant as they grow, aiming to cover the support evenly. Tie the shoots in place with raffia, soft garden twine or plastic-coated metal ties, taking care not to tie them too tightly— make a figure-of-eight loop with the tie to avoid damaging stems (**right**).

4 Several climbers are particularly attractive when allowed to scramble through the branches of trees and shrubs, but avoid very vigorous varieties which will smother their host. A classic combination is *Tropaeolum speciosum* (flame nasturtium) growing through a dark conifer.

# ornamental garden: *dividing and planting*

*As some of the earlier-flowering garden plants reach the end of their season, it is time to give them a new lease of life by dividing them. And now that the risk of frosts is over, tender bedding plants can safely be set outside in their flowering positions to provide lush colors.*

## Divide and replant irises

Flag irises make a large, spreading clump once they have been established for several seasons, and the center of the clump can become bare and woody. Once they have finished flowering, plants can be lifted and divided, improving their performance for the following year. Dig up the clump of rhizomes carefully. Identify sections of rhizome around the edge of the clump that have strong young shoots and plenty of fibrous roots, and cut these out using a sharp knife. Discard the old, woody portions. Trim the leaves back to a fan shape about 9in/23cm long and then replant the sections of rhizome in groups of three or five, spacing them some 6in/15cm apart. The top half of the rhizome should remain above ground when planted.

▲ *Once the blooms of flag irises have faded, established clumps of plants can be lifted and replanted to improve next year's performance.*

### LIFT AND DIVIDE NARCISSUS (DAFFODILS)

Daffodil bulbs are usually left in the ground from year to year, but those that have been growing undisturbed for several years may start to deteriorate, sometimes becoming "blind" when they produce foliage but no flowers. When this happens it's often because they have become overcrowded, in which case you should lift and replant the bulbs.

Once the foliage has died down, lift the bulbs carefully with a garden fork and shake off the soil. Many will have formed offsets—smaller bulbs around the edge of the main bulb that eventually separate. When the offsets are large enough they will come away easily from the main bulb and can be removed. Replant all the bulbs at the correct spacing, having dug over the planting site first and added a little slow-release fertilizer to the soil.

# plant out tender bedding

Many favorite bedding plants are frost tender, and they can't be planted outside until all risk of frosts is over. They are often on sale in garden centers much too early.

Tender bedding plants need to be hardened off (i.e. gradually acclimatized to outdoor conditions) before they are planted out in their flowering positions.

Keep them in a greenhouse, conservatory or other frost-free place at night, moving them outdoors during the day, until it is safe to plant them out.

1 Before planting, prepare the beds and borders where the plants are to grow by forking the soil over thoroughly, removing any weeds. Add an application of general fertilizer and work it into the top layer of soil.

2 Water the bedding plants well the evening before you intend to plant them. When planting, remove the plants from their pots or trays by giving the container a sharp knock on a firm surface to loosen the root-ball; tease the plants apart carefully if necessary (**right**).

3 Plant with a trowel immediately they have been removed from the container (**below**)—do not leave the roots exposed to the air because they will dry out quickly and this will delay re-establishment. Firm the plants into position thoroughly, using your knuckles.

4 Once the bed is planted, water the plants well using a fine rose on the end of the hose or watering can (**below**). Since the weather is often dry and warm at this time of year frequent watering may be necessary, especially in the days immediately after planting.

◄ *Nasturtiums and marigolds provide an attractive mixture of colors, especially highlighted when planted close together.*

# ornamental garden: *pruning and trimming*

*Several shrubs whose flowers are now finished will benefit from pruning. Other plants will also be bearing faded flowers, and deadheading is an important job from now on to keep the garden looking good. It's also time to give hedges a trim to keep them neat and tidy.*

### Prune early-flowering shrubs

There are several shrubs which flower in late spring and early summer whose season is now over. They include plants such as ceanothus, *Cytisus* (broom), deutzia, kerria, *Philadelphus* (mock orange), *Spiraea*, *Syringa* (lilac), *Viburnum opulus* and *Weigela*.

These shrubs do not need annual pruning, but if they are becoming overgrown and untidy, now is a good time to tackle them.

Start as always by removing dead and diseased stems, then prune out remaining stems which are old, weak or badly placed. Use pruners or a pruning saw to cut them off at ground level. Up to one-third of the stems can be removed to thin out the growth, and allow light and air into the center of the shrub.

DEADHEAD PLANTS AS NECESSARY

The aims of deadheading are threefold—to prevent the garden from looking untidy, to conserve the strength of the plant by preventing it setting seed unnecessarily, and to encourage the production of more flowers. Plants grown for their fruit, berries, or seedheads should obviously not be deadheaded.

Most plants should have the dead flower heads snapped off or cut with pruners just above a leaf joint; one exception is rhododendrons (including azaleas). They form new buds immediately behind the old flowers, so the dead flowers must be removed very carefully by hand.

◄ *Spring-flowering shrubs such as lilac should have old and weak stems removed to allow light and air into the center of the plant.*

► *Suckers from rose rootstocks can be identified by the larger number of leaflets. Dig right down to the root to pull the sucker off.*

# trim hedges

Hedge clipping is not the most popular garden chore, but it gives a very satisfying result when it is done properly, and it is worth taking a little time and trouble to get it right. Most hedges need trimming only twice a year, now and in late summer.

1 Clearing up will usually be quicker and easier if a tarpaulin or strong plastic sheet is laid beneath the hedge to catch the clippings (**right**). Where the hedge adjoins a flowerbed or border, a strip of paving slabs running directly alongside the base of the hedge is far easier to work from than the soil of the flowerbed, and, in addition, will help when it comes to clearing up.

2 For a formal hedge, stretch a piece of level twine tautly along the top of the hedge to make sure it is cut to a straight line (**above**). The top of the hedge can be left flat, but cutting it to a pointed shape (like a rooftop) is also attractive, and helps prevent damage from snow in areas that have severe winters.

3 Hand shears are satisfactory for small hedges, but powered hedge trimmers make the job quicker and easier (**above**). Electric trimmers are popular, but great care must be taken to insure that the power cable is kept safely out of the way of the blades, and that a ground-fault interrupter (GFI)—or circuit breaker—is fitted.

4 Begin cutting the hedge from the base, working upward. The sides should slope slightly toward the top, making a wedge shape (**above**). When trimming tall hedges, use a sturdy pair of steps set parallel to the hedge to reach the top. Avoid leaning ladders or steps against the hedge because they will ruin its shape.

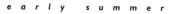

# ornamental garden: *plants in season*

The season of plenty is beginning now, with more and more
plants coming into flower by the day. Roses are among the top
favorites in bloom this month, but there are many other
flowering shrubs. Border plants are also looking particularly good.

▼ Papaver 'Patty's Plum': individual poppy
flowers tend to be short-lived, but there is
usually a long succession of blooms.

▲ *Cranesbills, or perennial geraniums, make soft mounds of attractively cut leaves topped by piercing purple-blue flowers.*

▼ *Elegant spires of flowers make the delphinium a classic border plant, perfect for a "cottage garden" effect.*

## PERENNIALS AND BEDDING PLANTS

*Achillea filipendulina* 'Gold Plate' (yarrow)
*Ageratum* (floss flower)
*Althaea*
*Aquilegia vulgaris* (granny's bonnet)
*Astrantia major* (Hattie's pincushion)
*Campanula* (bellflower)
*Coreopsis* (tickseed)
*Delphinium elatum* hybrids
*Dianthus* (carnation, pink)
*Dictamnus albas* (burning bush)
*Digitalis purpurea* (common foxglove)
*Fuchsia* (bedding varieties)
*Geranium*
*Heuchera* (coral flower)
*Iris*
*Lobelia erinus*
*Lupinus* (lupin)
*Nepeta* x *faassenii* (catmint)
*Paeonia* (peony)
*Papaver orientale* (oriental poppy)
*Pelargonium*

## BULBS

*Allium*
*Camassia leichtlinii, C. quamash* (quamash)
*Iris*
*Lilium* (lily)—pictured below

## TREES AND SHRUBS

*Abelia* x *grandiflora*
*Buddleja globosa*
*Buddleja alternifolia*
*Ceanothus* (California lilac)
*Cistus purpureus* (rock rose)
*Deutzia gracilis*
*Escallonia*
*Lonicera periclymenum* (common honeysuckle)
*Philadelphus* (mock orange)
*Potentilla* (cinquefoil)
*Pyracantha* (firethorn)
*Rhododendron*
*Rosa* (rose)
*Spiraea douglasii*
*Syringa* (lilac)
*Viburnum plicatum* (Japanese snowball bush)
*Weigela*
*Wisteria sinensis* (Chinese wisteria)

# lawns and water gardens: *general tasks*

*A well-kept lawn sets off the entire garden, so it is even more important to keep the grass up to scratch now that the rest of the garden is reaching its peak. The weather may be one thing that is working against you in your efforts to keep the grass lush and green; moles are another problem.*

## Water lawns as necessary

Grass is rarely killed by drought, but a parched, brown lawn ruins the look of the garden and often becomes overrun by weeds. With care, you can keep a beautiful green lawn without wasting water—an important consideration in these days of increasingly frequent water shortages.

Increase the turf's drought resistance by applying a bulky topdressing in the fall and by never cutting the grass too closely. Raise the height of the mower blades in dry weather. In dry spells, examine the grass closely. If it remains crushed where you walk instead of springing back up ("footprinting"), and the color of the grass is dull, it is time to water. Use an efficient sprinkler to apply a minimum of ½ in/12mm of water at a time and water late in the evening to avoid loss by evaporation.

▼ *Watering a lawn too lightly will do more harm than good by encouraging roots to form in the upper, more drought-prone layers of the soil.*

### DEAL WITH MOLE DAMAGE

Moles are one of the most frustrating garden pests. They can do terrible damage, particularly to lawns, and are almost impossible to control.  Mole scarers are rarely effective, and mole traps kill just one mole whereupon others move in to the vacant territory. The best thing to do is to grit your teeth until the mole has finished constructing his gallery of runs because tunneling then usually ceases. Sweep the molehills evenly over the lawn as soon as they appear—the soil makes a good top-dressing.

Treat anthills in the same way. They are less disfiguring but if they are squashed flat by the mower, patches of grass will be killed and weeds will colonize the area. Ant colonies can be treated with insecticide if really necessary.

# make a water feature

Water, especially moving water, is a great addition to any garden. A cobble or millstone water feature takes up little space, and is safe where there are young children. It also provides the sparkle and splash that makes water so entrancing. A competent electrician should provide the power supply to run the pump.

### WATER WITHOUT A POND

It is not always practical to have a pond in the garden, particularly if there are young children in the family or as frequent visitors—unsupervised toddlers can drown in seconds, even in shallow water. However, this does not mean that a gardener needs to be deprived of the pleasure of water entirely. Any water feature that does not include standing water should be safe, and many wall fountains are available as kits, though with a little imagination it is easy to make your own. Larger garden centers or water garden specialists can provide you with all you need, including practical advice.

1 Excavate a hole to provide the water reservoir, making it at least 16in/40cm deep with a diameter some 24in/60cm wider than the millstone, incorporating a shallow lip all round the edge. Line the excavation with butyl rubber. A rigid fiberglass mold or plastic tank could be used instead.

2 Set a submersible pump at the base of the reservoir. Build two or three columns of bricks or concrete blocks in the center of the reservoir to take the weight of the millstone, and lay a rust-proof steel mesh over the top of them (**right**). The edges of the mesh are supported by the lip at the top of the reservoir.

3 Run a flexible pipe from the pump up the center of the millstone, with a rigid pipe to deliver the water at the top. This pipe should be set below the surface of the stone to obtain a bubbling spout rather than a jet of water. Arrange cobblestones on the mesh around the edge of the stone (**left**).

4 Fill the reservoir with water and switch on the pump, adjusting the flow to achieve the right effect. Water will bubble out of the center of the millstone and flow over the pebbles back into the reservoir, but it will need frequent topping up to make up for evaporation. Switching the pump off and allowing the stone to dry out regularly will help prevent the formation of algae on the stone.

▶ *Water plays an important rôle in Japanese gardens. This bamboo water feature adds an effective Far Eastern note.*

# kitchen garden: *general tasks*

*A range of pests and diseases can ruin the appearance of home-grown vegetables and fruit, but if you act promptly it is possible to protect plants against some of them. If you do not want to use chemical pesticides there are usually more environmentally friendly alternatives available.*

### Protect fruit against pests and diseases

Codling moth is probably the most troublesome apple pest prevalent at this time of year. The small adult

▼ *The dense brown felt that forms on mildewed gooseberry fruits can be rubbed off before cooking, but it is a time-consuming job.*

moths fly at night and lay eggs on developing fruit and nearby leaves. When the larvae hatch, they make their way into the fruit and eat their way through it. Pheromone traps (see page 74) give some degree of control, but if you prefer a chemical remedy, an insecticide such as permethrin can be used in the

middle of this month and again at the beginning of midsummer.

Also look out for gooseberry mildew that starts as a furry white coating on the shoot tips and young fruits, and soon develops into a dense brown felt on the fruits. A range of fungicides can be used to protect plants against the disease.

## CATERPILLARS AND BRASSICA CROPS

Most gardeners like to see butterflies in the garden but few of them would welcome the cabbage white. It lays eggs on the leaves of any type of brassica, and they hatch out into ravenous caterpillars that can strip a plant bare in a few days. Hand picking and destroying the  caterpillars is possible, but not very practical. A better bet is a biological control that is generally very successful. It combines spores and toxins from a natural bacteria, Bacillus thuringiensis. Once infected, the caterpillars die within a few days, but they stop feeding and damaging the plants immediately they have ingested the spray.

# *earth up potatoes*

When the young shoots of potato plants first appear above ground, drawing soil over them gives protection against a late frost. As the plants grow, continuing to earth up prevents bitter green patches forming on the tubers.

1 In cold regions a late frost can still occur in early summer. If potato shoots are just appearing through the soil and frost is forecast, draw soil up to cover the shoots completely. Alternatively, cover the shoots with sheets of newspaper or row covers held in place with soil or stones, but remove this the following day.

2 As the top-growth develops, continue to draw soil up the sides of the stems at regular intervals to form a ridge (**right**). This prevents tubers near the soil surface from being exposed to light that will turn them green; green tubers are inedible as they contain poisonous solanine, which causes severe stomach upsets.

### HARVESTING PEAS

Early sowings of peas should now be ready for picking. They are best harvested as soon as the peas reach a useable size—don't leave them to become too big or they get tough and starchy. Wait until the shapes of the peas are just visible through the pod.

3 As an alternative to the process of earthing-up, potatoes can be grown under black poly mulch. Seed potatoes are planted in cultivated soil and black plastic sheeting is laid over the surface; as the shoots develop, slits are cut in the sheeting in the appropriate positions to allow the top-growth through.

4 The earliest potatoes are usually ready to harvest when the plants begin to flower. Scrape away a little soil to expose the tubers—they are ready to lift when they are the size of an egg (**above**). Yields are only small at this stage, but these early crops are particularly delicious.

# kitchen garden: *sowing and planting*

*The sowing season for vegetables is not yet over. In fact there are several types that can be sown now to extend the season and provide crops in late summer. It's also time to think even farther ahead and plant out some of the vegetables that will see you through the winter days.*

## Sow successional crops

Although the main sowing season is over, there are several vegetables that can be sown successfully over the next few weeks for picking in late summer or early fall. They include radishes, carrots, beets, corn salad, lettuces, kohlrabi, arugula, radicchio, turnips, rutabaga, and spinach. Care should be taken with the choice of varieties as the summer wears on because some are more suitable for late-season sowing than others, being resistant to bolting, or diseases such as mildew.

Lettuce often fails to germinate when sown in summer because it is subject to high temperature dormancy. This means lettuce should be sown with extra care in hot spells. Water the drills well immediately before sowing to reduce the soil temperature, and sow in the cool of evening for the best results.

### PLANT OUT WINTER CROPS

Winter crops such as Brussels sprouts, cabbages, kale, and leeks can be planted out now. All brassicas (members of the cabbage family) need to be planted very firmly because loose planting leads to loosely formed heads without a dense heart, and "blown" sprouts. In all but very heavy soils, firm newly-planted brassicas very thoroughly with the sole of your boot; firm again after watering. If you gently tug a leaf of the plant, the leaf should tear before the plant's roots move in the soil.

◄ *Fast-maturing radish can be sown at intervals all through the summer to provide a succession of young, tender roots.*

## *plant bell peppers outdoors*

Once the risk of frost is over, tender crops such as sweet bell peppers and tomatoes can be planted safely out of doors. Make sure the young plants are thoroughly hardened off before setting them in their final positions.

1 Sturdy young plants that are filling an 3½in/8cm pot with roots are the best size for planting out. Select vigorous, healthy plants with deep green leaves; white root tips should be just visible through the drainage holes at the base of the pot.

2 Remove the plant from its pot by placing two fingers either side of the plant's stem, inverting the pot and knocking the rim against a hard surface, eg, the edge of a table. The whole root-ball should slide out of the pot (**left**).

3 Dig a hole with a trowel in well-prepared soil in the vegetable garden and set the plant in it (**left**), covering the top of the root-ball with soil and firming in well with your knuckles. Water well immediately after planting.

4 If the weather should turn cool or windy after planting, young plants can be protected by covering them with a cloche. As the plants grow taller, two cloches can be turned on end to still provide some shelter.

5 Peppers and other tender vegetable crops also grow well when planted in growing bags on a patio (**above**), often a warmer, more sheltered position. Set two plants per bag for the best results. Cut a cross in the plastic and tuck the flaps under to make the planting hole. Plants in growing bags need regular watering and liquid feeding, particularly in dry or windy weather.

◀ *Green bell peppers are simply fruits picked when immature. If allowed, they will ripen to red, orange, or yellow, according to variety.*

# greenhouse: *general tasks*

*The greenhouse provides ideal conditions for pests, and they've got to be tackled promptly to stop them from multiplying out of control. Greenhouse food crops are developing well, but in order to continue they need to be given the correct fertilizers, especially if they are in pots or growing bags.*

### Feed greenhouse food crops

Greenhouse crops are likely to be growing either in a small area of border soil that is often depleted of plant food by continued cropping, or in restricted volumes of soil mix in pots or growing bags that cannot hope to supply all the nutrients

required throughout the growing season. This means that greenhouse crops need regular applications of fertilizer. The usual crops grown— eggplant, bell peppers, cucumbers, and tomatoes—are fruiting types. They are not normally given fertilizer until they start flowering to

avoid the production of leafy growth at the expense of flowers and fruit. Once flowering starts they can be given a compound fertilizer containing some nitrogen and phosphorus, with high levels of potash. Liquid tomato fertilizers are ideal for all fruiting crops.

▲ *Boost greenhouse crops by regular feeding. Liquid fertilizers are fast acting and rapidly absorbed by the plants.*

### KEEP PESTS UNDER CONTROL

The warm, protected conditions of the greenhouse encourage rapid, soft growth of plants and provide a paradise for many pests. They can often multiply so rapidly at this time of year that heavy, damaging infestations build up in a matter of days. It is necessary to be constantly vigilant, examining plants carefully for the first signs of a problem. Check the tender young shoot tips where aphids often

cluster, and the undersides of leaves where whitefly and red spider mite hide themselves.

Use either biological controls or one of the many insecticides suitable for greenhouse pest control. When using pesticides, read the directions carefully and follow them to the letter. And be sure to allow the necessary harvest intervals to elapse where food crops are being grown.

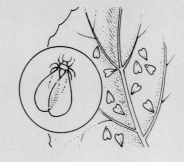

## SOW CINERARIAS

Cinerarias, with their bright, daisy-like flowers, make cheerful winter- and spring-flowering pot plants for the home. Sow seed now in a pot of seed and cuttings mix, scattering the fine seed as thinly as possible. Cover lightly with more mix or a thin layer of silver sand, fit a propagator top and germinate in the greenhouse or a cold frame. Seeds should germinate in 10–14 days, and plants sown now should flower in five or six months' time. Flowers are available in a good range of colors, including red, pink, purple, blue, and white, and there are often a good number of bicolors in seed mixtures.

# train cucumbers and tomatoes

These popular greenhouse salad crops should be growing strongly by now. Frequent, regular attention will keep their growth under control and make sure of good crops later on.

1 Greenhouse tomatoes are usually grown as single-stem cordons, trained up stakes or twine. If left to themselves they will form a bush of dense leafy growth; this takes up too much space in the greenhouse and makes the plants difficult to care for.

3 Greenhouse cucumbers produce the best fruits from unfertilized flowers; fertilization gives swollen, misshapen, bitter-tasting cucumbers. To prevent fertilization, male flowers should be removed from the plants as soon as they are seen.

4 Male and female flowers are easy to distinguish; females have a miniature fruit at the base of the flower right from the start (**left**). Even so-called "all-female" varieties produce the odd rogue male flower, which must be removed.

2 Side-shoots are removed as soon as they are large enough to snap off easily (**below**). Check each plant every few days; if the side-shoots become too large they are difficult to remove without damaging the plant. Early morning is the best time to snap them off cleanly.

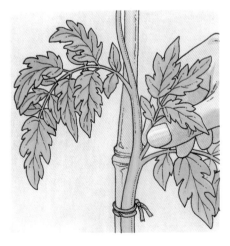

# midsummer

*Flowers are at their peak in most gardens now, and deadheading, watering, staking, and harvesting will keep gardeners busy. Make the most of the good weather to enjoy the garden, and on warm nights also make sure you stroll around after dusk to appreciate the night-scented flowers.*

### Lawns

Lawn grasses are among the first plants to show distress in dry spells. Continue mowing the grass frequently to keep it looking good, but raise the height of the mower blades a little to give the lawn more drought resistance. As long as the clippings are very short, they can be left on the lawn in dry spells to help conserve moisture.

### Plants

Rock garden plants and some early-flowering perennials will look better for being tidied up now, so once flowering has finished, cut them back hard. Continue to prune deciduous, flowering shrubs after flowering, too, to keep them to the required size. Many shrubs can also be propagated from semiripe cuttings this month and next.

▶ *Keep the flower borders looking their best by regular deadheading, feeding, and supporting throughout the summer.*

### Harvesting

In the kitchen garden there should be plenty to harvest, but successional sowings continue to extend the season. Keep fruiting plants such as beans, marrows, and peas well watered while flowering to insure a good crop. Watering throughout the garden is likely to take up a considerable amount of time in midsummer. Outdoor plants in containers, particularly, can start

suffering from water shortage within hours on hot, cloudless summer days.

### Pest and diseases

Fungus diseases can be a particular problem in warmer weather, and a routine of preventive fungicide sprays is a good idea for susceptible plants. Pests should be treated as soon as they are seen—preventive spraying is not generally applicable as far as insecticides are concerned.

## MIDSUMMER TASKS

**General**

- Check plants for pests and diseases and treat them early
- Continue watering without wasting water
- Install garden lighting

**Ornamental garden**

- Prune shrubs that have finished flowering as necessary; prune wisteria
- Continue trimming hedges
- Prick out perennials and biennials sown earlier
- Deadhead flowers and cut back rock plants that are becoming untidy
- Start to take semiripe cuttings of shrubs
- Look out for fall-flowering bulbs and Madonna Lilium candidum (lilies) and plant as early as possible
- Cut back early-flowering border plants to encourage a second flush
- Deadhead, prune, and water plants in containers
- Cut flowers for use indoors
- Stake and tie dahlias; disbud them if large blooms are required
- Check Aster novi-belgii (Michaelmas daisies) for mildew, and treat if necessary
- Order spring bulbs from mail-order catalogs

▲ *Garden lighting will add atmosphere and enable you to continue to enjoy the garden after dusk.*

**Lawns**

- Leave clippings on the grass occasionally
- Increase mowing height in times of drought

**Water garden**

- Top up ponds with fresh water as necessary
- Continue to feed fish to help build them up for winter

**Kitchen garden**

- Harvest vegetables regularly as soon as they are ready
- Check potatoes for potato blight
- Pick herbs for drying, freezing and use in pot pourri
- Thin seedlings
- Plant cold stored potatoes for a fall crop
- Continue planting winter vegetables
- Water beans when flowering
- Remove straw on strawberry beds after fruiting, and cut the foliage from strawberries not required for propagation. Root strawberry runners
- Cut off foliage affected by silver leaf on plums and other stone fruit
- Start summer-pruning of trained apples and pears
- Cut down summer-fruiting raspberry canes after fruiting

▲ *Sow herbs such as coriander ready for potting up for use over the winter months.*

**Greenhouse**

- Continue training food crops
- Renew shading as necessary; continue watering, ventilating, and damping down
- Use fan heaters to circulate cool air
- Prick off cineraria seedlings
- Pot up rooted cuttings
- Sow herbs for winter use
- Avoid blossom end rot on tomatoes by watering regularly to prevent plants flagging. Feed cucumbers, peppers, and tomatoes etc with high-potash fertilizer and pick fruits regularly as they ripen

# general tasks

*Watering is often vital during dry spells, but when incorrectly carried out it can do more harm than good. Most gardeners like to spend as much time as possible in their gardens now, and an outdoor lighting system enables gardens to be appreciated for that much longer each day.*

### Water garden plants with care

When watering any plants, it is important to make sure that the soil or compost is moistened right down to the main root area. If just a small amount of water is given it often penetrates only a shallow, top layer of soil; this encourages roots to form in this upper area, making the plant more prone to drought in the future. Water thoroughly or not at all!

Water can be applied in a number of different ways—with a watering can, through a hose pipe, by sprinkler or by seep hose. A seep hose is often one of the most efficient ways of watering because very little water is lost by evaporation. It is simply a length of tubing which is blocked at one end with holes at regular intervals along its length. It is laid on the soil alongside the plants and

attached to a hose; water seeps out of the holes on to the soil. If there is a ban on garden sprinklers, remember that the ban includes seep hoses, too!

◄ *A seep hose is a very efficient and virtually labor-free way of applying water to the soil; hardly any water is lost by evaporation.*

### STAKE BORDER PLANTS FIRMLY

At this time of year heavy storms are not uncommon, and rain and hail can flatten plants in minutes. Even if the flowering stems are not broken, insufficiently supported plants are unlikely to recover their shape fully after such a downpour. As long as border plants have been firmly staked and regularly tied in to their supports, they are more likely to survive without serious damage. Wet weather can cause buds to rot instead of opening fully; this is often seen on roses (particularly the full-flowered, old-fashioned varieties) and is known as "balling." Unfortunately there is little you can do to prevent it; cut off affected buds to encourage a second flush to form.

# prepare for vacations

The summer vacation season comes at just the wrong time for the garden, just when everything is growing lushly and needs regular attention to keep it looking good. However, it is worth spending a little time in preparation before you leave to prevent you from being confronted by a depressing jungle on your return.

1 Gather all planted containers, including hanging baskets, together in one spot (**below**). Place them in a sheltered, partially shaded position. Add water-retaining granules to the soil mix if this has not already been done. Give them a thorough soaking before you go, but if you're away for more than a long weekend, ask a neighbor to water them every couple of days.

2 Mow the lawn just before you go, but do not be tempted to cut it more closely than normal because this will damage the turf and make it more prone to drought. If it is overlong on your return, reduce the height gradually over several cuts (**right**).

3 Weed flowerbeds and the vegetable plot thoroughly, hoeing to remove all seedling weeds. Applying a mulch to the soil will help prevent new weed growth and also keep the soil moist.

4 In the vegetable garden, pick all fruiting crops such as zucchini, peas, and beans. Any left to mature on the plants will reduce future production, so arrange for a friend or neighbor to continue the harvest in your absence. Normally they are only to happy to oblige in return for the opportunity of a supply of fresh, home-grown produce!

## USE GARDEN LIGHTING TO ADVANTAGE

The garden can be a dramatic place at night with the imaginative use of lights. Spotlights can highlight particular plants or ornaments of interest or form interesting shadows or silhouettes, while underwater lights can make a garden pond a magical feature. Lighting on the patio enables meals to be enjoyed out of doors after dark, and well-placed lighting can be an important safety feature on potential hazards such as paths and steps. Garden lighting kits are generally easy to install (see page 106), but if you have any doubts, employ a qualified electrician to do the job.

# ornamental garden: *general tasks*

*Dahlias, one of the mainstays of late summer and fall, need attention now to produce prize-winning blooms. Another eye-catcher is the Madonna lily—look out for bulbs which will be on sale soon. And why not extend the amount of enjoyment you get from the garden by installing lighting?*

◄ *Low voltage garden lighting kits contain all you need to transform your garden to a magical place during the hours of darkness.*

### Install garden lighting

Low-voltage outdoor lighting systems are safe to use and easy to install. Complete kits are available containing everything you will need, including lamps, cables, and a transformer.

First, draw out a sketch of your lighting plan to estimate the amount of cable you will need, and to insure you have enough. Find a suitable position for the transformer (see the maker's instructions for precise details). Lay the lamps in their appropriate positions, then run the cable between them, leaving a long loop at each lamp. Attach the cable to the lamps as instructed, then assemble the rest of the lighting fitting and push the lamps firmly into the ground. When all the lamps are attached, test the system to insure it is working properly. If everything is in order, the cable running between the lamps can be buried under the soil, making sure it is not likely to be disturbed by future digging.

### STAKE AND DISBUD DAHLIAS

Dahlias are important plants for providing color and form in the late summer and fall garden. If large, eye-catching flowers are required, they can be obtained by disbudding the stems. Leave just the terminal bud on each stem, and remove all the buds from the leaf axils below it by snapping them off or rubbing them out. This will need to be repeated several times. Each flowering stem will need to be provided with a sturdy stake, and must be tied in regularly. Earwigs can be a problem, chewing at the petals and spoiling the flower shape. They can be  caught in traps consisting of a small pot filled with straw, inverted on the top of the stake. Inspect the traps each morning, and shake out and destroy any earwigs sheltering there.

# take semiripe cuttings

Now is a good time to take semiripe cuttings from many shrubs. They are less delicate than softwood cuttings, and need no special treatment. Most will be well rooted by the fall, but can be left in their pots in a sheltered place until the following spring.

1  Choose the current season's shoots which are still pliable, and just beginning to harden and become woody at the base. Cut the shoots with pruners or, if it is small enough, tear them off the stem with a small sliver of bark attached.

2  Remove the lower leaves and, if necessary, trim the stem to just below a node with a knife (**right**). The size of cutting varies from shrub to shrub, but is usually around 4in/10cm long.

3  Dip the base of the cutting in hormone rooting powder, tapping it once or twice to leave just a thin film on the stem (**left**).

4  Insert cuttings into prepared pots of cuttings soil mix topped with a layer of sharp sand (**right**). Place the pots in a cold frame if possible, or a well-ventilated greenhouse, or a sheltered position outdoors. Keep them lightly shaded for the first few days.

## PLANT FALL-FLOWERING BULBS

Bulbs such as amaryllis and colchicum, that flower in the fall, can be planted now. Most fall-flowering bulbs prefer a sunny spot in a sheltered situation. The Madonna lily (*Lilium candidum*) should also be planted soon: this is actually summer flowering, but needs to be planted as early as possible for flowers next year. It is a particularly striking lily with large, pure white, heavily scented, trumpet-shaped blooms. Look out for the bulbs appearing in garden centers from now on. Unlike most other lilies the Madonna lily requires very shallow planting, with just 2in/5cm of soil above the tip of the bulb.

# ornamental garden: *pruning and deadheading*

*Plants are working hard to produce magnificent displays of flowers at the moment, and can easily wear themselves out after a short time. With the correct care, however, it is possible to extend the season so that you can continue to enjoy a garden full of color for as long as possible.*

## Care for containers

Tubs, window boxes, and hanging baskets have become an indispensable feature of most gardens in summer, spilling over with plants to provide a feast of color.

Because the plants are crowded together in small volumes of soil mix, however, they soon begin to suffer from the effects of competition.

Containers need regular watering, feeding, and deadheading in order to keep the plants flowering for the longest possible period.

The amount of water they need depends on the type of mix in which they are growing and whether they are in a sheltered or exposed position, but it is often necessary to water small containers two or three times a day in hot, sunny weather. Add a dilute liquid feed to the water at every watering, or if you prefer you can incorporate some season-long, slow-release fertilizer granules into the soil. Deadheading (where practical) will help to encourage further flushes of bloom.

▼ *A number of border plants that flower in late spring and early summer will produce a second flush of blooms if cut back after flowering.*

---

### CUT BACK ROCK GARDEN PLANTS AFTER FLOWERING

Many of the rockery plants that were proving such a colorful spectacle a few weeks ago are looking rather bedraggled now that nearly all the flowers are over. Trim back species such as aubrieta, aurinia (alyssum), iberis and cerastium with pruners or a pair of well-sharpened shears, cutting the shoots to about half their length. This encourages fresh new growth and keeps the plants neat and compact. It can sometimes result in another flush of flowers to brighten up the rock garden later in the season, but should certainly improve the flowering of the plants next spring.

# prune wisteria

The glorious scented flowers of wisteria are over, but careful pruning now will help to insure a spectacular display next year. Wisteria can be a difficult climber to grow well, sometimes seeming reluctant to flower profusely, but the correct pruning will greatly improve its performance. Remember that further pruning will be necessary in winter.

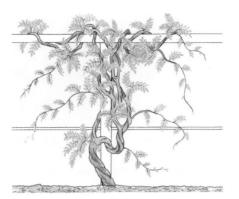

1 Wisteria flowers early, when the leaves are only just starting to open. By midsummer, however, the attractive pinnate foliage has made vigorous growth, and the leafy shoots may be getting out of hand (**above**).

2 Over the next few weeks, cut back nearly all the long shoots to about 6–10in/15–25cm from the main stem (**above**). Any stems needed to fill in the main framework can be pruned more lightly or left unpruned.

3 Climbing plants, including wisteria, always flower better when the flow of sap is slowed down by training the stems horizontally instead of letting them grow straight up. Pull wisteria stems gently into a near horizontal position and tie them to their support (**left**).

4 Summer pruning is only half the story; the shoots you have just cut back will need pruning again in winter, reducing them to three buds from their base. This will help promote the production of flowering spurs.

5 Once summer pruning is completed, make sure the soil around the roots is moist and apply a mulch around the base of the plant (**right**). Wisteria prefers moderately rich, moisture-retentive, loamy soil. In dry soils, the flower buds may drop from the plant before they open fully.

◄ *A second flush of flowers from plants such as perennial geraniums will be especially welcome in a few weeks.*

# plants for scent

A garden should not just be a visual delight but should give pleasure to the other senses as well. One of the senses that is most easily pleased is that of smell, and there are all sorts of garden plants with the most wonderful and intriguing scents.

Our sense of smell is actually very complex. Different fragrances can affect us in very different ways; they can also act strongly on our memories, with just one whiff of a particular smell being able to transport us instantly back to an event we had entirely forgotten. Certain scents can be very strong to one person but non-existent to another; similarly one person may find a fragrance wonderful while another finds it offensive.

When we talk of plant fragrance, it is flowers that spring to mind, and there are indeed many blooms that are strongly perfumed. Don't forget, though, that leaves can also be scented, and foliage often has a sharp, invigorating fragrance, never as sweet and heavy as that of flowers. The reason flowers are scented is to attract pollinating insects, particularly moths and butterflies, who use fragrance to locate the blooms—the sweet scent promises nectar. Other flowers are pollinated by flies, and give off a smell of rotting meat to attract them—*Sauromatum guttatum* (the voodoo lily) is well known for its foul scent. The purpose of fragrance in leaves is less clear, but presumably prevents animals from eating the foliage because strongly aromatic substances usually have an off-putting taste.

The way flowers and foliage give off fragrance varies. Some scents travel on the air for long distances, while some flowers need to be sniffed close up before their scent can be detected. Some fragrances are only released after light rain, and many flowers do not give off any scent until the cool of night in order to attract night-flying moths. Some fragrances, like that of violets, are tantalizing, disappearing after a few seconds no matter how hard we sniff the flowers. Most foliage scents are released only when the leaves are rubbed or brushed against.

*Fragrance in the garden*

It is always pleasant to walk around the garden and enjoy the mingling of pleasant scents, but many gardeners like to concentrate fragrant plants in one area where they

▲ *The Sir Edward Elgar rose not only looks beautiful, it also brings a particularly strong and pleasant scent to the garden.*

can most easily be appreciated—perhaps near the patio, around an arbor containing a seat or under a living room window. The spot should be sheltered so that the fragrance is not dispersed too rapidly on the wind, and be accessible after dark when many plants smell their strongest. Raised beds or tall containers help to bring smaller fragrant flowers to nose level.

Plants needing to be touched to release their scent should be placed where they are likely to be trodden on or brushed past, for example in cracks in paving or by a doorway. Leaves which are within easy reach will encourage passersby to pinch them as they walk past.

Don't try to cram too many strongly scented plants into a small area though, because the different fragrances may compete and lose their impact.

▲ *Hyacinths are among the most strongly scented spring-flowering bulbs, and are especially popular as house plants.*

▲ *There are several varieties of the familiar, sweet-scented honeysuckle, including the richly colored 'Dropmore Scarlet'.*

## PLANTS WITH SCENTED FLOWERS

*Brugmansia* (angel's trumpet)
*Buddleja*
*Chimonanthus praecox* *
    (wintersweet)
*Clerodendrum trichotomum*
*Clethra alnifolia* (sweet pepper
    bush)
*Convallaria majalis* (lily-of-the-
    valley)
*Cosmos atrosanguineus*
*Cytisus battandieri* (pineapple
    broom)
*Daphne odora* *
*Dianthus* (carnation, pink)
*Hamamelis mollis* * (Chinese
    witch hazel)
*Heliotropum* (helliotrope)
*Hyacinthus* (hyacinth)
*Iris unguicularis* *
*Jasminum* (jasmine)
*Lathyrus odorata* (sweet pea)
*Lavandula* (lavender)
*Lilium* (lily)
*Lonicera* (honeysuckle)
*Magnolia sieboldii*

*Mahonia japonica* *
*Matthiola incana*
*Narcissus poeticus* (poet's
    narcissus) and *Tazetta* hybrids
*Nicotiana* (tobacco plant)
*Osmanthus burkwoodii*
*Paeonia* (peony)
*Petunia*
*Philadelphus* (mock orange)
*Phlox paniculata* (perennial phlox)
*Polianthes tuberosa* (tuberose)
*Primula* (primrose)
*Reseda odorata* (common
    mignonette)
*Ribes odoratum* (buffalo currant)
*Romneya coulteri* (tree poppy)
*Rosa* (rose)
*Sarcococca* * (Christmas box)
*Syringa* (lilac)
*Viburnum x bodnantense*,
    *V. fragrans, V. farreri* *
*Viola odorata* * (English violet)

*winter flowering

# plants in season

Annuals are in full flower this month. Easy to grow, they make most effective, colorful garden plants. Summer bedding plants are also in their prime. Trees are looking majestic in full leaf, and there are plenty of flowering shrubs to brighten the garden.

▼ *Lavender not only brings a splash of color to the garden, it also contributes to the marvelous aromas found at this time of year.*

## PLANTS WITH SCENTED FLOWERS

*Achillea*
*Alstroemeria* (Peruvian lily)
*Althaea*
*Astilbe*
*Astrantia major*
 (Hattie's pincushion)
*Begonia semperflorens*
*Campanula* (bellflower)
*Chrysanthemum maximum*
*Coreopsis* (tickseed)
*Delphinium elatum* hybrids
*Dianthus* (carnation, pink)
*Digitalis purpurea*
 (common foxglove)
*Echinops ritro* (globe thistle)
*Erigeron* (fleabane)
*Fuchsia*
*Gaillardia* x *grandiflora*
*Geranium*
*Geum* (avens)
*Gypsophila paniculata*
*Helenium*
*Hemerocallis* (day lily)
*Heuchera* (coral flower)
*Kniphofia* (red hot poker)
*Lathyrus* (everlasting pea)
*Lupinus* (lupin)
*Nepeta* x *faassenii* (catmint)
*Nicotiana alata* (tobacco plant)
*Oenothera* (evening primrose)
*Pelargonium*
*Penstemon*
*Phlox paniculata* (perennial phlox)
*Romneya coulteri* (tree poppy)
*Scabiosa caucasica*
 (pincushion flower)
*Solidago* (Aaron's rod)

## BULBS
—

*Cardiocrinum giganteum*
*Crocosmia* x *crocosmiiflora*
*Eucomis bicolor* (pineapple flower)
*Gladiolus*
*Lilium* (lily)

## TREES AND SHRUBS

*Abelia floribunda*,  A. x *grandiflora*
*Catalpa bignonioides* (Indian bean tree)
*Ceanothus* (California lilac)
*Cistus* (rock rose)
*Clethra alnifolia* (sweet pepperbush)
*Cytisus battandieri* (pineapple bloom)
*Escallonia*
*Eucryphia*
*Fuchsia magellanica*
*Genista* (broom)
*Helianthemum* (rock rose)
*Hydrangea macrophylla*
*Hypericum calycinum* (Aaron's beard)
*Lavandula* (lavender)
*Lonicera periclymenum* (common
 honeysuckle)
*Olearia* x *haastii* (daisy bush)
*Philadelphus* (mock orange)
*Rosa* (rose)
*Vinca major* (greater periwinkle), V. *minor*
 (lesser periwinkle)

▲ *Lupins are particularly prone to damage by heavy rain if they are not adequately staked. This variety is 'Gallery Pink'.*

▼ *Free-flowering pelargoniums are a popular choice for hanging baskets and other containers. Deadheading will extend the flowering season.*

# kitchen garden: *general tasks*

*There are not too many plant diseases that have a really devastating effect on crops, but potato blight is one of them. Take action as soon as you see the first signs of this disease. Also, tidy up strawberry beds now that the crop is over, and propagate the plants by rooting runners.*

## Potato blight

This disease is common in wet summers, and is remarkable for the speed with which it develops. The first signs are brown blotches on the foliage, sometimes with a white mold on the underside. Symptoms spread rapidly, and within a few days the entire top-growth of the plants may have yellowed and collapsed.

Blight also affects the tubers, causing a dark brown rot. Spores infect the tubers when rain washes them off the top-growth into the soil. If the tubers are of a useable size, as soon as blight is identified on the foliage the top-growth should immediately be cut down and burned, removing all trace of it from the soil surface. Tubers may then escape infection. In damp summers, especially if blight has occurred the previous year, it is worth giving potatoes a protective fungicide spray from midsummer onward.

▼ *Keep a sharp look out for the first signs of potato blight on the foliage. If action is taken straight away, the crop can usually be saved.*

### STRAWBERRY BEDS

When strawberry plants have finished cropping it is time to give the bed some radical treatment. At one time it was common practice to set light to the straw as it lay around the plants; the ensuing blaze burned up the leaves and frazzled any lurking pests and disease spores. Risk of the flames getting out of hand is too great for this to be a popular method any longer, however. Instead, the leaves are cut from the plants, using either a pair of shears or a nylon line trimmer: be careful not to damage the new growth in the center of the crowns. Rake up the cut foliage together with the straw, and remove it for burning in a safe place.

# root strawberry runners

As long as established strawberry plants are healthy and vigorous, it is easy to produce new plants to extend the bed or to replace old, worn-out plants. Strawberry plants naturally produce a profusion of runners which root quickly and easily.

1 Strawberry runners are freely produced. Long, creeping stolons extend from the plants, bearing two or three plantlets along their length. If not required for propagation, runners are normally removed regularly to prevent a mass of tangled growth (**left**).

2 Select four or five of the strongest, most vigorous runners for propagation and remove the rest. Spread the runners evenly around the plant.

3 The plantlet nearest the parent is always the strongest on the runner, and the ones beyond it should be nipped off and discarded. Plantlets can be rooted direct into the soil around the plant—simply weigh down the runner with a stone or peg into the soil with a loop of wire to prevent it from being blown about (**left**).

4 Alternatively, the plantlets can be rooted into pots filled with either good quality garden soil or soil mix. Rooting the runners into pots makes the plants quicker to establish on transplanting as there is less root disturbance when the young plants are lifted. Either clay or plastic pots are suitable.

## TRAIN OUTDOOR TOMATOES

For a good crop of outdoor tomatoes it is essential to choose varieties specifically recommended for outdoor culture. They may be grown as cordons like greenhouse tomatoes, or as bushes, depending on the variety selected. Cordon varieties need regular side-shooting and tying in to their support, but bush varieties generally do not. Some bush varieties are specially bred for growing in patio pots or even hanging baskets, where the stems cascade over the sides. They need no training, but frequent watering and regular feeding are necessary, as for all container-grown plants.

Between mid and late summer, the tops of cordon-grown plants should be pinched out to encourage the fruits to ripen.

Bush varieties form a sprawling mound and do not usually need staking or side-shooting. They carry fruit trusses at the ends of the stems.

5 Half-bury the pots in the soil around the parent plant and peg the runners down into the mix (**above**). When pots are being used, it is important to make sure that the soil mix in them is not allowed to dry out.

# kitchen garden: *planting and harvesting*

*Herbs are valuable in the garden for their appearance and fragrance, and indispensable in the kitchen. While nothing beats the flavor of fresh herbs, there are several easy ways in which they can be preserved. Midsummer, while they are at their peak, is the time to pick them for storing.*

## Harvesting herbs

The best time to pick herbs is in the morning of a dry day, waiting until the dew has dried off the foliage. Pick young stems, and do not wash them unless it is absolutely essential.

The age-old method of preservation is drying; it is simple to do and gives good results. Tie the herbs in small, loose bunches—if they are too large, they will go moldy in the center. Hang them upside down in a warm, dry, airy place. The atmosphere in the kitchen is usually too moist and an airing cupboard (with the door ajar), spare bedroom, or garden shed may be more suitable. Once the stems and foliage are completely dry, the herbs can be crumbled and stored in tightly lidded jars.

For faster results, herbs can be laid on racks in a very cool oven overnight. They can also be dried in batches in a microwave, though it is often difficult to get the timing right with this method.

▲ *Select fresh, young shoots of herbs for preserving, picking them early in the morning, once the dew has dried off the leaves.*

## FREEZING HERBS

Freezing tends to give fresher-tasting results than drying, and is particularly useful for herbs that do not dry well, such as basil.

Pick over the herbs and remove tough stems, then place them (single varieties or a mixture) in an electric blender and almost cover with water. Whizz them in the blender until the herbs are finely chopped, then pour the resulting mixture of herbs and water into ice cube trays and freeze. Add one or two of the ice cubes to soups, sauces, or casseroles.

## *plant out leeks*

Leeks are an invaluable winter
vegetable, withstanding almost any
amount of cold weather. Seedlings from
sowings made in trays or a seedbed in
spring will now be ready for
transplanting to their final positions.

1 Prepare the ground for leeks thoroughly,
because they need to be planted deeply in
order to develop the maximum length of tender
white stems. The crop will benefit from some
well-rotted compost or manure worked into the
soil before planting.

2 Knock the underside of the seedflat smartly
to loosen the roots, and tease the young
plants apart carefully. Gather up a handful of
seedlings with the bases of the plants in line, and
trim the long, straggly roots and leaf tips with
a pair of sharp scissors to make the plants easier
to handle (**right**).

3 Make planting holes with a wooden dibble
some 6in/15cm deep and the same distance
apart. A leek seedling is simply dropped into each
hole, leaving the holes open (**left**). Make sure the
leek drops right to the base of the hole: that's why
it's best to trim back the roots.

4 Once planting is complete, water the plants
gently; this washes enough soil over the
roots to anchor them in place. Each planting hole
is filled with water and then left to drain (**right**).

5 If the weather is very dry shortly after
planting the seedlings may need to be
watered again once or twice, but otherwise they
usually need no further attention. They will be
ready for harvesting in fall and winter.

◄ *Continue to keep the vegetable garden free
of weeds as far as possible. Increasing numbers
of crops are approaching maturity now.*

# greenhouse

*Greenhouse food plants need regular feeding and watering, and there are still seedlings to prick off, rooted cuttings to pot up, and seeds to be sown. If you like the idea of an extra-early strawberry crop next year, now's the time to pot up a few strawberry plants for growing on in a warm greenhouse.*

### Feed and water food crops regularly

Greenhouse plants such as eggplant, cucumbers, melons, bell peppers, and tomatoes must be given adequate levels of water and plant food in order to keep producing heavy crops. All fruiting plants need high levels of potassium, and a high–potash liquid fertilizer is a convenient way to supply it. Follow the directions on the pack as regards frequency of feeding.

A common problem with tomatoes at this time of year is the appearance of a dark brown or black, dry, sunken area at the base of the fruit, known as blossom end rot. This is usually caused by the plants running short of water at flowering time, so that sufficient calcium cannot be transported to the developing fruit. It is too late to do anything for affected fruits, but guard against it happening again by keeping the soil adequately moist at all times. A handful of garden lime can be added to the can of water occasionally as an extra precaution.

▼ *To avoid blossom end rot on the fruits, make sure that container-grown tomatoes never run short of water at any time.*

### STRAWBERRY PLANTS

A heated greenhouse lets you pick ripe strawberries weeks before the outdoor crop is ready. Runners that you rooted earlier will provide plants for forcing if they are potted up now. Choose  the strongest growers and set them in individual 6in/15cm pots using a soil-based potting mix.

 Keep the pots in a sheltered corner of the garden or in a cold frame, and keep them watered for the rest of the summer. In the fall, protect them from excessive rain, and move into a frost-free greenhouse in midwinter.

## PRICK OFF CINERARIAS

Cineraria seedlings sown earlier should be pricked off into individual 3½in/8cm pots as soon as they can be handled easily. As with all seedlings, handle them by their seed leaves and not by their stems. Since cinerarias like relatively cool, airy conditions, free ventilation is essential; once established in their individual pots they can be placed in a cold frame. They like bright conditions but should be shaded from strong, direct sunlight which can scorch the large, soft leaves. Further batches of cineraria seeds can be sown now and in a few weeks time to give a succession of plants flowering through the early spring.

# herbs for winter

The aromatic flavor of fresh herbs is one of the great pleasures of summer. It is possible to continue to enjoy this through the winter, too, by sowing seeds now for growing in pots indoors.

1 Not all herbs will grow satisfactorily in pots, but basil, coriander, chervil, chives, dill, marjoram, and parsley are well worth trying. Sow enough for several pots in stages, to give a succession of young plants that can be brought from the greenhouse into the kitchen as they are needed.

2 Fill half-trays with moist sowing and cuttings mix and firm it well. Sow the seed thinly and cover it with a thin layer of more soil mix or sharp sand (**below**). Cover the completed tray with a plastic propagator top and set it in a slightly shady, evenly warm place until the seeds begin to germinate.

3 Once most of the seeds have germinated, remove the propagator top and bring the tray into full light. Grow the plants on in cool, airy conditions, pricking them out as necessary to give them more room to develop. When the seedlings are large enough, pot them up at two or three plants to an 3½in/8cm pot (**left**).

4 Some hardy herbs are evergreen or partially evergreen, and can continue to be used sparingly through the winter. Grow them in tubs and pots outside, but later in the fall move them near the kitchen door to make harvesting easier. Bay, rosemary, sage, thyme, and winter savory are good candidates.

# late summer

*The garden is at its best now, but despite the profusion of summer flowers and foliage, the first hints of fall soon make themselves felt. Dusk begins to come earlier, and in the mornings there is a hint of mistiness and heavy dew. It's time to start to prepare for the fall and winter ahead.*

In dry seasons, watering will be a priority in both the flower and kitchen gardens. Weeds may not be in such profusion as in early summer but must still be dealt with promptly if they are not to get out of hand.

Herbaceous and mixed borders can look splendid this month, but weeding, mulching, staking, and tying-in plants must continue. Staking is particularly important now because late summer storms can bring heavy rain and strong winds to wreck the display. Some of the border plants that were at their best earlier may now need to be trimmed in order to allow later-flowering subjects to be seen. Also take steps to control various pests and diseases before they have a chance to inflict too much damage—mildew on plants such as *Aster novi-belgii* (Michaelmas daisies) is very bad in

some years, but can be kept at bay by regular fungicide spraying of susceptible subjects.

In the kitchen garden there is often a glut as all the crops come to fruition at once. Picking must continue regularly because if pods or fruits of crops such as beans, peas, zucchini and squash are allowed to mature, the plants will stop producing further crops. Surplus

produce should be stored away for the winter and next spring, and now is the time for freezing, canning, and jelly and pickle making.

This is also the time of year when many gardeners take a couple of week's holiday, leaving the garden to fend for itself. This need not mean facing disaster on the return home; a little work put in before the holiday will be more than repaid afterward.

▶ *There should still be plenty of color from the flower borders for some weeks to come. Deadheading prolongs the flowering period.*

## LATE SUMMER TASKS

**Ornamental garden**

- Remove dead flowers from lavender and thyme, and clip plants
- Take cuttings of tender and dubiously hardy perennials to overwinter
- Continue to spray Michaelmas daisies against mildew
- Weed borders and tidy up the plants
- Feed late-flowering border plants

- Check dahlias and chrysanthemums for earwig damage
- Pot up mint for winter use
- Trim back border plants to allow late-flowering varieties to be seen
- Order bare-root shrubs and trees for fall planting
- Plant container-grown shrubs and border plants, keeping them well watered

- Clear out faded window boxes and hanging baskets, and replant them for winter interest; continue to feed and water others
- Trim evergreen hedges for the last time
- Remove annuals that have finished flowering
- Plant Lilium candidum (Madonna lily) bulbs
- Continue to take semiripe cuttings of shrubs

**Lawns**

- Prepare the site for sowing grass shortly

**Water garden**

- Aerate ponds in sultry weather

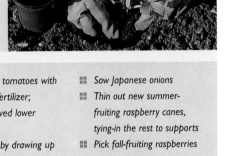

◀ Firm strawberries well when planting, and make sure the soil remains moist.

**Kitchen garden**

- Make a herb garden and take cuttings of shrubby herbs
- Plant strawberries
- Summer prune trained fruit
- Pick early apples as they ripen
- Continue to harvest vegetables and soft fruit, freezing or storing gluts for later use

- Feed outdoor tomatoes with high-potash fertilizer; remove yellowed lower leaves
- Blanch leeks by drawing up soil around the stems
- Sow prickly seeded spinach or spinach beet for a spring crop
- Sow spring cabbages in a seedbed

- Sow Japanese onions
- Thin out new summer-fruiting raspberry canes, tying-in the rest to supports
- Pick fall-fruiting raspberries as they ripen
- Provide squash and pumpkins with straw to keep fruits off wet soil
- Ripen onions by bending their necks

▼ Early apples are ready for picking when the fruit separates easily from the spur.

**Greenhouse**

- Pick melons as they ripen. Continue to pick tomatoes and other food crops
- Regulate watering of food crops carefully
- Watch weather forecasts and close down vents on cooler nights

- Sow cyclamen seed for houseplants; start old cyclamen tubers into growth
- Take cuttings of pelargoniums
- Pot up freesia corms for scented winter flowers

- Check greenhouse heaters are in good working order

# summer- and fall-flowering bulbs

*Flowering bulbs*

Spring is the season that instantly comes to mind whenever flowering bulbs are mentioned, but there are plenty of bulbs that carry magnificent flowers in late summer, and often on into the fall, making a spectacular show right at the end of the season.

Many of these bulbs like a warm, sunny position, and a nicely sheltered site—against the base of a warm wall, for example—is ideal. In areas with cold winters, some need to be lifted once they have finished flowering and stored under cover for the winter. Other types are quite hardy, and can be left in the garden all year round.

*Agapanthus campanulatus* and *Agapanthus* hybrids (African lily)

Striking, round heads of bright blue, funnel-shaped flowers held above clumps of strap-shaped leaves. Likes a sheltered spot; may need moving indoors for winter in particularly cold gardens.

*Canna* hybrids (Indian shot)

Bold, exotic-looking plants with large, paddle-shaped leaves, sometimes in bronzy shades, and spikes of brilliantly colored flowers often streaked and speckled. Lift rhizomes in the fall and store under cover.

*Colchicum autumnale* (fall crocus)

Not a crocus at all, but with similar looks. Pink, lilac, or white goblet-shaped flowers in late summer and fall on fragile-looking, translucent stems. Fully hardy.

*Crinum* x *powelli* (swamp lily)

Sturdy stems carry clusters of large, fragrant, funnel-shaped pink blooms (white in the variety 'Album'). Rather tender; protect the planting area with a mulch of dry leaves or peat, but in very cold areas overwinter plants in pots under cover.

*Cyclamen purpurascens*

Magenta flowers with typical upswept petals and a delicate fragrance. Leaves are rounded and attractively marbled with silver. Fully hardy.

◄ *Agapanthus, with its striking, round heads of bright blue flowers, gives height and color to summer displays.*

▲ *These magnificent deep red canna lilies bring a richness to the color scheme in the garden.*

### Eucomis bicolor (pineapple flower)

Densely packed spikes of flowers are pale green edged with purple; stems are topped off by a pineapple-like tuft of leaves. Frost hardy, but appreciates a winter mulch of dry leaves or similar in cold, exposed sites.

### Galtonia candicans (summer hyacinth)

Tall stems with widely spaced, pendulous white bells rising above long, strap-shaped leaves. Frost hardy.

### Gladiolus callianthus (acidanthera)

Lopsided, star-shaped white blooms with deep purple markings at the center. Sweetly scented. Lift corms in the fall and store in dry mix over winter.

### Schizostylis coccinea (kaffir lily)

Open, star-shaped flowers with satin-textured petals; usually bright scarlet, though pink varieties are available.

Usually a flush of flowers in late summer, followed by the main flowering in mid- to late fall. Frost hardy.

### Tigridia pavonia (peacock flower)

A long succession of short-lived flowers composed of three large and three small petals, usually strikingly marked with contrasting bright colors and patterns. Lift the bulbs in the fall and store in dry mix under cover over winter.

▶ *Indian shot (canna) makes a splendid specimen plant with its striking colors and boldly shaped foliage.*

### FEEDING BULBS

If bulbs are to be kept from year to year, it is important that they are able to build up a good food reserve during the growing season. Most varieties of bulbs will benefit from being given regular applications of fertilizer from the time they start to show their buds until the leaves begin to yellow and die down. This is particularly important for bulbs that are being grown in containers. A general, balanced fertilizer is best; it should have at least as much potash and phosphorus as nitrogen.

# ornamental garden: *general tasks*

*Walls and fences often mark the boundary of a garden, but they also have several other purposes. They provide protection from cold winds, keep out stray animals and trespassers, give privacy from neighbors and passersby, and camouflage eyesores that detract from the pleasure of the garden.*

### Choosing the barrier

The type of screen that is most appropriate depends on the main purpose for which it is required. For protection against strong winds a solid barrier is not a good choice— the air rips over the top of the barrier and comes down the other side in gusts and eddies, often making the problem worse rather than curing it. A permeable barrier such as trelliswork with a light covering of plants, screen block walling or a post and rail fence is better in this situation, because it filters the wind and slows its speed.

For privacy, a solid barrier may be a better choice, though this depends on exactly how the garden is overlooked and by whom—a light, permeable screen may be sufficient to obscure the view from outside. The same applies to views that you wish to obscure from within the garden. Careful positioning of a screen is therefore very important. Moving the screen backward or forward between the object to be disguised and the viewpoint will make a substantial difference to the height or width the screen needs to be.

▼ *A light wooden garden screen may be all that you need to provide some privacy in a garden that could be overlooked.*

# overwintering non-hardy perennials

Many popular garden plants are not frost hardy or not reliably so. They are often described as "slightly tender" or "dubiously hardy," and will die in a hard winter. Take some cuttings now and you will have young plants to act as an insurance policy against winter losses.

Plants that may be severely damaged by frost include pelargonium, many varieties of fuchsia, argyranthemum (marguerite), lantana, heliotropium (heliotrope) and *Helichrysum petiolare* among others. Cuttings usually root quickly at this time of year to provide plants for overwintering.

1 Select vigorous, healthy, preferably non-flowering shoots and either snap them off or cut them with pruners (**right**). Trim off the lower leaves, and make a cut with a razor blade or sharp knife just below a leaf node.

2 Insert the prepared cuttings into sandy soil mix in a seedflat or around the edge of a pot (**below**). Water them well using a fine spray, and cover with a clear plastic propagator top. Keep them in a warm, lightly-shaded position.

3 The propagator top can be removed or its ventilators opened once the cuttings show signs of rooting. They can remain in a frost-free greenhouse or conservatory, or a cool, bright room in the home, over the winter months.

## EARWIG TRAPS

Check chrysanthemum and dahlia flowers for signs of earwig damage. These flowers are particularly prone to attack from earwigs which eat holes in the petals, and distort the flowerheads by damaging the buds as they open. Night is the main feeding time, when most of the damage is done; during the day the earwigs seek a convenient place to hide. Earwig traps can be set up by inverting a flower pot loosely stuffed with straw on the end of a garden stake near the flowers. This provides an irresistably attractive daytime roost for the pests that can be shaken out of the straw and disposed of.

# ornamental garden: *planting and potting*

*It's time to look ahead and replant exhausted summer-flowering containers for winter interest. Trees and shrubs can be planted now, too, but remember they need special care after planting in hot weather. And if you fancy some fresh mint for winter, this is the time to pot up a few roots.*

### Container-grown specimens

Both shrubs and border plants can continue to be planted right through the summer if they have been grown in containers, but it is important to remember to water them regularly. Water the plants in their containers several hours or the day before planting. This makes sure that the top-growth is fully charged with moisture and is able to cope with any disturbance with minimum wilting; it also aids the removal of the root ball from the pot without root damage.

In hot, sunny weather, avoid planting during the middle of the day when the planting site is in full sun; it is better to wait until the relative cool of evening. Water the soil thoroughly immediately after planting: another watering a couple of hours later may be necessary to insure the water penetrates right down to the roots.

▲ *Containers come in many shapes and sizes; these stylish containers are made from old car lights.*

### POT UP MINT FOR WINTER

A few sprigs of fresh young mint are very welcome during the winter months, and potted roots are easy to encourage into growth while outdoor plants are completely dormant.

The spreading roots of mint can be found just below the soil surface: using a trowel, lift a few long sections. They break easily, but even small portions of the roots will grow, and their removal will not harm the parent. Fill a seedflat with potting mix, firm it well, and press the lengths of mint root into the soil mix surface until they are covered. Cover with another layer of soil and water until it is just moist. Keep the flat in a moderately warm place, either in the greenhouse or on a light windowsill in the home. Once the shoots start to appear, give them as bright a position as possible.

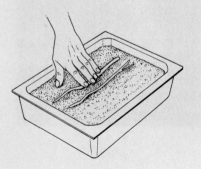

# plant a winter window box

By late summer, many containers of plants are starting to look a little jaded and past their best. Once this stage is reached it is a good time to replant some containers to give interest through the winter, when it will be especially welcome.

1 Remove and discard the worn-out bedding plants and soil. Clean out the inside of the window box, replace crocks over the drainage holes and refill the box loosely with fresh soil mix (**right**).

2 Select plants to give color, form, and flowers over the fall and winter. Suitable choices include winter-flowering heathers and viola (pansies), skimmia, dwarf conifers, variegated hedera (ivy), and small bulbs such as galanthus (snowdrops) and early-flowering crocus.

3 Set your chosen plants, still in their pots, in the window box until you have arranged them to your satisfaction. It is usually best to have taller, upright plants to give height toward the center of the box, and some trailers at the sides to soften the outline (**left**).

4 Remove the plants from their pots and set them in the windowbox using a trowel, adding more mix as necessary. Firm in lightly but thoroughly, using your knuckles. Bulbs such as snowdrops can be planted last, pushing them to the correct depth with a dibble (**right**).

5 Water the completed window box and put it in a sheltered place to establish for a few weeks: it can then be moved to its permanent position. Choose a place which will not be exposed to extreme cold or biting winds; plant roots in a container have less protection from cold than when they are buried in the ground (**right**).

◀ *Plant up a hanging basket to cheer up the winter months; this one includes colorful pansies, ivy, and skimmia.*

# ornamental garden: *plants in season*

Herbaceous borders are perhaps at their peak this month, being filled with color and flowers. Hanging baskets, windowboxes, and tubs should still be looking good, too, though they may be running out of steam if watering and feeding have not been kept up.

▼ *Among the best of the late-flowering border plants are the aromatic, flat, colorful heads of achillea.*

## TREES AND SHRUBS

*Buddleja davidii*
*Campsis radicans* (trumpet creeper)
*Clerodenrum bungei*
*Eucryphia*
*Fuchsia*
*Hebe*
*Hibiscus syriacus*
*Hydrangea macrophylla*
*Hypericum* (St John's Wort)
*Lonicera* (honeysuckle)
*Rosa* (rose)

## BULBS

*Crocosmia* x *crocosmiiflora*
*Cyclamen purpurascens*
*Eucomis bicolor* (pineapple flower)
*Gladiolus* hybrids
*Lilium* (lily)

▼ *The sweet scent of lilies continues*
*to be a major feature of the garden.*

▲ *Many rose varieties have several flushes*
*of bloom to carry them through the summer*
*and into early fall.*

## PERENNIALS

*Acanthus* (bear's breeches)
*Achillea* (yarrow)
*Aconitum* (aconite)
*Anemone hybrida*
*Aster*
*Begonia semperflorens*
*Chrysanthemum*
*Gazania*
*Helenium*
*Helianthus annuus* (sunflower)
*Hemerocallis* (day lily)
*Kniphofia* (red hot poker)
*Phlox paniculata* (perennial phlox)
*Romneya coulteri* (tree poppy)
*Rudbeckia* (coneflower)

# lawns and water gardens: *general tasks*

*As long as the weather has not been too dry, lawns should still be looking good. Next month is the best time to start a new lawn from seed—prepare the ground for it now. Water gardens should also be in good condition, with plenty of color and interest from both floating plants and marginals.*

## Keeping ponds healthy

Now that floating plants such as *Nymphaea* (water lilies) have spread their leaves to shade much of the water surface from direct sun, any problems with green water due to algae that occurred earlier in the summer should be over. Lilies and similar plants should still have plenty of flowers to add color to the water garden scene, but some of the older leaves will be yellowing and starting to die back. Remove these from the water as soon as you notice them; it is important to keep decaying plant refuse out of the pond as far as possible. Also continue to check the undersides of lily leaves for the transparent blobs of snails' eggs, and remove any found. Water snails can be a serious plant pest, and snails or eggs are often introduced unwittingly when new plants are bought. The ramshorn snail is the only satisfactory species for garden pools.

### AERATE POND WATER

Normally, the water in a pond takes in oxygen and releases carbon dioxide at the surface, but in sultry, thundery weather this process becomes very slow or may stop altogether. Fish in the pool can be badly affected, and can sometimes be seen at the surface of the pool gulping in air: if nothing is done they may die. The effect is worst at night, when pond plants are adding to the carbon dioxide content of the water.

The simple remedy is to stir up the water to increase its surface area and allow some of the carbon dioxide to escape. This can be done by leaving fountains or waterfalls running, by stirring the water vigorously with a stick or aiming a forceful jet from a hose into the pool.

▲ *Waterfalls not only look and sound attractive, they can help to keep the water in a pool well aerated—often vital in thundery weather.*

▶ *A well-established, well-kept lawn sets off the whole of the rest of the garden. It will soon be time to start making new lawns.*

# prepare sites for sowing grass

Early fall is the best time to sow seed for a new lawn, but now is the time to start preparing the soil. Remember that the grass is going to be a permanent feature for years to come, so it is well worth making sure that the basic preparation is thorough. This is your only chance to get soil conditions right.

## PREPARING FOR A NEW LAWN

Turf is the quickest way to make a new lawn, giving virtually instant results. Although soil preparation for turf does not need to be quite as painstaking as for seed sowing, it is still worth cultivating the area to be turfed thoroughly well in advance, removing perennial weeds, stones etc. and adding a long-lasting fertilizer to get the grass off to a good start.

1 Clear the site of existing turf, cultivated trees, shrubs and plants and weeds. It is especially important to get rid of perennial weeds because they will be very difficult to control once the lawn is established. Use a weedkiller such as glyphosate where necessary.

2 Once the site is cleared of plant growth, remove any other obstructions there may be, such as large stones, paving slabs and so on (**right**). The cleared site can then be leveled, filling in dips and flattening out bumps.

3 If the site slopes steeply it may be necessary to reduce the gradient or construct terraces. Where this sort of work is essential, remove the topsoil and stack it nearby, adjusting the levels by moving subsoil. Respread the topsoil evenly once the work is completed.

4 Check the structure and condition of the soil. Add well-rotted organic matter such as garden mix to improve heavy and light soils. Give it a final once-over before sowing (**left**).

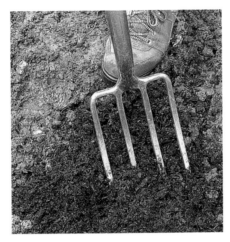

# kitchen garden: *sowing and planting*

*The reward for all your work in the vegetable garden becomes apparent as more and more crops are ready to harvest. It's still time to be thinking ahead, however; there are crops to be sown or planted now for next season, and winter crops to look after for the more immediate future.*

## Spinach for spring

The tender green leaves of spinach make a very welcome vegetable in the spring, and plants sown now are less likely to run to seed than crops sown in the spring for summer use. Traditionally, prickly-seeded varieties of spinach are the ones to sow in late summer and early fall, using round-seeded types in spring. Many modern hybrids are equally good for both seasons, however.

Sow seeds thinly in drills about 12in/30cm apart; water the soil the day before if conditions are dry. Once the seedlings emerge, thin them to around 9in/23cm. Depending on the weather, there may be leaves to harvest from late fall right through the winter, but the most reliable flush of foliage will be in early spring. Earlier cropping can be obtained if the seedlings are covered with cloches.

### JAPANESE ONIONS

Onion varieties such as 'Express Yellow' and 'Senshyu Semi-globe Yellow' are specially bred for sowing in late summer. They are winter hardy, and will give the earliest crop next year in early to midsummer. The timing of sowing is fairly critical, however. Plants that are sown too soon often run to seed prematurely in the spring, whereas those which are sown too late either give a disappointing crop of small bulbs or die out over winter. Gardeners in cold districts need to sow one or two weeks ahead of those in milder areas.

Sow in rows 9–12in/23–30cm apart, and leave the seedlings until spring; then thin them to 4in/10cm apart. Water the drills before sowing, and damp them down frequently in the days following if the weather is hot, to cool the soil and improve germination.

◀ *Sow plenty of rows of spinach. The leaves shrink so much when they are cooked that you always need more than you think you will.*

## *plant strawberries*

The yield and quality of strawberries usually drops off after three years of cropping, and it is advisable to think about replacing the bed with new plants after this time. Replacing one-third of the plants in the strawberry bed each year means that you will continue to have strawberries to harvest every year.

1 Strawberry plants are prone to a number of virus diseases that reduce their yields, and it is a good idea to buy certified virus-free stock to give them the best possible start.

3 Well-rooted runners in small pots or peat blocks can be bought from garden centers, or by mail order from specialist suppliers. They should be planted as soon as possible after arrival, spacing them around 12–18in/30–45cm apart in rows 3ft/90cm apart (**below**).

2 Prepare the soil well before obtaining the plants, adding well-rotted organic matter and clearing away all traces of weeds, so difficult to control in any well-established strawberry bed.

4 Plant with a trowel (**above**), firming the plants in thoroughly with the sole of your boot. The crown of the plant should be just level with the soil surface. Water after planting, using a medium fine spray on the watering can or hose to avoid disturbing the roots (**below**).

◀ *Crops for harvesting in winter, such as cabbages, should be coming along strongly. Keep them weed free, and water them in dry weather.*

133

# kitchen garden: *gathering the harvest*

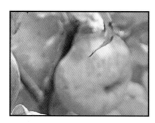

*In late summer and early fall crops are ripening daily, and much of the produce may go to waste unless it is picked regularly and stored correctly. Some crops need to be consumed as soon as possible after picking, but others will keep for some time as long as the right storage method is used.*

### Harvesting and storing produce

The best time for harvesting is early in the day, before crops lose their moisture in the warm weather. Handle the produce carefully so that it is not bruised; any damaged crops should be put to one side for immediate consumption. Once picked, keep fruit or vegetables for short-term storage in a cool, dark place; the salad box of a refrigerator is usually ideal if there is room.

Root vegetables can be left in the ground over the winter, or stored in boxes of almost-dry mix or in paper sacks. Dense-hearted cabbages, ripe squash and pumpkins, and many varieties of apples and pears will keep well in a cool, airy shed; onions and shallots can be plaited into ropes or stored in trays somewhere dry. Don't forget to make jellies and pickles, as these are good, traditional preservation methods for a wide range of fruit and vegetables.

## FREEZING

Freezing is probably the most popular method of long-term storage, and is appropriate for soft fruit, or any crop that deteriorates quickly once picked. It preserves the color and flavor of the fruit well, though the texture may suffer in some cases.

Pick over the fruit well; wash it only if essential. It can be open-frozen (ie spread on trays), frozen in containers packed with dry sugar, or frozen in sugar syrup—whichever is most appropriate. Fruit normally cooked (cooking apples and gooseberries, for example) can be cooked before freezing. Remember to label the packs because fruit is difficult to identify once frozen. Most well-prepared fruit will keep in excellent condition for over a year in the freezer.

◀ *Gooseberries for cooking are picked as soon as they are large enough. Dessert varieties, for eating raw, must be left on the bushes to ripen.*

▶ *Pick early-maturing varieties of apple as soon as they separate easily from the tree. Eat them within a few days; they do not store well.*

# pruning fruit in summer

Apples and other fruits grown as cordons, fans, or espaliers need pruning in the summer to control their growth. Correct pruning is a vital technique for keeping these forms under control so that the plants remain both attractive and fruitful.

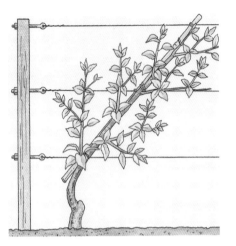

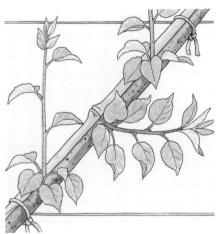

**1** Summer pruning should be carried out over a number of weeks as the shoots reach the correct stage. Shoots which are ready for pruning are about pencil thickness, and becoming woody and dark in color at their base (**above**).

**2** The first leaves from the base on each shoot are known as the basal cluster and usually consist of three leaves growing in the same place. This basal cluster is ignored when counting the number of leaves on the shoot (**above**).

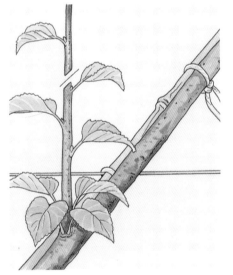

**3** The severity of pruning depends on the type of shoot. New lateral shoots which are more than 8in/20cm long, and growing from the main stem, are cut back to three leaves above the basal cluster. Cut just above the bud in the leaf axil, angling the cut slightly so that it slopes away from the bud (**above**).

**4** Side-shoots that are growing from existing laterals or fruit-bearing spurs should be cut back harder, reducing them to just one leaf above the basal cluster. This pruning system improves the cropping potential of the tree by encouraging the development of fruiting spurs, and checking excessive leafy shoot production (**above**).

# making a herb garden

There's no doubt that fresh herbs make all the difference to home-prepared food, and no keen cook would want to be without them. But herbs are worth growing for many other reasons besides their culinary value, including their wonderful scents, attractive appearance, and their fascinating history.

Because herbs are so special, they are frequently grouped together in a specialist herb garden. Traditional herb gardens are formal, often with very intricate designs. While this is an attractive way of growing them, informal herb beds are also popular and sometimes fit more naturally into the overall garden design. It's all a matter of personal choice.

Before making a final decision on the style and position of the herb garden, consider the following factors. An open, sunny sheltered position is essential. This encourages the strongest growth from the plants, and makes the herb garden a more attractive place for the gardener to linger, enjoying the fragrances wafting on the still, warm air. If herbs are being grown primarily for cooking, site the herb garden near the kitchen so that it is possible to gather a few herbs quickly even when it is wet or cold. For the same reason, make sure that the main herbs are accessible from a path or firm surface to avoid treading in the mud when gathering them.

Once you have chosen the site, it's time to think about the design. There are many traditional options, from the complicated ribbons and twists of a knot garden to a simple checkerboard of alternate paving slabs and planting spaces. Herbs do seem particularly

◀ *When making a herb garden, include stone slabs to step on in order to make it easier to pick the herbs in wet weather.*

### HERB OILS

Pick a handful of strongly aromatic herbs, eg, fennel, marjoram, rosemary, tarragon or thyme, and crush them lightly. Put them in a jar or bottle with a well-fitting lid and pour lightly warmed, good quality oil over them. Olive oil is a favorite, though it does have a strong flavor of its own; grapeseed oil is more neutral, allowing the herb's own flavor to come through. Put the lid on and let the oil stand in a warm place for two or three weeks, shaking frequently. Strain the oil into another jar of fresh herbs and repeat. Use in salads, marinades and rubbed over fish and meat before cooking.

suited to formal arrangements: two intersecting paths dividing a small, square garden into four equal beds is a popular option, especially with a sundial or statue placed at the center to form a focal point.

▲ *Choose healthy, well-established young plants from a garden center or, for more unusual varieties, a specialist herb nursery.*

## Selecting the plants

Choose the plants according to your own preferences, but remember to include some evergreens such as bay, rosemary, sage, and winter savory to add interest to the garden in winter. Mix and match plants with variegated, silver or dark foliage, and set plants with broad, bold leaves, such as angelica or lovage, to contrast with the fine, feathery textures of leaves such as fennel and dill.

The majority of herbs prefer light, free-draining soil; their roots may rot in wet soils. They also need soil that is not too rich in nutrients because the best flavors and aromas do not come from soft, lush plants. Dig the site well, as deeply as possible to promote good drainage. If necessary, add some coarse sand or fine grit to the soil to improve drainage around the plants' roots. On poor soils, add a light dressing of bonemeal fertilizer to keep the plants growing steadily through the season.

Buy young, vigorous, container-grown plants from a garden center or specialist nursery. Firm them in thoroughly after planting, and don't forget to label them. Let them become well established before taking too may cuttings, though it will not do any harm to pinch out some of the shoot tips to encourage branching.

▲ *A dressing of gravel around the plants will help to keep the soil surface free-draining as well as finishing off the herb garden attractively.*

# greenhouse: *general tasks*

*Increasingly the evenings and nights are becoming cool, providing ideal conditions for diseases such as gray mold unless dead and dying plant material is removed promptly. Now's also the time to check that greenhouse heaters are in working order, ready for when they are needed.*

## Harvest greenhouse crops

Keep picking eggplants, cucumbers, melons, bell peppers, and tomatoes as they ripen. Take care with the watering of tomatoes; when plants are watered after a dry period the fruits are prone to split. Keep the soil just moist at all times. Remove lower leaves from tomatoes as they yellow; they are of no further use to plants.

Peppers can be harvested while they are still green, or left on the plants to ripen. Pick them just as they begin to turn color, and they will carry on ripening after picking. It is sometimes difficult to judge when melons are ready to harvest, but it is best to rely on your sense of smell.

Ripe melons give off a heady, almost alcoholic aroma from the stem end, and the fruits' skin starts to crack slightly around the base of the stem. Once ready, cut them and eat them as soon as possible because they soon become overripe if left.

▼ *Melons can become very heavy as they mature, and often need to be supported in nets attached to the greenhouse framework.*

### TAKE PELARGONIUM CUTTINGS

Pelargonium plants can be cut down in the fall and overwintered in their pots in the greenhouse, but young plants raised from cuttings taken now often do better in the long run.

Use vigorous, healthy shoots, preferably non-flowering. If flower buds are present in the growing points of any suitable shoots, just pinch them out as you prepare the cutting. Follow the procedure for softwood cuttings (see page 77), keeping them in a humid atmosphere until they are rooted. If space is at a premium in the greenhouse get rid of the parent plants once you are sure that these cuttings are well rooted.

# start new and old cyclamen

Cyclamen, with their graceful, upturned petals on long flower stems, are very popular winter-flowering pot plants. Now is the time to start old tubers into growth after their summer rest, and to sow seeds for new plants.

1 Cyclamen tubers that have been stored in pots of dry soil mix over the summer will probably be producing tiny clusters of leaves on the surface by now. They should be tipped out of their pots and the old mix crumbled away.

2 Very large tubers can be cut into two or more sections, each with a growth bud; dust the cut edges with fungicide powder. Repot into fresh, moist potting mix, so that only the lower half of the tuber is buried.

3 Cyclamen seed is sometimes slow to germinate. Speed up the process by soaking the seed in tepid water for 12 hours, then rinse it under gently running water for 30 minutes to wash away natural germination inhibitors (**above**).

4 Sow the seed in pots of sowing and cuttings mix, pushing it just below the surface (**left**). Seedlings develop with long leaf stalks and a tiny, translucent tuber on the soil surface. Handle carefully when pricking out.

## POT UP
## FREESIA CORMS

Freesias have wonderfully scented flowers, and corms that are potted up now will give elegant, fragrant plants for the home in the middle of winter. But check when buying them that they are scented varieties, as some of the modern cultivars have unfortunately lost their fragrance.

Plant the corms in gritty mix so that their tips are around 1in/2.5cm below the mix surface, setting six corms to a 5in/13cm pot. Water sufficiently to make the mix just moist. Stand the pots outside in a sheltered place in the garden until frosts are likely, when they should be moved to a garden frame or cool greenhouse.

# fall

Enjoy the garden's final, colorful fling of flowers and foliage before the darker days and cool, dull weather of the fall take hold. There's plenty of tidying up to do after the summer, but it's also time to look ahead and start making preparations for the spring to come.

# early fall

*Many of the early fall tasks involve clearing away the debris of the summer season, but there's also plenty of sowing and planting to do. Warm, sunny days and an abundance of bright flowers, foliage, and fruits make the melancholy job of tidying up after the summer a much more pleasant affair.*

Although fall marks the end of the main growing season, it is a busy time in the garden. There are crops to be gathered, leaves to sweep up and tender plants to be protected before the first frost arrives. Misty mornings, heavy dew, and cool weather combine to make ideal conditions for fungus diseases; regular checks and prompt treatment where appropriate are necessary to prevent plant losses.

The dying leaves of deciduous trees and shrubs often make a remarkable display of brilliant color, but all too soon the show is ended by gales which bring the leaves tumbling down. Dead leaves must be removed from garden ponds, lawns, alpine plants, paths, and patios before they can do damage or become a nuisance, and leaf clearing can be a major job in large gardens.

Beds and borders should still be putting on a show with late-blooming plants if varieties have been chosen wisely. Tidy spent border plants and old stems to show off these late-flowering plants to advantage. Weeds continue to thrive and need removing regularly.

Fall is an excellent time for planting both bare-root and container-grown plants. It is also time to plant spring bulbs, always a pleasant task, as we can look forward to their flowers signaling that winter is over in a few months' time.

There are seeds to be sown in early fall, too. Some hardy annuals will brave the winter cold and produce early flowers next summer if sown outdoors now. In the vegetable garden peas and some beans can be tried, and fall is the perfect time to sow a new lawn.

◀ *Border plants such as the architectural, steely-blue* Eryngium *continue to make a bold display well into the fall months.*

## EARLY FALL TASKS

**General**

:: *Watch out for fungus diseases around the garden*
:: *Deal with fallen leaves*
:: *Clean and put away garden furniture*

**Ornamental garden**

:: *Plant spring bulbs*
:: *Sow hardy annuals to overwinter*
:: *Take cuttings of evergreens and plant hardy evergreen shrubs*
:: *Move tender plants under cover before the frosts. Provide outdoor protection for slightly hardier ones*

:: *Replace annuals and summer bedding with spring bedding as they fade*
:: *Continue to clear containers and replant with bulbs and spring bedding*
:: *Clear and weed around fall-flowering bulbs and perennials*

:: *Prepare sites for fall planting of bare-root trees and shrubs*
:: *Protect decorative berries from birds*
:: *Take cuttings of old-fashioned and shrub roses*
:: *Check ties and stakes on trees, and adjust if necessary*

▲ *Daffodils bulbs should be planted as soon as they become available in the stores.*

**Lawns**

:: *Sow new lawns*
:: *Rake and aerate lawns, and give them a fall feed*
:: *Repair bald patches, broken edges, bumps and dips*

:: *Deal with toadstools*
:: *Water garden*
:: *Net ponds against falling leaves*

:: *Remove tender pond plants before the frosts*

**Kitchen garden**

:: *Plant spring cabbage*
:: *Harvest maincrop potatoes*
:: *Support winter brassicas if necessary*
:: *Lift maincrop carrots and beets*
:: *Thin out seedlings*

:: *Pick outdoor tomatoes and clear away plants*
:: *Harvest pumpkins and squashes before the first frosts*
:: *Sow winter lettuce under a cloche or tunnel*

:: *Plant onion sets for an early crop*
:: *Continue picking apples and pears*

▼ *Prick off cyclamen seedlings as soon as they are large enough to handle.*

**Greenhouse**

:: *Ventilate the greenhouse and water plants with care*
:: *Bring pot plants such as azaleas and solanums back indoors*
:: *Pick remaining food crops (such as peppers and tomatoes) and discard the plants*

:: *Clean the framework and glass where appropriate*
:: *Plant bulbs in pots and bowls for forcing*
:: *Pot up cineraria and cyclamen seedlings*
:: *Continue to take cuttings of tender outdoor plants as an insurance against winter losses*

# ornamental garden: *general tasks*

*Even when late flowers have faded, the fall garden need never be dull. Deciduous foliage can provide some spectacularly brilliant colors; berry-bearing plants continue the show for months, provided birds don't eat the lot. Evergreen plants also start to come into their own in the fall.*

## Enjoy fall color

Shortening day length triggers off brilliant reds, oranges, and yellows in some deciduous leaves. Plants vary in the intensity of color produced. Acer (maple), berberis (barberry), cercidiphyllum, fothergilla, nyssa (tulepo), parthenocissus (Virginia creeper), hamamelis (witch hazel),

▼ *Fall color from deciduous trees and shrubs can makes a brilliant spectacle. Select varieties specially bred for their colorful foliage.*

and many others provide some reliably colorful species and varieties.

Climate and soil conditions have a major part to play, too. The more marked the contrast between day and night temperatures, the better the leaf color. Wet, mild weather, when the leaves tend to remain green and hang on the trees for longer, can also spoil the show. But other factors are more within our control. Prevent fall leaves from being prematurely blown from trees by planting them in a sheltered

position. Provide fertilizers during the growing season to promote plenty of lush leaf growth to turn color later. For lime-hating plants, acid (rather than neutral) soil greatly intensifies their leaf color.

### PROTECT BERRIES FROM BIRDS

Bunches of brightly-colored berries can decorate the garden right through fall and winter, but often the first sharp frost brings flocks of birds to strip the berries from the plants.
Netting (provided it is supported away from the plants to prevent birds pecking through it) protects the berries but usually spoils the appearance of the plants. Bird-deterrent sprays are an alternative; they use a harmless but bitter-tasting compound to make berries unpalatable. Yellow and orange berries are far less likely to be attacked than bright red ones, so try planting varieties such as *Pyracantha* 'Orange Glow' and *Ilex aquifolium* 'Bacciflava'.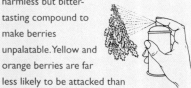

## TAKE CUTTINGS OF EVERGREENS

Shoots to be used as cuttings should have ripened at the base and be around 6in/15cm long. Pull them away from the main stem with a small heel of bark at the base; treat them with a rooting hormone combined with a fungicide to prevent rotting, and insert them into trays of sandy sowing and cuttings mix. Overwinter the cuttings in a cold frame or unheated greenhouse; they should have rooted by the following spring.

# protect non-hardy plants

A number of garden and patio plants are not reliably hardy in many gardens and need a little help to survive the winter. If you have taken cuttings from these in late summer (see page 125) you will at least have some plants in reserve in case the worst happens.

1 Herbaceous plants die down in the fall and spend the winter below soil as a dormant root-stock. Tender plants may not survive frost and cold penetrating the ground, but an insulating mulch of dry leaves, dead bracken or chipped bark heaped over the root area will help them survive.

2 Small trees and shrubs can be protected from low temperature damage by surrounding them with insulating material such as straw or bracken. The material must be dry to avoid fungus disease, and it must be loosely packed so that air can circulate through it.

3 Surround the shrub with a circle of wire netting supported on stakes, and loosely pack the wire cage with the insulating material. A piece of plastic sheeting over the top will keep the material dry (**below, left**).

4 The roots of plants in containers are particularly prone to cold weather damage. Lag the container with straw or a similar material; bubble wrap sheeting is useful for wrapping around tubs and pots in a double layer (**below**).

145

# ornamental garden: *planting and sowing*

*It's time to prepare for a colorful spring, by replacing summer bedding plants and annuals that are past their best, and by planting spring-flowering bulbs in lawns. New evergreen shrubs can also be planted safely now, as long as they are not likely to be damaged by cold winter weather.*

## Plant hardy evergreens

Because evergreen plants carry their full complement of leaves at planting time, extra care must be taken to protect them from adverse weather. Strong winds carry moisture away from the leaf surfaces, leading to scorching and leaf fall, and leaf tips and margins can be damaged by hard frosts. Make sure that evergreens planted now are quite hardy; more tender types will do better if they are planted in late spring.

Prepare the soil for evergreens in the normal way, digging deeply and adding some slow-release fertilizer such as bonemeal to the base of the planting hole. Make sure you firm in plants thoroughly; because they have leaves to catch the wind, root rock can be a problem. They should also be firmed back in thoroughly with the ball of your foot after windy or frosty weather. If cold, windy weather strikes after planting evergreens, protect them with a windbreak while they get established (see page 168).

▼ *Evergreen shrubs and trees really come into their own during the fall and winter months, providing color and interesting shapes.*

### REPLACE SUMMER BEDDING

Summer bedding and annual flowers will soon be past their best. Over the next few weeks it's time to replace them with spring bedding for some early interest next year.

Put spent plants on the compost pile. Dig the vacant soil over well, removing weeds, and add some slow-release fertilizer: refill containers with fresh potting mix. Plant up beds and containers with spring bedding plants such as *myosotis* (forget-me-not), *viola* (pansies), *primula* (primroses), and *erysimum* (wallflowers), interplanted with spring bulbs such as tulips and hyacinths for an effective display.

# naturalizing spring bulbs

Bulbs growing through grass always look particularly attractive during the spring flowering season. Daffodils and crocus are the two subjects most popular for growing like this, but several others are also successful, including *Colchicum* (fall crocus), *Fritillaria meleagris* (snakeshead fritillary), *Muscari* (grape hyacinth) and *Scilla* (squill).

1 Informality is the key to success when naturalizing bulbs. To look as natural as possible, handfuls of the bulbs are scattered randomly over the area, and planted as they fall, with one or two minor adjustments (**above**).

2 Removing plugs of turf and soil to plant the bulbs individually is hard work (**above**). The lawn area should be watered deeply two or three days before planting to soften the turf; a long-handled bulb planter makes the job much easier.

3 Drop a bulb at the base of the hole and replace the soil plug, treading it down lightly with the foot. Make sure the bottom of the bulb is in firm contact with the soil at the base of the hole, not wedged half-way up.

## SOW HARDY ANNUALS OUTDOORS

Hardy annuals such as *nigella* (love-in-a-mist), *calendula* (marigolds), *limnanthes* (poached-egg plants) and *helianthus* (sunflowers) can be sown where they are to flower to overwinter outdoors.

4 When planting small bulbs such as crocus it is often easier to fold back a section of turf and plant direct into the soil below. Cut an H-shape with an edging iron (**left**), undercut and fold back the two flaps of turf. Plant the bulbs randomly into the soil (**below**), water, then fold the flaps back into place and firm thoroughly.

5 Before planting bulbs in lawns, remember that the grass cannot be mown in spring until the bulb leaves have died. Choose an informal area of the garden where this will not matter.

# bulbs, corms, and tubers

Plants need certain conditions in order to be able to grow—they must have suitable temperatures, sufficient light and an adequate supply of nutrients and water. If some or all of these requirements are not present, the plants must have some strategy for coping with the problem or they will die.

Many plants become dormant in order to survive until conditions become suitable for growth again. The most successful plants do not just become dormant, however,

they also have a store of nutrients and water to help them over the difficult period once they begin to regrow. Bulbs, corms, and tubers are all underground storage organs that hold a reserve of nutrients and water to enable them to start into growth and flower in the appropriate season. Many gardeners think of all these structures as "bulbs," and they are often grouped together and referred to as "bulbous plants" for convenience. However, there are differences between them and the way they grow.

Bulbs are modified leaves with leaf bases attached to a short stem. The leaves are very fleshy and contain food reserves, and the small stem is cone or disk shaped. In the center of the bulb, surrounded by the fleshy leaves, is the flower bud and the immature foliage leaves that will emerge from the bulb when it starts to grow.

On the outside of the bulb there are usually firm, dry scales forming a tunic that helps protect the bulb from moisture loss and damage by pest or diseases. Not all bulbs have these, however; lily and fritillaria bulbs have no papery tunic, and the overlapping leaf scales are very obvious. This makes these bulbs particularly prone to damage and drying out, and they need more careful storage and handling than bulbs with a tunic. The structure of a bulb can easily be examined by slicing an onion in half. The separate, fleshy leaves, cone-shaped basal stem, central embryo flower bud, and protective outer scales are all easy to recognize.

Corms are modified stems. On the outside they are surrounded by the dried remains of the previous year's

◀ *Dahlias have clusters of tuberous roots which carry their growth buds on a short section of the plant's main stem.*

▲ *The daffodil is one of the most familiar true bulbs. Bulbs increase by producing offsets from the base, which eventually separate entirely.*

▲ *Corms are surrounded on the outside by the dried remains of the previous year's leaf bases, so they sometimes look like bulbs.*

leaf bases, making them look superficially like bulbs, and under these leaf bases they have parallel ridges that are the leaf nodes. A new corm is formed on top of the old one every year, and the old one withers away. If a corm is sliced in half, you will see a solid structure, that is not composed of separate leaves like a bulb.

## PLANTING THE RIGHT WAY UP

If a bulb, corm, or tuber is planted upside down, this will not stop it growing; however, the stems will have to do a U-turn to grow up to the soil surface, and this bend in the stem will be a weak point that's vulnerable to damage. It is usually fairly easy to tell which is the top of the structure—look for a growth bud or buds at one end and the remains of roots at the other. Some tubers are more difficult because they have a dished surface, but tiny growth buds should be visible. Fritillarias and lilies, without a protective tunic, often have hollow centers where water may collect and cause rotting. It is safer to plant the bulbs on their sides to avoid this happening.

A tuber is another swollen storage organ which may be formed from either the stem or the roots, depending on the plant. The potato is a very familiar stem tuber, while dahlias have clusters of root tubers. On potato tubers, axillary growth buds are found toward one end. These are the "eyes" that grow into shoots from which form roots and eventually, more tubers. The original tuber withers away as its food reserve is used up. Since root tubers usually have their growth buds only on a short section of the plant's stem to which they are attached, each tuberous root must have a small piece of main stem attached to it if it is to grow. Tubers are also solid throughout if sliced through.

The food reserves within bulbs, corms, and tubers exist to help the plant survive its dormant period. This may be in winter when conditions are too cold for growth, or in summer when they are too dry—the timing varies according to species.

# ornamental garden: *plants in season*

*Early fall may mark the beginning of the end of the growing season, but it is still filled with color and interest. Late-flowering perennials and bulbs, bright fruit and berries abound; and, depending on the weather conditions, the first of the fiery fall leaf tints from deciduous trees and shrubs make themselves evident.*

▲ Perovskia atriplicifolia *'Blue Spire'* has attractive, aromatic, gray-green foliage as well as panicles of strikingly blue flowers.

▶ *The butterfly's favorite, Sedum spectabile. The variety 'Iceberg' has pure white flowers instead of the more familiar pink.*

▼ *The dainty flowers of Cyclamen hederifolium are held above attractively marbled leaves that persist right through the winter.*

## TREES AND SHRUBS

*Caryopteris* x *clandonensis*
*Ceanothus* (California lilac)
*Clerodendrum bungei* (glory bower),
    *C. trichotomum*
*Erica* (heath)
*Hebe*
*Hydrangea macrophylla*
*Leycesteria formosa*
    (Himalayan honeysuckle)
*Malus* (crab apple)
*Perovskia atriplicifolia*
*Rosa* (flowers and hips) (rose)
*Vinca major* (greater
    periwinkle), *V. minor* (lesser periwinkle)

## PERENNIALS AND BEDDING PLANTS

*Achillea* (yarrow)
*Aconitum napellus* (aconite)
*Anemone hybrida*
*Aster*
*Eryngium* (sea holly)
*Helenium*
*Hemerocallis* (day lily)
*Kniphofia* (red hot poker)
*Rudbeckia* (coneflower)
*Schizostylis coccinea* (kaffir lily)
*Sedum spectabile* (ice plant)
*Solidago* (Aaron's rod)

## BULBS

*Amaryllis belladonna*
*Colchicum* (fall crocus)
*Crinum* x *powellii*
*Crocosmia crocosmiiflora*
*Crocus* (fall-flowering species)
*Cyclamen*
*Nerine bowdenii*

◀ *The daisy-like flowers of helenium brighten fall borders with their gloriously rich shades of red, bronze, and yellow.*

# lawns and water gardens: *general tasks*

*Mild, damp fall weather encourages toadstools—an unwelcome sight in the middle of the lawn—but is ideal for the germination of grass seed. Garden ponds need care now to prevent the water from being polluted with decaying plant matter, and pond fish need help to face the winter ahead.*

### Remove tender pond plants

Some floating pond plants make an attractive contribution to the pool in the summer, but will not survive a cold winter out of doors. They include the water hyacinth (*Eichhornia crassipes*) and the water lettuce (*Pistia stratiotes*). Remove them from the pond well before the first frosts are due. Overwinter them in a frost-free greenhouse, placed in a washing-up bowl or similar container filled with pond water, with a lining of mud at the bottom. Put them back in the pond in early summer. *Trapa natans* (water chestnut) is also frost tender but is an annual that will not survive the winter anyway. It should also be removed from the pond to prevent the decaying foliage from polluting the water.

### NET PONDS AGAINST FALLING LEAVES

It is vital to keep fall leaves out of the pond. Decaying plant material gives off toxic gases which will poison fish and turn the water stagnant. Use fine mesh plastic netting to cover the surface of the pond, insuring that it is pegged down securely all around the edges.

Before putting the net in position, cut down excess growth of oxygenating plants and remove this, together with all dead and dying foliage and flowers from water and marginal plants.

## sow a new lawn

Seed is the cheapest way of making a new lawn, and allows most control over which grass varieties are used. Although lawn seed can also be sown successfully in spring, early fall, while the soil is still warm and the conditions moist, is the best time for the job.

1 Give the prepared site a final raking to level it and break down the clods of soil to a fine, even, crumbly texture (**right**). If the soil is loose and puffy, shuffle over the whole site to firm it gently with your feet before raking.

2 Weigh out the correct quantity of seed for the area to be sown (sowing rates should be given on the packs, and are usually about 1–1½ oz per sq yd/35–50 g per sq m). Split the total quantity of seed into two.

3 Sow the first half of the seed mixture over the whole lawn as evenly as possible, working from top to bottom; then sow the second half working from side to side (**left**). This double sowing helps to even out any inconsistencies in the sowing rate.

4 Use a spring-tine rake to scratch the seed lightly into the soil but do not try to bury it (**below**). Using seed treated with a bird repellent will cut down the bird nuisance; if necessary, the lawn area can be protected with plastic netting supported on stakes.

### REMOVE TOADSTOOLS FROM LAWNS

Crops of toadstools are common on turf at this time of year, appearing magically overnight. There are many different types of fungi. Most of them grow on organic matter in the soil and are quite harmless. If their appearance spoils the look of the lawn, they can simply be picked off and thrown away—they appear for only a short time each year.

One type that is more serious is *Marasmius oreades* (fairy ring fungus) that can cause obvious, unsightly green rings in the grass. Although various fungicides may be suggested, this fungus is almost impossible to treat successfull; remaking the lawn may be the only answer. The deep green rings may be disguised by treating the lawn with fertilizer to green up the rest of the grass.

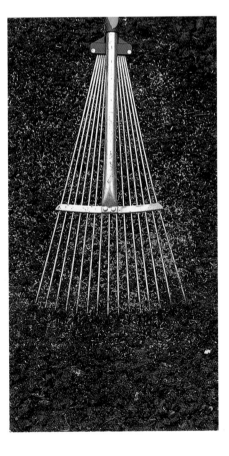

◀ *The water hyacinth (*Eichhornia crassipes*) is a serious invasive pest in frost-free areas, but is killed off in the fall in cold climates.*

# kitchen garden: *general tasks*

*There are sowings and plantings to be made in the kitchen garden, and harvested crops need to be stored away carefully. Make sure winter vegetables are progressing satisfactorily, and give them the protection they need from the bad weather that may be around the corner.*

### Harvest pumpkins

Pumpkins and winter squashes should be cut and brought under cover before the first frosts. As long as they are fully ripened, they can be stored for many weeks in a cool but frost-free, dry shed. Check the fruit has no signs of damage or rot before storing, particularly where it has been resting on the soil.

Maincrop potatoes should also be lifted now. On a dry, sunny day, fork the potatoes out of the soil and leave them on the surface of the ground for several hours to dry. Store them in burlap or heavy-duty paper sacks, or wooden or sturdy cardboard boxes. Do not use plastic sacks; they retain moisture and cause rotting. Store in a cool, dark place and cover the potatoes to exclude all light.

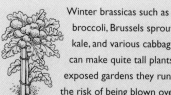

## SUPPORT WINTER BRASSICAS

Winter brassicas such as broccoli, Brussels sprouts, kale, and various cabbages can make quite tall plants. In exposed gardens they run the risk of being blown over because they have relatively shallow root systems. In windy areas, provide each plant with a sturdy wooden stake.

The earliest varieties of Brussels sprouts will now be ready for picking. Start harvesting from the base of the stem, where the largest buttons are, and gradually work upward.

▶ *Winter squashes should store well for weeks, but any that are damaged should be used up straight away as they will only rot in store.*

# lift root vegetables

Some root crops will happily stay in the soil right through winter, but others are best lifted at the end of the growing season and stored above ground, especially in areas where the soil is heavy and inclined to remain wet in winter. Wet conditions are likely to cause the roots to rot.

1 Carrots are at their tastiest pulled young (**right**) and eaten straight away, but maincrop varieties make a useful crop for eating throughout the winter. If left in the soil too long they tend to split, which can make them unusable.

2 Fork up the carrots carefully to avoid spearing them, and shake off loose earth. Cut off the foliage (**below**), and layer the carrots in boxes of fine, almost dry soil, sand or peat. Store the boxes in a cool, dark place, eg, shed or garage. Use up any damaged carrots straight away.

## PROTECT SUMMER-PLANTED POTATOES

If you planted a few cold-stored potatoes in summer to give you new potatoes in the fall and winter, it will soon be time to protect the plants from cold weather, depending on the climate in your area. Use a mulch of straw, dry bracken or similar material along the rows. The first tubers may be ready for harvesting in mid-fall, but in reasonable conditions can be kept in the ground until mid or late winter.

3 Beets are often pickled in vinegar, but are also delicious if cooked and eaten like any other fresh root vegetable. The golden variety will not stain pink any other food with which it comes into contact, as the standard red varieties do.

4 Beets are lifted and stored in the same way as carrots, but the leafy tops should be twisted off, not cut with a knife, to avoid bleeding. Lift the roots before they become too big because they are inclined to go woody (**below**).

# kitchen garden: *planting and sowing*

*As well as harvesting the abundance of crops in the kitchen garden now, keep some continuity of cropping going with further plantings and sowings. A little extra protection from the weather can be gained by sowing under cover. Seedlings from earlier sowings need thinning out or transplanting.*

### Plant onion sets

Onion sets planted in the fall will give an early crop next year, several weeks before maincrop varieties are ready for harvest. Varieties available for fall planting have been chosen for their hardiness and disease resistance, and include 'Early Yellow Globe', 'Yellow Spanish', 'Snow White hybrid', and the red-fleshed 'Red Hamburger'. Prepare the soil thoroughly and mix in some coarse sand or grit to lighten it if necessary, as fall-planted sets need free-draining conditions. Plant the sets in rows 14in/35cm apart, spacing the sets 4–6in/10–15cm apart in the row. Always plant onion sets with a trowel, because simply pushing the sets into the soil can compact the ground immediately beneath them, making it difficult for the roots to penetrate. Fall-planted onions can be ready to harvest as early as late spring, but they can be stored for only a few weeks.

## THIN OUT SEEDLINGS

Seedlings from late sown crops, including lettuce, radish, spinach, and turnips, among others, should be thinned out as soon as they are large enough. This thinning is best carried out in progressive stages to allow for plant losses—thin to half the final recommended spacing first, then remove every other plant later on, as necessary.

Where seedlings are very crowded, great care is necessary to avoid disturbing the roots of the plants which are to remain after thinning. If the weather is dry, water the row of seedlings before thinning to make it easier to tease away the unwanted plants.

◄ *Fall-planted onion sets should produce a crop that is ready for harvesting very early the following summer.*

## lettuce for winter

It's great to have been able to cut fresh salads straight from the garden through the summer, and it's something that will be sadly missed over the next few months. However, it is possible to have a supply of winter lettuce from the greenhouse—the plants won't be as succulent and full hearted as summer varieties, but they're still worth growing. Sow the seed now; once the seedlings are large enough, they can be transplanted into growing bags, or direct into the greenhouse border.

1 It's important to choose the right variety of lettuce for growing in the greenhouse in winter because only a few are suitable. Check with your local garden center to see what is the best choice.

2 An unheated greenhouse is quite suitable for growing winter lettuce, although heated greenhouses will give a faster-maturing crop. Cold frames and polytunnels can also be used successfully for growing winter salads.

▲ *Transplant cabbages to their cropping positions. If preferred, space the young plants closely to obtain "greens" rather than densely hearted cabbages.*

3 Sow the seed thinly on a prepared flat of moist soil mix and cover lightly. Lettuce seed becomes dormant in very hot conditions, so it is important to keep the flat in a well-ventilated, lightly shaded position after sowing.

4 Once the seedlings are showing through, move the flat to full light. Water very carefully to avoid fungus disease. Prick out the seedlings to wider spacings as soon as they are large enough to be handled easily.

# sprayers and spraying

An efficient, easy-to-use sprayer is an essential piece of garden equipment. Pests and diseases are very common, particularly in the kitchen garden, and most gardeners are likely to find themselves needing to spray plants at one time or another. Even organic gardeners need sprayers, for they are used to apply organic remedies and fertilizers.

A sprayer enables a liquid to be applied as a spray of fine droplets, usually by forcing it through a nozzle under pressure. This enables the operator to achieve good, even coverage of the plant being treated. Where just a few plants are involved, a small, inexpensive hand-held sprayer holding about 1pt/500ml is sufficient. Although a small hand-held sprayer is useful for houseplants and treating individual plants in the garden, it has its limitations. It is often difficult to mix pesticides in such small quantities, and it is a nuisance to keep refilling the sprayer for larger jobs. Also, operating the trigger action is very tiring during prolonged use.

The next step up is a compression sprayer holding about 1–1¾ gallons/5–8 litres. Typically, this has a hand pump on top, and once the sprayer has been filled and the top screwed on tightly, a few strokes of the pump supply enough pressure to send the liquid through the nozzle in a fine, penetrating spray. This type of sprayer generally has a spray lance attached to plastic tubing to give a long reach. When the pressure of the spray starts to fall, a few more strokes of the pump are required to restore it. This type of sprayer is ideal for most medium to large gardens.

◀ *This type of sprayer is pressurized by a few strokes of the pump every few minutes. A long spray lance is a practical addition.*

▼ *A small hand-held sprayer is fine for occasional use, but is not practical where there are a lot of plants to be treated.*

For even larger spraying jobs, a backpack sprayer is useful. This holds 2 gallons/10 litres or more of liquid and comes with straps so that it can be worn like a backpack. A lever on the side is operated with one hand while the lance is held in the other; the lever is pumped up and down gently and continually during spraying. Backpack sprayers are expensive and are only likely to be necessary for very large vegetable gardens or orchards, although they can be useful for lawns or treating large areas of vacant soil with weedkiller. When filled with liquid, a backpack sprayer is very heavy and is unsuitable for those with bad backs.

### Sensible spraying

The fine drops from sprayers can travel long distances on the breeze. Never spray on a windy day, when other plants or even neighboring gardens could be unintentionally on the receiving end.

Always follow the instructions for diluting and applying pesticides to the letter, and dispose of any unused solution as advised on the pack. The best times to spray are in the early morning, or in the late afternoon or evening when there is no strong sun to scorch the leaves, and beneficial insects are less likely to be harmed.

▲ *Backpack sprayers are excellent for large-scale spraying jobs, but a smaller, cheaper sprayer is adequate for the majority of gardens.*

If you use a sprayer to apply weedkiller, label it clearly with an indelible marker pen and keep for applying weedkiller only. Never use it to spray cultivated plants with pesticides or fertilizer because traces of the weedkiller may remain, however well it is washed out.

## SAFE USE OF GARDEN CHEMICALS

- Store chemicals safely, out of the reach of children and pets, in the original packaging complete with instructions
- Use the most suitable chemical for the job, choosing the least persistent type where there is an option
- Read the application instructions and follow them carefully
- Mix up just enough chemical for the job, avoiding surplus spray solution
- Keep pets and children away while the spray is being mixed, applied, and until it has dried on the treated plants, unless the label advises differently
- Wash out the sprayer thoroughly after use, disposing of the rinsing water on to bare soil or gravel paths
- Use gloves when handling concentrates and solutions, and wash all exposed skin thoroughly when spraying is finished

# greenhouse: *general tasks*

*Now that the days are shortening, greenhouse plants need all the daylight that they can get, and washing the glass can make an enormous difference. Extra space will be needed for seedlings and tender plants; make room for them by clearing out the remains of summer crops such as tomatoes.*

## Indoor azaleas

Azaleas should have spent the summer outside in a partially shaded bed, with their pots plunged in soil to prevent them drying out. Their summer holiday is over now so dig them up, clean the pots and bring them back into the greenhouse before the cold weather arrives.

Plants can be repotted if necessary, but don't be in too much of a hurry to move them up a size because they flower best if the roots are slightly cramped. Traditionally azaleas are grown in soil-based potting mix and clay pots, but they also do well in plastic pots and soilless mix as long as you are careful with the watering. The mix should be just moist at all times. Keep the plants in a cool room when they are in flower.

### CLEAN THE GREENHOUSE

Even though greenhouse glass may look clean, it will have collected a surprising amount of grime over the summer months, which cuts down the amount of light able to reach the plants inside. Wash the outside of the glass thoroughly with a stiff broom and warm, soapy water, or use a pressure sprayer.

On a mild, dry, preferably sunny day, move the plants outdoors while you clean the inside—scrub down the glass, staging, and framework. This helps to combat overwintering pests and disease spores while making the place look neat and tidy. Don't slosh too much water about inside, and leave the doors and ventilators open to air and dry the greenhouse before moving the plants back in.

# pot up flower seedlings

Seedlings of cineraria and cyclamen that were sown earlier should now be ready for potting up. Both are invaluable winter-flowering plants for the home, bringing color and cheer into the house just when it is most needed. Cinerarias that were sown in late spring and early summer will be in flower by early or midwinter; those sown later will flower in spring. Cyclamen usually take around 14 months to reach flowering size.

## REMAINING TOMATOES

Greenhouse tomato plants have come to the end of their useful life now, and should be cleared away. Pick any unripe fruit that remains on the plants. Keep the best-developed fruits in a cool, dim place indoors and they will slowly ripen over the next few weeks. Storing a ripe apple or banana with them in an enclosed space, like a drawer or cupboard, will speed up ripening. Small, firm fruits are unlikely to ripen satisfactorily like this, but if there are enough of them they make terrific green tomato chutney.

◄ Azaleas make attractive winter-flowering pot plants, and are not too difficult to keep successfully from year to year.

1 Since cyclamen seed germinates over an extended period, not all seedlings from the same sowing will be at the same stage of growth, and not all will be ready for transplanting. Select the largest for moving on, and extricate them carefully from the tray to avoid damaging the rest.

2 Handle the seedlings gently, because they are very delicate. Hold the young plants by the leaves and not by the slender, fragile stems; pot them up so that the tiny developing tuber is sitting on the surface of the compost (**right**). Firm in the roots very lightly.

3 Cineraria seedlings are more robust, and their development should be more even. Depending on their stage of growth, the seedlings can be pricked out into trays, into individual 3½in/8cm pots, or moved to larger pots (**below**). Keep the soil mix just moist at all times.

4 Shade newly-transplanted seedlings from direct sun for a few days, using horticultural blanket or a sheet of newspaper to protect them if necessary (**below**). Both cyclamen and cineraria need cool conditions; be prepared to ventilate the greenhouse in sunny weather when necessary.

# mid-fall

*The tidy-up continues as more and more fall leaves hit the ground and late season flowers fade. As the weather becomes increasingly cold, it's time to protect the more delicate plants. Remain on the alert for frosts, though with luck you may find yourself enjoying a warm and sunny Indian summer.*

## Tidying up

This is often the time when fall leaf color is at its glorious best, but it won't be long before a windy spell brings the leaves to the ground in drifts. Fallen leaves are not so bad when they are dry and crisp, but once rain turns them to a slimy brown sludge they pose a danger to both plants and people. Remove them from lawns and small, vulnerable plants like alpines before the leaves smother them; also clear them from paths and steps before somebody slips in the decomposing mush and injures themselves.

Cut down spent flowers and dying foliage in herbaceous borders, but don't be too enthusiastic. Some dead, brown stems and leaves have an architectural value, and seed heads can be particularly decorative.

## Cold snap

At what time the first frost arrives, and just how bad the weather might be, depends largely on your particular location. Some regions can rely on mild falls and winters, while others can guarantee that freezing conditions will arrive in the near future. Only experience can tell you what to expect, but always be prepared for the worst. Better to prepare your dubiously hardy plants for icy weather that does not arrive, than leave them to be killed by a single unexpected cold snap.

## Future plans

As more plants in the kitchen garden finish cropping and are removed, vacant soil begins to appear, ready to be dug over for next spring. The earlier winter digging can start the better, allowing you maximum time to complete a task which can be backbreaking if rushed. If the fall weather is too depressing, cheer yourself up by continuing to plant spring-flowering bulbs and spring bedding to give you something to look forward to at the end of the winter, and start thumbing through new seed catalogs to plan next year's sowing program.

◀ *The deep pink flowers of* Nerine bowdenii *stand out in the fall sunshine. The bulb's foliage does not appear until spring.*

## MID-FALL TASKS

**General**

- Remove fallen leaves from paths, patios, steps and lawns and turn them into leaf mold
- Clear away all garden debris to avoid pests and diseases
- Protect vulnerable plants from rain and cold; beware of early frosts

**Ornamental garden**

- Tidy herbaceous borders and divide border plants; apply bonemeal to borders and around shrubs and trees
- Plant tulips and hyacinths; plant lily bulbs as they become available
- Remove and burn diseased leaves fallen from roses
- Plant bare-root trees and shrubs
- Lift and store dahlia roots when the leaves have been blackened by frost
- Lift and store gladioli and tuberous begonias
- Finish planting spring bedding
- Protect newly-planted shrubs from strong winds

▲ This is the ideal time to plant tulips. If planted too early, they start into premature growth.

**Lawns**

- Lay turf for new lawns
- Continue to sweep up leaves and repair damaged areas of grass. Mow as necessary, raising the cutting height of the mower from its summer setting
- Apply bulky top-dressing

▼ Turf establishes quickly in fall conditions, providing a virtually instant new lawn.

**Water garden**

- Remove submersible pumps from ponds; clean and store them under cover
- Tidy pond plants and marginals, removing dead leaves from the water

**Kitchen garden**

- Continue harvesting crops, and store fruit and vegetables. Pick remaining apples and pears. Check fruit and vegetables already in store
- Remove vegetable plants as they finish cropping; begin digging and adding organic matter to soil. Start a new vegetable plot if required
- Finish planting spring cabbages
- Start to fill in seed orders for next year when the catalogs arrive
- Take hardwood cuttings of soft fruit
- Plant new rhubarb crowns
- Prune blackcurrants, blackberries, and hybrid berries

**Greenhouse**

- Remove shading and clean the glass if this has not already been done
- Sow Lathyrus odoratus (sweet peas) for early flowers outdoors next year
- Take care not to overwater, or splash water about. Remove dead and dying foliage, flowers, and fruit promptly
- Ventilate whenever possible to maintain an airy atmosphere
- Heat the greenhouse as necessary to maintain a suitable temperature for the plants

# general tasks

*Clean up fall leaves and plant remains and transform them into valuable compost and leaf mold for the garden. A number of garden plants need protection from fall and winter weather now. It is not just cold that is the problem; excess rain can have serious effects, too.*

## Cold protection for plants

Continue to provide protection for plants that may not be reliably hardy in your area (see page 145). It is often difficult to know just how well a particular plant will survive local conditions, but any plant that is described as "rather tender," "dubiously hardy," "half-hardy" or "suitable for favored areas" should be given extra care in regions where there are penetrating frosts. This is particularly important for young plants, or recently planted subjects that have not had a chance to establish properly and become acclimatized to the conditions. Plants such as agapanthus (African blue lily), cordyline (cabbage palm), phygelius, yucca, eucalyptus, passiflora (passion flower), and acacia (wattle) are among many that may need protection.

Remember that many plants that will happily survive overnight frosts where the temperature rises during the day, are likely to be killed by cold spells where freezing conditions persist for several days at a time.

### KEEP OFF EXCESS RAIN

It is often excessively wet rather than cold conditions that kills plants during the fall and winter. Plants with furry leaves, such as verbascum, are particularly prone to rotting in wet weather because the fur on the foliage holds on to moisture. Silver-leaved plants are also at risk; they are adapted to dry growing conditions and are often badly affected by a damp atmosphere.

Susceptible plants can usually be protected by covering them with an  open-ended cloche, which keeps water off the foliage but still allows air to circulate to help prevent fungus disease from developing.

◄ *It is important to protect susceptible plants against overnight frosts at this time of year. One option is the horticultural blanket.*

## how to build a compost pile

Virtually all types of soil benefit from the addition of plenty of rotted organic matter, but the problem is usually finding a handy supply of suitable material. Composting your garden refuse has two benefits — it provides a convenient and valuable supply of the organic matter your soil needs, and is also a means of disposing of awkward, bulky waste.

1 A compost pile is simply somewhere waste material can be gathered together to rot down (**left**). Confining it within a wire, plastic, or wooden bin (it can be either a proprietary composter or a home-made one) keeps it neat, and helps to encourage rapid decomposition by providing the most favorable conditions.

2 Anything organic (i.e. anything that has once lived) can be composted, but avoid animal products and cooked items because these attract vermin. Young weeds, plant refuse, fruit and vegetable peelings are all suitable. Lawn mowings can be added to the heap if they are well mixed with bulkier, more open waste. Add a layer of garden soil to the heap every so often.

### SWEEP FALLEN LEAVES FROM PATHS

It is surprising how quickly fallen leaves become slippery when they have been lying around in damp weather. On patios, paths, and particularly on steps they can pose a real danger to pedestrians. Sweep them up regularly; apart from anything else, they are easier to gather up when they are still dry. Pack the leaves into plastic sacks, tie the tops and pierce some holes in the sides of the sack with a garden fork. Leave the sacks in a corner of the garden and eventually the contents will rot down into valuable leaf mold.

3 Once the bin is full, cover the top with a piece of old carpet or cardboard to keep in the heat and keep out excess rain, and allow the contents to decompose to a dark brown, crumbly, sweet-smelling mass (**above**). Occasionally turning the sides of the heap to the middle is hard work, but it does speed up the rotting process.

4 The traditional fall bonfire is a wasteful and polluting affair, but can be used for woody prunings and other material that is too hard to rot down. Diseased plant material and seeding weeds are also best burned rather than composted, as disease spores and weed seeds may not always be killed by the composting process.

# ornamental garden: *general tasks*

*Even though the summer is over, the ornamental garden still contains plenty of interest for the weeks ahead. Some plants need to be lifted now and stored under cover for the winter. Flower borders can be tidied, and many perennials can be given a new lease of life by being divided and replanted.*

## *Decorative seed heads*

When clearing up the flower border, it's all too easy to cut down plants that have a valuable role in providing fall and winter interest. Many seed heads are highly decorative, and have strong architectural shapes that are very attractive. Don't be too rigorous about deadheading—leave the final flush of flowers to set seed.

Flowers worth growing for their seed heads include acanthus (bear's breeches), allium, briza (quaking grass), cynara, eryngium (sea holly), festuca (fescue), *Iris foetidissima*, lunaria (honesty), nigella (love-in-a-mist), papaver (poppy), *Physalis alkekengi* (Chinese lantern), scabious (especially 'Paper Moon'), and typha (bullrush). Many border plants also have "everlasting"-type flower heads that are worth preserving when they are dead, including achillea (yarrow), carlina (carline thistle), hydrangea and *Sedum spectabile*. Their russet-brown shades are more subtle than their summer colors, but produce a pleasing effect, especially when lightly iced with frost.

### APPLYING BONEMEAL

Bonemeal is a natural slow-release fertilizer that gradually supplies its nutrients to the soil. It provides some nitrogen and a much larger proportion of phosphates, and is useful for applying around perennials, trees, and shrubs during the dormant season.

Always wear gloves when applying bonemeal. There is a slight risk of the fertilizer being contaminated with animal diseases, particularly anthrax, though this risk is extremely small and should not be a concern provided the bonemeal has been properly sterilized. However, if you have any small cuts or abrasions to your skin, bonemeal—and other powdered fertilizers—will make them sting unpleasantly.

## *divide border plants*

Division is an easy way to increase your stock of herbaceous perennials. Not only does it give you a new supply of plants, but it actually improves the performance of plants that have been in place for more than a couple of years. Border plants can also be divided in spring, but mid-fall is generally the best time of year to do the job.

1 Popular border plants such as Campanula (bell flower), hosta, Achillea (yarrow), Echinops (globe thistle) and Papaver (poppies) are all suitable subjects for division. Dig up the whole clump carefully with a garden fork, and place it on a spare piece of weed-free soil or on a plastic sheet on the lawn or path (**right**).

2 Often the center of the clump will be woody and hard, with the strongest shoots growing around the edge. Splitting the clump up will enable you to discard the unproductive center and rejuvenate the plant by replanting the more vigorous sections.

3 Use two forks back to back to prise tough clumps apart (**left**), or cut them with a knife. Smaller plants may be teased apart by hand. As a guide, each portion should be large enough to fit comfortably in the palm of the hand, and must have good roots and strong growth buds,

4 Replant the new portions straight away; the roots will dry out if they are exposed to the air for too long. If replanting in the same place, dig the soil over quickly with a trowel, removing any weeds, and incorporate a little bonemeal or similar slow-release fertilizer.

◄ Sedum spectabile *is one of a number of border plants whose dead flower heads remain attractive through the fall months.*

### LIFT AND STORE DAHLIAS

Dahlias in the border need to be protected from cold, wet winter weather in order to survive until spring. As soon as frosts have blackened the foliage, cut down the main stem to about 6in/15cm and lift the tuberous roots. Store them upside down for a few days in order to allow any moisture to drain from the hollow stems, then clean the soil off the tubers and pack them into flats, covering them with almost-dry compost. Store the flats in a cool but frost-free, dry place (such as a garage or shed) over the winter. Gladioli corms and begonia tubers should also be lifted now, and cleaned and stored in boxes of compost in a dry, frost-free place, like the dahlias.

# ornamental garden: *planting*

*Fall is an excellent time for planting, but in windy areas, it is worth providing a temporary windbreak as protection for newly planted subjects. Bulbs pose no such problems. While many spring-flowering types should have been set out last month, there are one or two that prefer later planting.*

### Bare-root trees and shrubs

Bare-root plants have been lifted from nursery beds in the open ground, and have to be sold in the dormant season when they are more resilient to the disturbance of transplanting. They are usually cheaper than container-grown plants, and there is often a better choice of varieties available. They are also easier to transport than plants in containers, and can be bought by mail order.

Care should be taken not to let the roots dry out any more than is necessary. Try not to expose them to the air but keep them covered by plastic bags, paper, or burlap sacks during transportation. Ideally bare-root subjects should be planted immediately, but if that is not possible they can be heeled in to a spare piece of ground temporarily, just covering the roots with fine soil. Inspect the roots immediately before planting, and trim back with pruners any that show signs of damage.

▲ *Bare-rooted conifers (here wrapped in burlap for transportation) are best transplanted now during the dormant season.*

### PROTECT NEWLY-PLANTED SHRUBS FROM STRONG WINDS

Shrubs that have been planted in exposed positions are at risk of damage from the windy weather that is common at this time of year. Evergreens are most vulnerable because they are still carrying their leaves, but even deciduous plants can be damaged by root rock caused by wind catching the branch framework, or the branches may be snapped off.

Reduce the possibility of damage by erecting a temporary windbreak on the windward side of the shrub. Drive two or three stakes into the ground, and tack windbreak netting, sacking, or even old plastic sacks to the stakes to provide shelter. The windbreak can be removed in late spring next year, provided the plants are sufficiently well established.

▶ *Some of the most attractive tulips are the smaller varieties, such as* Tulipa kaufmanniana *hybrids, with their striking, mottled foliage.*

## plant tulips and hyacinths

Spring bulbs such as narcissus (daffodils) and crocuses should have been planted in early fall, but it pays to wait until now, or even until late fall, before planting tulips and hyacinths. If planted too early they make premature growth that may be damaged by cold weather.

### CONTAINER BULBS

Tulips and hyacinths are also ideal for planting in tubs and windowboxes. The best effects are always obtained by planting only one variety in each container because different varieties flower at different times.

1 Tulips and hyacinths make good subjects for the flower border, especially when mixed with spring bedding plants such as wallflowers and forget-me-nots. Dig the soil deeply and add a slow-release fertilizer such as bonemeal.

2 Dig planting holes with a trowel or use a special bulb planter (**right**). Make the holes sufficiently deep for the tops of the bulbs to be covered with twice their own depth of soil. Shallow planting leads to poor flowering.

3 Drop the bulbs into their holes making sure that they are the correct way up, and that the base of the bulb is in contact with the soil at the bottom of the hole. Return the soil to the hole and firm it lightly.

4 Because there will be no sign of the bulbs until next spring, it is easy to forget where they are planted and to damage them by cultivating the ground in winter. Label the area where they are planted to avoid this (**below**).

# growing variegated plants

The term variegated means marked with two or more colors, usually in an irregular pattern, and as a gardening term it is nearly always applied to leaves. The most common colors on a variegated leaf are green and yellow, or white, though several other colors can be involved, such as pink, red, purple, and orange.

Variegated foliage obviously adds color and pattern to the garden in much the same way as flowers do. It is valuable because it tends to be longer lasting than flowers, and on evergreen plants is present through the fall and winter when flowers are scarce and the garden could easily look dull and uninteresting. Variegated evergreens that merge into the background during the summer stand out splendidly in the dormant season,

seeming to glow with a special brightness. Gold-variegated subjects, particularly, give the appearance of sunshine even on the cloudiest, most miserable days.

Because the green pigment (chlorophyll) in leaves is necessary for efficient photosynthesis (the process by which plants manufacture their own energy), variegated plants, with less green pigment, tend to be at a bit of a disadvantage. This means they are usually slower growing and less vigorous than all-green varieties, and they generally need a position in bright light where they can receive as much sun as possible. If they do not receive sufficient light the variegation may disappear as the plant tries to compensate by producing more green pigment.

Variegated plants should be positioned carefully from a design point of view, too. When planted near each other, they lose their impact and can cause uncomfortable clashes of color and tone. For the best effect, a variegated variety should be surrounded by plain-leaved subjects, preferably of a darker shade, against which the brighter variegation will stand out.

True variegation takes the form of an irregular pattern, but the term is generally used to include more regular markings on leaves, too. There may be a central blotch, often at the base of the leaf near the leaf stem, or a yellow or silver margin of varying widths. Sometimes the leaf is speckled with a contrasting color or is irregularly marbled, while the variegation may have distinct edges or merge into the contrasting shade. Many variegated leaves have just two colors, but others have more and some hedera (ivies) are green, pale green,

◀ *Euonymus fortunei 'Emerald 'n' Gold' has an intense golden variegation that sometimes becomes flushed with pink in cold weather.*

◄ Ilex aquifolium *'Aurea Marginata'*, with gold-margined leaves, has the added bonus of being a berry-bearing female cultivar.

margined), "variegata" (variegated), "maculata" (spotted), and "picturata" (painted).

The following variegated evergreen varieties are attractive and reliable:

- *Aucuba japonica* 'Crotonifolia', 'Picturata', 'Variegata' and others (spotted laurel)
- *Cornus alba* 'Elegantissima', 'Spaethii' (dogwood)
- *Elaeagnus* x *ebbingei* 'Limelight', 'Gilt Edge'
- *E. pungens* 'Maculata', 'Frederici' and others
- *Euonymus fortunei* 'Emerald 'n' Gold', 'Emerald Gaiety', 'Silver Queen' and others
- *Hedera colchica* 'Dentata Variegata', *H. helix* 'Gold Heart Eva', 'Glacier' and others (ivy)
- *Ilex aquifolium* 'Golden Queen', 'Silver Milkmaid' and others (holly)
- *Osmanthus heterophyllus* 'Aureomarginatus'
- *Pieris japonica* 'Variegata'
- *Viburnum tinus* 'Variegatum' (laurustinus)
- *Vinca major* 'Variegata' (greater periwinkle)
- *Vinca minor* 'Argentiovariegata' (lesser periwinkle)

cream, and white, for example, while plants such as *Solenostemon* (coleus) may have four or more colors on the same leaf. Occasionally no green pigment is visible at all—*Berberis* 'Rose Glow', for example, is purple marbled with pink. In these cases, chlorophyll (the green pigment) is still present but is masked by other pigments.

The fact that a species or cultivar is variegated is often reflected in its botanical name. Look for words like "aureomarginata" or "argenteomarginata" (gold or silver

◄ Aucuba japonica *'Variegata'* is an attractive and reliable feature in the garden at any time of year.

## DEALING WITH REVERSION

Variegated varieties have often arisen as mutations or "sports" of a plain-leaved species, and can be unstable—they tend to "revert" to the plain-leaved state. If a plain-leaved branch is produced, it is more vigorous than the variegated shoots because it contains more chlorophyll and will eventually overtake the entire plant. As soon as a plain-leaved shoot is seen, it should be pruned out, cutting it right back to where it joins the main stem. The production of reverted branches sometimes indicates that the plant needs brighter growing conditions.

# ornamental garden: *plants in season*

In most areas, fall color is now at its peak, but it will not be long before the leaves fall. Seed heads and fruit have an ever-increasing role to play in providing interest, but late-flowering perennials and bulbs are still providing color in many gardens.

▼ *The vigorous climber* Parthenocissus quinquefolia, *commonly known as Virginia creeper, has outstanding fall foliage.*

## TREES AND SHRUBS

Acer (maple)
Berberis (deciduous) (barberry)
Cercidiphyllum japonicum
    (katsura tree)
Cotoneaster
Erica (heath)
Euonymus alatus (burning bush),
    E. europaeus and others
Fothergilla major
Hamamelis
Hippophae rhamnoides (sea buckthorn)
Hydrangea quercifolia
Malus (apple, crab apple)
Parthenocissus (Virginia creeper,
    Boston ivy)
Gaultheria mucronata
Pyracantha (firethorn)
Rosa (hips) (rose)
Skimmia
Sorbus
Vitis coignetiae, V. vinifera
    (grape vine)

## PERENNIALS

Aconitum napellus (monkshood)
Anemone hybrida
Aster
Gentiana sino-ornata
Liriope muscari (lily turf)
Physalis alkekengi var. franchettii (Chinese
    lantern)
Sedum spectabile (iceplant)

## BULBS

Amaryllis belladonna
Colchicum (common crocus)
Crinum x powellii
Cyclamen
Galanthus reginae-olgae (snowdrop)
Nerine bowdenii
Schizostylis coccinea (kaffir lily)

▲ Schizostylis coccinea, the kaffir lily, is one of the latest flowering border plants. The variety 'Sunrise' has delicate shell-pink flowers

▶ Purple-leaved Rosa glauca, usually grown for its purple foliage, has the bonus of bunches of glossy red rose hips through the fall.

# lawns and water gardens: *general tasks*

*Ponds still need attention to insure that the water is not being polluted by fallen leaves and other plant debris. If you are planning a new lawn, this is an ideal time to lay turf; if you just want to improve the condition of your existing lawn, a bulky top-dressing applied now will work wonders.*

## Pond plants and marginals

A water garden can look rather depressing by this time of year with untidy, yellowing foliage and dead and dying flowers of marginals spoiling the pond's appearance.

It is now a good idea to cut the stems right back to just above water level, taking care not to drop any plant material in the water.

If you have not already cut back underwater oxygenators, do so now. These plants produce rampant growth during the spring and summer, and much of it will die back during the fall and winter. It is best to anticipate this by using pruners to reduce the tangle of stems by up to two-thirds. Make sure the cut plant material is removed from the water.

Pond fish may still benefit from feeding, depending on the weather and the number of fish in the pool. If it is still relatively warm, try giving a small amount of food to see how interested they are; continue feeding only if they clear up the food given within 5 or 10 minutes.

### REMOVE SUBMERSIBLE POND PUMPS

A submersible pump is the simplest method of powering water garden features such as fountains and waterfalls. If the pump has not already been removed from the water, do so now, cleaning it thoroughly (especially the filter). Store it in a dry place under cover for the winter months.

If it is not convenient to remove the pump—when it is in the centre of a large pond and is not easy to reach, for example—it can be left in place, but it should be switched on and run for a short while every few weeks throughout winter, unless the pond is frozen. Removing the pump in fall will prolong its life, though.

▼ *Tidying pond plants and marginals using pruners will cut down on the amount of tangled stems when the plants die back now the summer months have ended.*

## a new lawn from turf

Turf is far more expensive than grass seed but it has one great advantage—it provides an instant effect. It is now easy to obtain special lawn turf made up of fine-leaved grass varieties for high quality, luxury lawns. Meadow turf is cheaper; although the lawn will not be of bowling green quality it will be adequate for most family gardens. Don't underestimate the amount of work involved in laying turf; it is a hard, heavy job, so round up as much help as you can.

### BULKY TOP DRESSING

Mix peat (or peat substitute), good quality, sieved loamy soil and medium horticultural sand (but not yellow builders' sand). The proportions of ingredients depend on the underlying soil type—increase the amount of sand on heavy soils, and use more loam and peat on light soils. Spread the top-dressing all over the grass, working it in between the blades with the back of a rake or a stiff broom. It will make the lawn look very messy to start with but will soon disappear, encouraging strong, dense grass growth next spring and summer.

1 Prepare the lawn site in advance, as you would for a new lawn from seed (see page 153). Turf needs to be laid within a day or two of delivery, so make sure you will be able to start laying it straight away.

2 Unfold or unroll the first length of turf and lay it flat on the prepared soil, using a taut line to act as a guide for a straight edge where necessary (**right**). Use the back of a spade or a special turf beetle to firm down the turf and insure good contact with the soil.

3 Lay the next length of turf, butting the short edges closely together, and continue like this until the first row is complete (**right**). Lay the second row tight against the first, staggering the short joints like bricks in a wall. Stand on a plank on the new turf to spread your weight evenly. Continue until the whole area has been covered.

4 Once the turfing is complete, cut the edges of the lawn to shape with a half-moon edging iron, using a taut line (for straight edges) or piece of hosepipe (for curves) as a guide. Trickle a mixture of peat and sand, or some fine soil, into the cracks between the turfs to encourage them to knit together (**left**).

# kitchen garden: *general tasks*

*Rhubarb is really a vegetable, although it is always thought of as a fruit. In early spring, tender young rhubarb stems are a real delicacy, and this is the ideal time to plant new crowns. Some soft fruit crops are due for pruning, and hardwood cuttings can be taken to increase or replace stock.*

▲ *Rhubarb can be planted at this time of year for harvesting in the early spring. Make sure you grow it from certified virus-free crowns.*

### Plant new rhubarb crowns

Rhubarb is best grown from certified virus-free crowns (also known as sets). They are available from good garden centers or by mail order, and consist of a clump of fleshy roots topped by a knobbly crown with one or more large, plump buds. Dig plenty of well-rotted garden compost or manure into the planting site. Do not add any lime because rhubarb prefers slightly acidic soil conditions.

Plant the crowns so that the buds are only just covered with soil; if planting more than one crown, set them 3ft/90cm apart. Do not pull too many stems in the spring following planting. 'Cherry Red' and 'Macdonald' are good varieties. Plant the herb sweet cicely nearby, and include a handful of the foliage when cooking the stems. It reduces the acidity, and you won't need to add so much sugar.

### WINTER ROOT CROPS

Root crops such as parsnips, salsify, and rutabaga can in most areas be left in the ground overwinter to be pulled as required, but once the foliage has died down there is nothing to show where they are. Mark the rows clearly now. When you start harvesting, begin at one end of the row and move up the marker to show where you finished lifting the crop, so that you know where to dig next time. In very cold weather, when the soil is frozen, it will be impossible to get at the roots, so some should be lifted and stored in boxes of soil in a shed when an icy spell is forecast.

## take hardwood cuttings of soft fruit

Soft fruit, such as currants and gooseberries, are easy to propagate by hardwood cuttings. The cuttings can be left in the open garden all winter, and need very little skill to root successfully. The most important point to remember is not to insert the cuttings upside down—it's easier than you might think to make a mistake unless you prepare them carefully.

1 Cuttings are taken in the dormant season, using fully-ripened wood of the current year's growth. Wait until all the leaves have died before cutting the stems with pruners. Use strong, healthy stems of pencil thickness.

2 Each stem can be cut into lengths to give several cuttings; it may be easy to forget which end of the cutting is which. Use sharp pruners to cut stems into 6–10in/15–25cm portions (**right**), making a straight cut at the base of each length and a sloping cut at the top. Treat the bases with rooting hormone.

3 Dig over a suitable piece of moist soil, adding some sharp sand unless it is already free-draining. The cuttings will need to be left in place undisturbed for one year. Make a narrow slit trench with a spade, and insert each cutting so that just the top 2in/5cm is above ground.

4 Firm the soil back against the cuttings with the ball of your foot, and label the row (**left**). Apart from occasional weeding, the cuttings need little further attention. Over winter, corky callus tissue forms over the bases of the cuttings, and new roots should grow from this next spring.

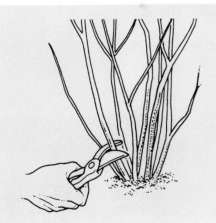

### BLACKCURRANTS AND BLACKBERRIES

Blackcurrants carry most of next year's crop on the wood that has been produced this season. Cut to the ground all the branches that carried fruit this year, leaving the strong new growths. The older wood can be recognized because it is gray or black while new wood is pale brown. If you have trouble differentiating between the two, prune at harvest time next year, cutting out the branches carrying fruit as soon as the

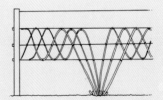

currants are ripe. Blackberries should also be pruned now, again removing the canes that carried fruit but retain the current season's canes. Tie-in the canes which are to be retained to their supports. Damaged, spindly, or weak growths should be removed.

# kitchen garden: *harvesting and digging*

*Most varieties of apples ripening now are suitable for storing for a few weeks but some will keep until next spring, given the right conditions. In the vegetable garden digging continues as crops are cleared from the ground. If you do not yet have a vegetable plot, this is a good time to get started.*

### Harvest apples and pears

A few apple and pear varieties may need to be left until late fall, but the majority will have been picked by the end of this month. A number of

apple varieties store well, in some instances remaining in good condition until late spring. 'Arkansas Black', 'Golden Delicious', 'Gold Rush', and 'McIntosh' are among the good keepers. Choose unblemished specimens, wrap them individually in sheets of wax paper and store in a single layer in boxes in a cool garage, cellar, or shed.

An alternative method is to place six apples in a strong plastic bag, punch a few holes in the bag with a pencil and tie the top loosely, leaving a small gap. This method is good for varieties that tend to shrivel. Pears do not store for very long though, and need inspecting daily because they must be eaten immediately they are ripe—they spoil within a day or two.

### CLEAR VEGETABLE CROPS

—

By now, crops such as runner and French beans, summer cabbages, marrows and so on will be more or less finished, and the plants can be cleared away.

Unless the spent crop plants are badly diseased, add them to the compost heap to rot down. Tough, woody stems, like those of some brassicas, are very slow to rot and can either be shredded before being added to the heap, or be burned instead. As rows of crop plants are removed, dig the soil over and add compost or manure as available.

▶ *Apples are ripe and ready for picking once the stalk separates easily from the spur when the fruit is lifted gently.*

◀ *Wrapping apples separately before storing will help to prevent rot spreading if one of them starts to decay. Only unblemished fruits should be stored; damaged apples will not keep.*

## start a new vegetable plot

Home-grown vegetables are always welcome, and are very rewarding to grow. While a few vegetables can always be grown in containers on the patio or among the flowers, a dedicated vegetable plot will give you a lot more scope for trying out new, exciting varieties. Make the plot as large as is practical for you to look after.

1 If the vegetable plot is to be made in the lawn, it will be necessary to strip off the turf. This can be done by cutting parallel strips in the grass with a half-moon edging iron, and undercutting the turf with a sharp spade (**left**). Hiring a turf cutter is worthwhile for large areas.

2 If the turf that has been removed is good quality, it can be relaid elsewhere, or perhaps sold. Otherwise, it can be stacked upside down to rot, when it will make an excellent loam for potting or for mixing with growing soil mixes.

3 The newly-exposed soil should be well cultivated, either digging it by hand (**left**) or using a mechanical cultivator. Although the cultivator is quicker and easier, double digging allows deeper cultivation and gives better results in the long run—as long as you have the necessary time and stamina to do it. Spread the job over several weeks if necessary.

4 While digging, incorporate as much rotted garden compost or manure into the soil as possible; this improves fertility and soil structure, allowing heavy soils to drain more freely and light soils to become more moisture retentive. The plot should be left roughly dug over winter to allow frost to break down the clods into finer crumbs.

5 A soil testing kit is a worthwhile investment, giving you an idea of the acidity and nutrient levels in the soil (**above**). Acidity (pH) testing is usually quite accurate and will indicate whether an application of lime is necessary. Nutrient analysis is rather less reliable, but will still give a guide to your soil's fertility.

# greenhouse: *general tasks*

*Fungus diseases are rife in cool, damp conditions prevalent at this time of year. Poor light levels can be a problem, too; make sure that the maximum amount of light can penetrate the glass. Also, look ahead to spring and summer by sowing sweet peas and planting bowls of bulbs for forcing.*

### Sow sweet peas for early flowers next year

Fall-sown sweet peas come into flower some four or five weeks earlier than spring-sown ones, and continue blooming for just as long at

the other end of the season. The tough coats of the seed can sometimes delay germination, especially in the case of the dark brown or black seeds.

Before sowing it pays to nick the seed coat lightly with a sharp knife, on the side opposite the lighter colored eye where the seedling will emerge.

Sow the seed in pots, or special sweet pea tubes that allow the long roots to develop fully. They do not

need warm conditions—59°F/15°C is suitable for germination. Seedlings do well in a cold frame or an unheated greenhouse where they can develop into sturdy plants ready for planting out in their flowering positions in early to mid-spring. Choose paler colored varieties for the best fragrance. 'Unwin's Striped Mix', 'Old Spice Mix', 'Royal Mix', 'Noel Sutton', and 'Quito' are among those recommended for their scent.

▲ *The fragrant flowers of sweet peas (Lathyrus odoratus) can be appreciated that bit earlier next year if some seeds are sown now.*

### VENTILATION AND WATERING

Fall is a tricky time in the greenhouse. On a chilly, misty morning, it seems obvious to leave the ventilators tightly closed and be very sparing with the watering, but a few hours later fall sunshine can have sent the temperature soaring and leave plants gasping for a drink. If you are away from the house all day, fit an automatic ventilator that will open when the temperature reaches a pre-determined level. Water plants when the surface of the soil feels dry but avoid overwatering because it leads to root and stem rot at this time of year. Also take care not to splash the foliage or crowns of plants, and keep the atmosphere on the dry side to avoid fungus disease such as botrytis.

# prepare forced bulbs

Many gardeners find winter a dull and frustrating season, and are impatient for the first signs of spring. It's easy to bring a touch of spring into your home much earlier with bowls of forced bulbs. Plant an assortment of varieties now and you will be enjoying their blooms in the depths of winter, just when you need a fillip.

## SHADING

The shading that was essential to prevent foliage being scorched by summer sun is no longer necessary now; greenhouse plants need all the light they can get. Paint-on shading can be removed on a dry day with some elbow grease and a dry cloth, while blinds and netting can be cleaned, rolled up and stored for next year. Clean the greenhouse glass underneath the shading thoroughly.

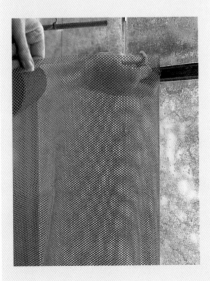

1 The earliest flowers are obtained from treated or prepared bulbs that have been given special cold treatment to alter their flowering time. Ordinary bulbs can also be forced for early flowering, but they will only be a short time ahead of outdoor ones.

2 Plant the bulbs closely together in bowls or pots of moist, soilless potting mix (**above**)—bulb fiber can be used, but has no special merit over normal mix. The extreme tips of the bulbs should be just visible through the soil when the bowl is filled.

3 The planted bowls now need to be placed somewhere cool and dark for several weeks. The ideal temperature is 35–40°F/2–5°C; a cool garage, basement, shed, or shaded cold frame are suitable. Plunging the bowls in a deep bed of sand or ashes is traditional, and helps keep them evenly cool, moist, and dark. Placing the bowls in an old, still functioning refrigerator in a utility room or garage is a more modern approach, and works well.

4 The bulbs must be left in their cool, dark position for between 10 and 16 weeks, according to variety, to form a good root system. Check them regularly to make sure that the soil does not dry out—water when necessary to keep the compost just moist, never wet (**left**).

# late fall

*Tidying up and preparing plants for the colder weather ahead continues, but planning for next season starts in earnest now, with new plantings to be made and seed orders to be filled out. This is also a good time to have the lawn mower overhauled so that it is ready for next spring.*

At this time of year we really notice how the days are shortening. For many gardeners, the only time the garden can be seen in daylight is at weekends, and all the tasks that need to be done have to be crammed in to two short days, provided the weather allows. Fortunately there are few really pressing jobs.

It's important though, that you protect the more tender plants before the coldest weather arrives. Night frosts will already have struck in many gardens, but the most damaging, sustained freezing temperatures are usually a feature of the winter. Don't forget to lag outdoor taps and water pipes, too.

Any damage to plants and garden structures caused by fall gales should be repaired quickly. Fences are particularly prone to problems, so check that fence posts and panels are sound. Garden sheds may also be showing signs of wear and tear. Secure roofing felt that has been loosened, and check for leaks inside, carrying out repairs as necessary. It is vital to have dry storage conditions available for many items including tools and machinery, fertilizers and chemicals, as well as produce such as tree fruit and root vegetables.

Weeds seem to keep growing whatever the weather, and weeding should be carried out as necessary. Since many chemical herbicides need weeds to make rapid growth to work most efficiently, hand weeding is generally the best approach in late fall and winter.

◄ *Make the most of late flowers like sedums. A drab time of year is approaching, with fall color finally extinguised by wind and rain.*

## LATE FALL TASKS

**General**

:: Note gaps in the borders and make plans to fill them
:: Protect outdoor faucets and water pipes from freezing
:: Check bonfire piles for hibernating animals before lighting

▼ *Floating a ball on the water surface can help to delay the pond freezing.*

**Ornamental garden**

:: Continue tidying borders. Leave top-growth for winter protection in cold areas. In exposed gardens, prune roses lightly to prevent root rock
:: Continue planting bare-root trees and shrubs

:: Take hardwood cuttings from shrubs
:: Protect alpines from rain
:: Lift chrysanthemums and box roots to provide cuttings in spring
:: Finish planting tulips and hyacinths

:: Continue to remove weeds
:: Tidy alpines and rock gardens

**Lawns**

:: Give a last cut if necessary, then send mower for service and blade sharpening
:: Aerate compacted areas
:: Continue turfing in mild spells

**Water garden**

:: Protect ponds and fish from cold. Stop feeding fish

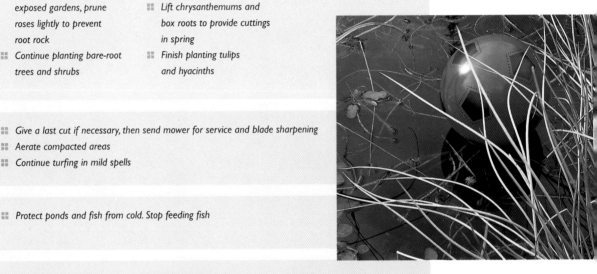

**Kitchen garden**

:: Sow beans and hardy peas for overwintering
:: Continue digging spare ground
:: Begin harvesting parsnips and Brussels sprouts. Lift some root crops for use in case the soil becomes frozen

:: Check summer-planted, cold-stored potatoes and lift when ready. Order new seed potatoes from catalogs for the best choice of varieties
:: Plant new fruit trees and bushes; begin winter pruning of fruit

:: Continue weeding as necessary
:: Protect winter brassicas from birds

**Greenhouse**

:: Ventilate and water with care; use fungicides where necessary
:: Bring bulbs for forcing into the light as they develop. Check that plunged bulbs remain moist

:: Insulate greenhouses and frames with bubble wrap
:: Pinch out the tips of fall-sown Lathyrus odoratus (sweet pea) seedlings at about 4–6 in/10–15 cm

:: Plant Narcissus 'Paper White'
:: Sow sprouting seeds for salads

▲ *Late fall is an excellent time to plant new fruit trees.*

# ornamental garden: *general tasks*

*If you want to repeat the display of bright, late summer and fall color from chrysanthemums, it's time to lift the roots and box them up for winter, ready to provide cuttings next spring. You don't have to wait until spring to take hardwood cuttings, though; they are easy to root and can be taken now.*

### Chrysanthemum roots

Some varieties of the so-called florists' chrysanthemum are hardy enough to overwinter in the garden, but the best quality plants are produced from cuttings taken in the spring. As the plants finish flowering now, they can be cut down to around 6in/15cm and the roots lifted carefully with a garden fork. Shake off some of the soil clinging to them, and box up the roots in almost-dry peat or potting mix.

Store the boxes of roots in a frost-free greenhouse or cold frame, garden shed, garage, or similar place. In mid to late winter they will be brought into a heated greenhouse and watered in to start them into growth, but for now they should be kept virtually dry. If you grow a number of named varieties, tie a label around each stem to identify them.

▼ *Chrysanthemums stop flowering at this point in the year; it is time to cut them down and lift their roots with a fork.*

## PROTECTING ALPINES FROM RAIN

Low-growing alpines will often stand any amount of cold, but many will not tolerate wet weather in winter. Susceptible alpines can be protected by suspending a sheet of glass or clear plastic horizontally over the plants, holding it in place by sliding it into notched wooden stakes, or lay it on top of bricks (weight it down to prevent the wind blowing it away). Free air circulation around the plants is vital.

# take shrub cuttings

Many garden shrubs can be propagated by hardwood cuttings that usually root easily and need very little care. A cold frame is an ideal place to overwinter the cuttings, but a sheltered position in the open garden will do as long as it has some protection from excessive rain. Some cuttings may be rooted by the following spring, but others may take 12 months or more before they are rooted sufficiently to be planted out in their growing positions.

1 Select strong, healthy growth which has been made in the current season. The shoots should be of around pencil thickness; thin, weak stems do not make good cuttings.

2 On deciduous shrubs, most leaves will have fallen, but any remaining can be brushed away (**right**). Cut the stems into 6in/15cm pieces, discarding the thinner tips. Make sure you know which is the top and bottom of each section.

3 With evergreen shrubs, remove the leaves from the lower two-thirds of the stem on each cutting. Dip the bases of the cuttings into hormone rooting powder or liquid (**below**), and insert them into pots of moist, sandy cuttings mix. Then you should place the pots in a cold frame or sheltered spot in the garden.

4 Shrubs that can be increased by this method include aucuba, buddleja, *Buxus* (box), *Cydonia* (quince), forsythia, *Philadelphus* (mock orange), sambucus, spiraea, viburnum and weigela. Climbers such as *Vitis* (grapevine), and trees such as *Salix* (willow) and *Populus* (poplar) also grow well from hardwood cuttings.

## TIDY BORDERS

Continue to tidy flower borders, cutting down dead stems and removing dead and dying foliage. If left, they provide handy overwintering sites for a range of garden pests, especially slugs and snails. These can cause an enormous amount of damage in the spring when they feast on the succulent new shoots that start pushing up through the ground.

# pleasure from berries

Berry-bearing plants make a brilliant contribution to the fall garden, and their display can last right through the winter too, if you are lucky.

For a plant species to be successful, it needs to reproduce itself freely and colonize as large an area as possible. Each berry contains a seed or number of seeds with the potential for reproduction: some seeds will germinate from berries that ripen and fall to the ground, but this limits the spread of the plant to the immediate area. In order to colonize new ground, the seed must somehow be transported more widely.

In the case of berries, birds and small wild mammals provide the means of transport. They eat the berries, the seed passes unharmed through their digestive system, and is later deposited, often a considerable distance away. The most successful plants are therefore likely to be those that produce the tastiest, most tempting, highly visible berries, which accounts for their showy forms and bright colors—factors also making them desirable decorative garden plants.

## Poor show

When a plant has been specially chosen for its berries, it is obviously disappointing when they fail to appear. This event is not all that uncommon, and can be due to a number of reasons. Many species, including *Ilex* (holly) and skimmia, have separate male and female plants. Only the female bears the berries, and only when the flowers

▲ Berberis wilsoniae: *the point of berries is to be eaten by birds, so it is not surprising that beautiful displays may quickly be eaten.*

POISONING BY GARDEN BERRIES

With berries often being brightly colored, highly visible, and similar to edible currants and other soft fruits in the garden, they are very tempting to young children, sometimes with unpleasant or even fatal results. The following plants are grown for their decorative berries, but the berries are poisonous when ingested: lords and ladies (*Arum maculatum*), spindle tree (*Euonymus europaeus*), holly (*Ilex aquifolium*), stinking iris (*Iris foetidissima*), pokeweed (*Phytolacca decandra*), snowberry (*symphoricarpos*), and guelder rose (*Viburnum opulus*). Other plants such as yew (*Taxus baccata*), bird cherry (*Prunus laurocerasus*), privet (*Ligustrum ovalifolium*) also bear poisonous berries, though they are not grown specifically for this feature.

▼ Pyracantha *'Orange Glow'* provides
a stunning show of rich color in the late fall,
making it a desirable decorative plant.

## RELIABLE BERRY-BEARING SHRUBS

\* *Aucuba japonica* 'Rozannie', 'Salicifolia' and others (spotted laurel)

*Berberis* x *carminea* 'Barbarossa', 'Buccaneer' and others (barberry)

*Callicarpa bodinieri* var. *giraldii* (beauty berry)

*Celastrus orbiculatus* (oriental bittersweet)

*Cotoneaster* 'Cornubia', *C.* x *watereri* 'John Waterer'
    and many others

*Crataegus* x *lavalleei* 'Carrierei' and many others (hawthorn)

*Euonymus europaeus* (spindle tree)

*Gaultheria procumbens* (checkerberry)

*Gaultheria mucronata*

\* *Hippophae rhamnoides* (sea buckthorn)

\* *Ilex* x *altacleriensis* 'Camelliifolia', *I. aquifolium* 'J. C. Van Tol' and many
        others (holly)

*Iris foetidissima*

*Leycesteria formosa* (Himalayan honeysuckle)

*Mahonia aquifolium* and others

*Photinia davidiana, P. glabra*

*Pyracantha* 'Mohave', 'Orange Glow' and many others (firethorn)

\* *Ruscus aculeatus* (butcher's broom)

\* *Skimmia japonica* 'Nymans', 'Veitchii' and others

*Symphoricarpos albus* var. *laevigatus* (snowberry), *S.* x *doorenbosii* 'Mother
of Pearl' and others

*Viburnum opulus* (guelder rose), *V. wrightii* var. *hessei*

\* Separate male and female plants are needed

have been pollinated by a male. This means that you need a female variety, and there must be a suitable male variety within insect-flying distance. It usually pays to buy and plant both male and female varieties at the same time to be on the safe side. Take care when choosing varieties though; things are not always what they seem— for example, *Ilex aquifolium* 'Silver Queen' is a male variety, while *I.* x *altacleriensis* 'Golden King' is a female.

A poor show of berries can also be caused by dry soil conditions at flowering time; regular organic mulches will help here. And of course, plants that produce only a few flowers can only bear a few berries. For plants that fail to flower freely, an application of sulfate of potash in the spring and fall can sometimes work wonders.

As far as the plant is concerned, the whole purpose of a berry's existence is to be eaten by a bird, so it is hardly surprising that birds make short work of many attractive displays. There are several ways to protect plants from birds (see page 144). Red berries are the most highly visible against a green background, while species and varieties with yellow, orange, purple, pink, or white fruit tend to be longer lasting.

▲ *Berberis* × *ottawensis* *'Superba'*
*(purpurea)* offers interestingly shaped berries
and leaves to the general garden display.

# ornamental garden: *plants in season*

As flowers and fall foliage fade, evergreens assume an increasingly important role in bringing interest to the garden. Fruits and berries continue to provide color, and there are still flowers on show as long as the right species have been planted.

▶ *The deep blues of Gentiana sino-ornata enrich the garden's color scheme.*

▼ *Viburnum tinus 'Eve Price' offers a frothy interest to the fall garden.*

## PERENNIALS

Aster

Helianthus (sunflower)

Gentiana sino-ornata

Iris unguicularis

Liriope muscari (lily turf)

## BULBS

Colchicum (fall crocus)

Crocus (fall-flowering species)

Cyclamen

Galanthus reginae-olgae (snowdrop)

Nerine bowdenii

Schizostylis coccinea (kaffir lily)

Sternbergia lutea (fall daffodil)

▼ *Sunflowers provide bold, bright splashes of color and dramatic interest.*

## TREES AND SHRUBS

*Aucuba japonica* (spotted laurel)

*Berberis* (barberry)

*Callicarpa* (beauty berry)

*Clematis orientale, C. tangutica*

*Cornus alba* (red-barked dogwood)

*Cotoneaster*

*Fatsia japonica* (Japanese aralia)

*Gaultheria mucronata*

*Jasminum nudiflorum* (jasmine)

*Leycesteria formosa* (Himalayan honeysuckle)

*Malus* (apple, crab apple)

*Prunus* x *subhirtella* 'Fallalis' (fall cherry)

*Pyracantha* (firethorn)

*Rosa* (hips) (rose)

*Salix alba* var. *vitellina* 'Britzensis' (white willow)

*Skimmia*

*Sorbus*

*Symphoricarpos* (snowberry)

*Vaccinium* (bilberry)

*Viburnum*

# Lawns and water gardens: *general tasks*

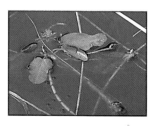

*Lawns now start to show signs of wear on heavily used routes as the soil becomes compacted in wet weather. The grass may need a final cut before the mower is sent away for servicing, ready for next spring. Garden ponds should need little attention unless the weather turns particularly cold.*

▲ *Aereating compacted areas of lawn is important to help surface water drain away. It is easily achieved with a garden fork.*

### Aerating turf

When the soil is moist it is easily compacted. A frequently trodden route across the lawn will soon become muddy now, with its covering of grass gradually thinning and being worn away. Since it is important that air can reach the roots of the grass and that surface water can drain away at all times of the year, action should be taken as soon as worn patches are noticed. If the damage is not corrected, moss is likely to develop in place of the grass.

Try to redirect foot traffic away from the worn places if possible. Use a garden fork to spike the compacted areas, driving the prongs into the turf some 3–4in/7.5–10cm deep. Waggle the fork backward and forward gently to enlarge the holes slightly before removing it. Repeat over the whole area to leave the rows of holes evenly spaced in both directions.

### LAWN MOWERS

If the grass has continued to grow, give it a final cut with the blades set high before sending the lawn mower away for its annual service. It is far better to get this done now than wait until next spring—that's when everyone else has the same idea, meaning you have to wait weeks before you get it back. Alternatively, service the mower at home if you have a basic knowledge of mechanics.

After a season of grass cutting, the blades will need resharpening and adjusting so that they cut cleanly and do not tear the grass. Although this can also be carried out at home, it is not an easy job and is best done professionally.

# protect ponds from cold weather

If a garden pond freezes over for more than a couple of days, fish may be killed by the toxic gases trapped beneath the ice. The easiest way to prevent this is to install a pond heater.

## STOP FEEDING FISH

As the water temperature drops, fish become inactive and will not take food until the water warms up again in the spring. They live off stored body fat through the winter, so it is important to build them up in the early fall. Any food given from now on will sink to the bottom of the pool and rot, polluting the water.

1 At this time of year it is very important to keep the water free of any kind of decaying vegetation, whether this is dead leaves from water plants or fall leaves from nearby trees. Remove dead and dying leaves regularly, and cover the pool with a net if necessary.

2 Remove the pond pump if one is installed, and clean and service it before storing it for the winter (**left**). If the pool is within reach of a power supply, install a pond heater. This keeps only a small area of the pond free of ice, but allows the air in and toxic gases to escape.

3 If it is not possible to use a pond heater, a ball floating on the surface of the water will delay freezing as it moves about in the wind (**above**). And if the water does freeze, boiling water poured around the edge of the ball enables it to be removed leaving a hole in the ice. Hollow polystyrene packaging material can also be used.

4 Most sunken garden ponds are in no danger of freezing solid, but miniature ponds in half barrels are a different matter—they lack the insulation of the soil around them. In all but mild areas, fish from barrels should be moved under cover. Lagging the barrels with several layers of bubble wrap helps protect water plants.

# kitchen garden: *general tasks*

*Harvesting the winter vegetable crops usually begins now, once the first few frosts have bitten; protection from hungry wild birds may be necessary, too. Although many gardeners find the whole subject of fruit pruning mystifying, it can be kept quite simple, and will insure maximum crops.*

## Prune fruit trees

Apple and pear trees that are grown as open-centered bushes or small trees are not difficult to prune. The object is to maintain a well-shaped tree that carries as much fruiting wood as possible, while also bearing young branches to provide replacement fruiting wood in future seasons. Start by pruning out any dead, dying, or diseased branches. Then remove crossing branches, and branches that are growing into the center of the tree. Now cut back strong-growing young laterals (side-shoots) by about half to two-thirds of the current season's growth, depending on how vigorous the growth is (the more vigorous the shoot, the more lightly it should be pruned because winter pruning stimulates growth). The tips of the leaders (main branches) should be pruned more lightly, cutting back the current season's growth by about one-quarter. Finally, remove some of the older branches which have borne fruit to encourage the production of new replacement shoots.

▼ *Long-arm pruners are very useful for reaching high fruit tree branches; you may be able to avoid using a stepladder.*

### LIFT ROOT CROPS

Many root crops such as parsnips, rutabaga, maincrop carrots, salsify, and scorzonera are usually hardy enough to stay in the ground all winter, where they will keep in better condition than in store. However, if the weather becomes really cold and the soil freezes, it can be impossible to prise the crops from the icy ground. Lift a small supply now and store them in boxes of soil near the house so that they are easily accessible in cold weather. A few leeks can be stored alongside them because these are also difficult to harvest in freezing weather.

# keep birds at bay

A well-planned vegetable plot should contain a variety of vegetables that can be harvested through the winter, but wild creatures will be hungry too, and only too ready to take advantage of a free meal from your garden. Some form of deterrents are often necessary to obtain your share of the harvest.

### BRUSSELS SPROUTS AND PARSNIPS

There is a saying that it is not worth harvesting Brussels sprouts and parsnips until they have had a good touch of frost to improve their flavor. Whether frost actually does improve the flavor is open to question, but it is certainly true that they are both hardy enough to withstand severe frosts without damage, allowing the harvest to be extended right through the winter.

1 Brassicas such as cabbages and Brussels sprouts provide invaluable winter fare, but the plants are prone to damage by pigeons. In a cold spell, a crop can be reduced to a skeleton of veins within hours, so choose some protection.

2 Bird scarers can help to deter pigeons though their effect is often disappointing (**right**). Moving, glittery or noisy objects are best. Strips of foil or unwanted CDs can be hung from stakes to shine as they twist in the wind, while children's windmills on sticks provide noise and movement. Tautly stretched tape from old audio or video tapes makes a low hum in the breeze.

3 A physical barrier can be provided by stretching twine between stakes in a criss-cross fashion over the top of the crop, or using horticultural blanket draped over the tops of the plants. This needs to be secured at the edges to prevent it being blown away (**below**).

4 Growing brassicas in a fruit cage is the most reliable answer where pigeons are a real problem. In cold regions, the netting over the top will need to be replaced with large mesh netting for the winter to prevent snow from collecting—its weight would tear the net.

# kitchen garden: *planting and sowing*

*An out-of-season treat of new potatoes may be available from specially-treated seed potatoes planted in the summer; remember to order potatoes from the catalogs for more conventional planting in spring. Unlikely as it seems, it is also time for sowing some vegetables outdoors for next year.*

## *Sowing beans and peas*

As long as you sow the right varieties, both beans and peas will overwinter as seedlings to give early crops next year—you could be picking beans and peas by late spring. Choose a reasonably sheltered site for sowing, on free-draining soil. On heavy soils there is a risk of the seeds rotting, and in this case it is better to sow them in pots or boxes in an unheated greenhouse for planting out in the spring. The crop will not be so early, but it will be more reliable.

Sow beans 4–6in/10–15cm apart in rows 12in/30cm apart; peas are sown rather more closely in the row, at 2–3in/5–7.5cm apart. Depending on your climate zone and prevailing local conditions, your local garden center should be able to advise on the most appropriate varieties to sow in your garden or greenhouse.

▲ *Certain varieties of beans can be sown at this time of year to give a crop late the following spring.*

### SUMMER–PLANTED POTATOES

Specially-prepared, cold-stored seed potatoes that were planted in the summer produce a crop some two or three months after planting. Check them now, by scraping away some soil to expose the developing tubers. As long as the majority are large enough to eat they can be lifted when you want to use them. If the weather is mild, the tubers may continue to swell, but most of them will have finished developing by now. Do not lift the entire crop as you would for maincrop potatoes; they keep best if left in the soil up to midwinter, insulated from freezing weather with a mulch of straw or dry bracken.

▶ *Cherry trees grow particularly well if they are trained against a reasonably sheltered wall or fence. Morello types are most popular.*

## plant fruit trees and bushes

With the development of dwarfing rootstocks, it is possible for fruit trees such as apples and pears to be grown even in small gardens. Soft fruit bushes such as currants and gooseberries are also easy to grow and provide very welcome crops in the summer.

1 Choose from the wide variety of fruit trees available from specialist nurseries. The plants are often supplied bare root, by mail order, and should be planted as soon as possible after delivery. Most garden centers stock a reduced but reasonable selection, usually container grown.

2 Dig out a planting hole wide enough to take the roots of the tree without cramping, and deep enough for the tree to be planted at the same depth it was growing in the nursery. Fork over the base of the hole and add some well-rotted garden compost or planting mixture.

3 Hammer the stake in position before planting the tree to avoid damaging the tree roots. A short stake is all that is necessary. Check that the size of the hole is correct for the tree, then spread the tree roots out in the base of the planting hole (**above**).

4 Return the excavated soil to the hole, gently jiggling the tree up and down while you do so in order to insure that the soil sifts between the roots. Then you should tread the soil firm with the ball of your foot as you proceed (**above**).

5 When the hole is refilled, attach the tree to the stake with an adjustable tree tie (**above**). Fruit bushes are planted in the same way. If container-grown, remove the root-ball carefully having watered it well a few hours before, put it in the base of the hole and firm the soil around it.

# fruit tree rootstocks

It is possible to grow a fruit tree in almost any size garden, no matter how small it might be—apples, pears, and many other tree fruits can even be kept small enough to grow in a tub on a patio.

The method by which the size of the tree is controlled is grafting the fruiting variety onto a separate rootstock that determines the rate of growth. Size is not the only aspect of growth that is governed by the

rootstock; the number of years between planting and fruiting are also affected. Trees on the more dwarfing rootstocks do tend to crop earlier, another benefit for the home gardener.

A great deal of research has been undertaken into dwarfing rootstocks, and still continues, with large numbers of new rootstocks under evaluation. The research is aimed at commercial fruit growers, but new

and improved rootstocks can eventually find their way onto the amateur market.

Small trees are more suitable for gardens where space is limited, and are easier to prune, harvest, and spray. Using ladders and long-handled pruners is awkward and time-consuming; a tree that allows all parts to be reached from the ground is easier to look after.

However, dwarfing rootstocks have some drawbacks. They need staking in their early years, and some need permanent support throughout their lives. Fertile, moisture-retentive soil is also necessary or the crop will be very disappointing .

Really small, dwarfing rootstocks are not necessary for most gardens. A compromise will usually be a better choice, such as the semidwarfing apple rootstock M26 rather than the very dwarfing M27. The trees will still be relatively compact and quick to bear fruit but will put up with poorer soil conditions, be self-supporting after a few years and carry a much bigger crop. The most dwarfing rootstocks are necessary only if you want to grow trees in pots, or train them in very restricted forms such as step-overs.

While, some garden centers have a good choice of rootstocks, it is usually necessary to go to specialist fruit producers to obtain the most recent introductions. Most specialist nurserymen will be happy to discuss your requirements with you, and give you advice on the best rootstock to meet your needs. Some of the newest rootstocks, particularly for cherries, have not yet been grown for long enough to have entirely proved themselves, and some growers have reservations about their hardiness, disease resistance, and compatibility with other fruiting varieties. Rootstocks that do not live up to expectations usually disappear from fruit growers' catalogs within a year or two.

◀ *Fruit trees are a major boon to any garden and the good news that they can be grown in almost any size garden.*

## FRUIT TREE ROOTSTOCKS

| Rootstock | | Approximate size | Years to come into cropping |
|---|---|---|---|
| **Apples** | M27 | under 6ft/18m | 2 |
| | M9 | 6–9 ft/1.8–2.7 m | 2–3 |
| | M26 | 10–12 ft/3–3.6 m | 2–3 |
| | MM106 | 12–13 ft/3.6–4 m | 3–4 |
| | MM111 | 13–15 ft/4–4.5 m | 4–5 |
| **Pears** | Quince C | 12 ft/3.6 m | 3–4 |
| | Quince A | 13 ft/4 m | 4–5 |
| **Plums** | Pixy | 6–10 ft/1.8–3 m | 3 |
| | St Julien A | 12 ft/3.6 m | 4–5 |
| | Brompton | 13 ft/4 m | 4–5 |
| | Myrobalan B | 13 ft/4 m | 4–5 |
| | Mariana 4 | 15 ft+/4.5 m+ | 4–5 |
| **Cherries** | Gisela | 6–10 ft/1.8–3 m | 3 |
| | Colt | 13 ft/4 m | 4–5 |
| | F12/1 | 16 ft+/4.8 m+ | 5–6 |

## GRAFTING ONTO ROOTSTOCKS

Established gardens often contain very large, old fruit trees of unknown origin that can sometimes cause problems. You may want to remove the tree because it is too big, or perhaps need to replace it because it is diseased or reaching the end of its useful life, but you are reluctant to destroy it because it bears crops of attractive, well-flavored fruit that you cannot identify in order to obtain another of the same variety.

In this case it is possible to preserve the stock by grafting stems of the original tree on to a suitable rootstock for replanting. Grafting is a fairly skilled job but if you do not feel confident of being able to do it yourself, one or two specialist nurseries will do it for you for a fee and a supply of suitable dormant stems (scion wood).

# greenhouse: *general tasks*

*As the weather grows colder, tender plants in the greenhouse are at greater risk of damage. Some plants need only a little protection, and insulating the greenhouse may be sufficient to keep them alive without any artificial heat. Even when heat is required, insulation will help reduce fuel bills.*

## Insulate greenhouses and frames

Do-it-yourself insulation is a useful way of maintaining temperatures and helping to keep down fuel bills in the greenhouse.

The fact that plants need the maximum amount of light limits the materials that can be used: the favourite is bubble wrap because it is cheap, and easy to obtain as well as work with.

It comes in rolls and can be cut to fit the inside of the greenhouse, keeping each strip as long as possible to minimize the amount of joins. It is usually best to run the strips horizontally around the greenhouse. Fix the polyethythene in position with pins in a wooden structure, or special clips in an aluminum frame.

Bubble wrap can also be used to insulate the insides of the glass on garden frames.

▼ *Special clips are available to fix an insulating layer of bubble polyethythene to greenhouses that have an aluminium frame.*

### FORCED BULBS

Bulbs that are being forced for early flowering should have been kept in total  darkness after planting to encourage good root formation. The average dark, cold periods required are 12 weeks for crocus, 12–13 weeks for *Narcissus* (daffodils), 10–12 weeks for *Hyacinthus* (hyacinths) and 15–16 weeks for *Tulipa* (tulips). When the required number of weeks have elapsed and shoots have reached around 1in/2.5cm high, it is time to bring them into full light.

A greenhouse with a temperature of about 50°F/10°C is ideal; relatively cool temperatures are necessary for the leaves and flower buds to develop properly. Wait until the buds are starting to show color before moving the bulbs into a cool position in the home for flowering.

# heating the greenhouse

A greenhouse is infinitely more valuable if it can be heated sufficiently to keep it frost free. There are many different types of heaters available to suit a range of different situations and budgets—spend some time over choosing the best type of heater for your particular requirements.

## SWEET PEA SEEDLINGS

Sweet peas which were sown earlier in the fall should have germinated and be growing strongly. When the seedlings reach 4–6in/10–15cm tall, pinch out their growing tips. This insures stocky, healthy plants with plenty of side-shoots to bear flowers. Give the seedlings cool, well-ventilated conditions; a cold frame is the best place for them.

1 It is well worth considering running an electricity supply to the greenhouse, but this must be installed by a qualified electrician, using armored cabling and waterproof sockets. If the greenhouse is not too far from the house, it need not be very expensive (**above**).

2 Electric heaters have many advantages. They can be thermostatically controlled, switching on automatically as necessary at any time of the day or night, saving fuel and trouble. Fan heaters provide good air circulation, and a healthy atmosphere for plant growth (**above**).

3 Mains gas can also be installed in the greenhouse where available, but this tends to be unusual (**above**). Greenhouse heaters using bottled propane gas are more common but this is not so convenient because the gas bottles need to be changed regularly. Propane gives off water vapor as it burns, and the moist atmosphere produced can encourage plant diseases.

4 Kerosene heaters are cheap to buy and can be used where mains gas and electricity are unavailable (**above**). They are labor intensive and messy; they need frequent filling with kerosene. Because they are not thermostatically controlled they waste fuel and can be expensive to run. They also give off water vapor and fumes while burning, making greenhouse ventilation essential.

# winter

Despite short days and chilly weather, the garden can be a soul-lifting place to be in the winter months. There's evergreen foliage, winter flowers and berries, and the starkly beautiful, architectural shapes of trees and shrubs to enjoy. Add some silver highlights from a sparkling frost and you've a truly magical scene before you.

# early winter

*The weather is often entirely unpredictable now. Penetrating frosts and icy winds; continuous dull, depressing rain; or mild, calm, sunny days more like early fall: anything is possible. It may not be the best time of year to be working outside, but seize your opportunities when they arise.*

A greenhouse is a real boon for a keen gardener now—whatever the weather, you can get on with growing plants in comparative comfort. In contrast to the often bleak scene outdoors, the greenhouse can be full of color from bulbs and pot plants, and given there's enough heat, some seed sowing can begin.

Although the grass has stopped growing and the mower has been put away for the winter, that doesn't mean you can entirely ignore the lawn. This is the time of year when it is most likely to suffer wear and tear, so be prepared to act promptly in order to prevent damage from occurring.

Wild birds can be a nuisance at times, but most gardeners appreciate the life they bring to the garden in winter, and are happy to encourage them. The fall season with its fruit, seeds, berries, and insects is over, and it's time to start putting out food on the bird table. But once you start feeding, you must keep it up because the birds will come to rely on you. Remember to provide water for drinking and bathing, too, particularly in freezing weather.

If the garden is looking dull, cheer it up by planting some containers of hardy winter plants like flowering Viola (pansies) and heathers, and variegated foliage plants. In the kitchen garden there will probably still be winter digging and fruit tree pruning to get on with, and don't forget to send off those seed orders before the spring rush.

◀ *Variegated evergreens like* Hedera colchica *'Sulphur Heart' are particularly valuable for brightening the garden in the winter months.*

## EARLY WINTER TASKS

**General**
- Continue winter digging
- Make paths to avoid wear on lawns
- Cover compost piles to keep out rain

**Ornamental garden**
- Continue to plant containers for winter and spring interest
- Firm newly-planted trees and shrubs after frosts
- Protect the blooms of Helleborus niger (Christmas rose) with straw on the ground
- Check trees and shrubs for root rock or lifting after frosts, refirming them if necessary
- Order flower seeds from catalogs, especially those needing an early start
- Protect young trees against rabbits with tree guards

**Lawns**
- Avoid walking over frosted grass. Turfing is still possible in mild spells

**Water gardens**
- Thaw holes in frozen ponds

**Kitchen garden**
- Protect fall-sown bean and pea seedlings
- Order seeds from catalogs
- Prune fruit trees

**Greenhouse**
- Check the temperature regularly with a maximum/minimum thermometer
- Bring forced bulbs indoors as the flower buds show color
- Sow seeds such as onions and pelargoniums in a heated propagator
- Clean pots and seedtrays ready for the bulk of spring sowing
- Remove faded flowers on cyclamen
- Move cyclamen, primula (primroses) etc., from the home to the greenhouse when they finish flowering. Spray Indian azaleas with plain water regularly
- Plant more Narcissus 'Paper White' (daffodils) for a succession of flowers

▲ Make a firm path on well-used routes across lawns to avoid regular treading wearing the grass.

▼ Bulbs of Narcissus 'Paper White' planted now should be in flower in about six weeks.

# plant names

The use of the correct botanical or scientific names for plants is always a contentious subject. Many gardeners find the scientific names unwieldy, impossible to pronounce or spell, and nowhere near as good as the common names they've been using all their life.

Many of these criticisms are true, but there are very good reasons for using scientific names. The first is that common names are not all that common—they vary according to where you live, and often apply to more than one plant. And, of course, different countries using different languages also use different common names.

The scientific names, on the other hand, are controlled by the International Code of Nomenclature

to insure that each plant has its own unique name, and that the name denotes its family origins correctly. The names are international, being based mainly on Latin (though Greek and other languages are also used). Once the language of scientific names is understood, the names themselves can convey a great deal of information.

We still use the system of classification of plants developed in the 18th century by Linnaeus, who organized plants into genera and species. The botanical name of a plant is generally in two parts; the first part is the genus (as in *Crocus*) and the second part is the species (as in *chrysanthus*). Included in the name may also be a variety (a naturally occurring, stable variation in the species) or cultivar (a variation which has been selected or bred by man).

For greater clarity, the way the name is written follows set rules. The genus begins with an upper case (capital) letter, the species with a lower case letter, and both are in italics. A naturally occurring variety is also written in italics, with the abbreviation var. in front of it, while a cultivar name is written in Roman type (i.e. non italics), and enclosed in single quotation marks. We therefore have names such as *Ficus benjamina* var. *nuda*, or *Lonicera japonica* 'Aureoreticulata'. A hybrid (cross) between two species or genera is signified by an 'x' before the name, as in x *Cupressocyparis leylandii* (a cross between two genera, *Cupressus* and *Chamaecyparis*) or *Ceanothus* x *veitchianus* (a cross between two species, in this case *C. rigidus* and *C. thyrsiflorus*).

The species names generally provide most

◀ x Cupressocyparis leylandii: *the 'x' denotes that this tree is a cross between two genera; in this case,* Cupressus *and* Chamaecyparis.

▶ Lithodora diffusa: *improved techniques of plant identification have meant that it is now known as* Lithospermum diffusa.

information about a particular plant, often denoting its color, size, growing habit, flowers, or place of origin. Names containing folius describe the leaves, and florus the flowers—as in *albiflorus* (white flowered) or *cordifolius* (having heart-shaped leaves). A few common descriptive species names are given in the box below. (Remember that the spelling will alter according to whether the genus name is masculine or feminine, following the rules of Latin grammar.

One point that many gardeners do find annoying is the way the botanical names of plants are sometimes changed. This is not done on a whim but because new and improved techniques of plant identification have enabled botanists to discover that some plants have been incorrectly classified. *Lithospermum diffusum* has in recent years become *Lithodora diffusa*, for example, and *Coleus* has been reclassified under *Plectranthus* or *Solenostemon*. Irritating as these changes are, they are inevitable as our knowledge of the plant kingdom becomes more accurate and refined.

▲ Coleus *was originally wrongly classified; it has recently been correctly reclassified under* Plectranthus *or* Solenostemon.

## DESCRIPTIVE BOTANICAL NAMES

*alatus:* winged

*albus:* white

*alpinus:* alpine

*angustifolius:* narrow-leaved

*arachnoides:* spider-like or with the appearance of a cobweb

*baccifera:* bearing berries

*candidus:* shining, white

*chinensis:* from China

*citriodorus:* lemon scented

*denticulata:* toothed

*dissectus:* deeply cut

*foetidus:* having a fetid smell

*fragrans:* scented

*glaucus:* blue-gray

*grandifolius:* large leaved

*hispidus:* spiny or bristly

*laciniatus:* deeply cut into narrow segments

*laevigatus:* smooth

*lanuginosus:* wooly

*maculatus:* spotted

*maritimum:* growing near the sea

*meleagris:* speckled

*nanus:* dwarf

*nummularia:* like coins

*nutans:* nodding

*officinalis:* having medicinal use

*pictus:* boldly marked, painted

*procumbens:* prostrate

*pumilus:* dwarf or small

*repens:* creeping

*scandens:* climbing or scrambling

*sempervirens:* evergreen

*spectabilis:* showy

*tenax:* tough, strong

*tortuosus:* twisted

*utilis:* useful

*variegatus:* variegated

*vernalis:* of spring

*vulgaris:* common

*xanthocarpus:* with yellow fruits

# general tasks

*Encourage birds into the garden now by providing them with regular, easy meals, and they may stay around to keep down insect pests in the spring and summer. Take care of other animals too—the fish in ponds will be badly affected if the pond stays frozen over for more than a day or two.*

## Feeding garden birds

As soon as the weather turns cold, birds begin to find it increasingly difficult to obtain sufficient food. Not only are there fewer insects, berries, and fruit in the garden, but there are increasingly fewer daylight hours in which to eat. Supplying food regularly for birds can make all the difference to their survival, especially the smaller species.

Use a bird table placed in the open, and protected as far as possible from cats. A roof over the table helps to keep the food dry. Do not put out more food until the birds have cleared up what is there because excess food falls to the ground and attracts vermin. Suitable foods include peanuts, soaked brown breadcrumbs, apples and other fruit, suet and shortening, oatmeal, fresh (not desiccated) coconut, seeds and so on. Special feeders are available for different foods and species of birds, including models that prevent the food being taken by squirrels.

▲ *Put out a supply of bird food regularly all through the winter months. Once birds start to visit a bird table, they will come to rely on it.*

### WINTER DIGGING

Digging is best done a little at a time to avoid back strain, so continue steadily with the job over the next few weeks. Incorporate as much  organic matter into the ground as possible while digging, especially on light or heavy soils. Garden compost, stable manure, spent mushroom compost, spent hops and similar

 materials will all help to improve the texture of the soil, enabling light soils to retain more moisture and heavy soils to drain more freely. If you find digging too hard or time consuming, a mechanical cultivator can be used instead once a whole plot is cleared for cultivation.

## protect lawns from wear

Cold, wet conditions increase the likelihood of damage to turf as the soil is easily compacted and the grass is unable to make new recovery growth. A frequently walked route over the lawn—from the house to a garden gate or shed, for instance—will soon become obvious in winter, with the grass becoming thin and eventually bare patches appearing.

Encouraging alternative routes that do not cross the lawn is one solution, but the quickest, most straightforward route is always the one most likely to be used. If this route crosses the lawn it may be best to accept the situation and make a firm path.

An informal stepping-stone path is often an appropriate style; it appears less intrusive than a solid path. A slightly curving route is good, but it should not deviate too much from the more direct, trodden pathway or it will not be used.

1 Insure the stones are placed the correct distance apart to give an easy walking pace. Lay the first slab in place and cut around it with a half-moon edging iron (**below, left**). Undercut the turf with a spade to remove it; excavate the soil and replace with a 1in/25mm layer of sand.

2 Drop the slab into place; its surface should end up just below that of the surrounding grass so that mowing can take place over the top of it. Check the level and settle the slab into place by tapping firmly with the handle of a lump hammer or similar tool (**below, right**).

### THAWING HOLES IN FROZEN PONDS

If ponds remain frozen over for more than two days, thaw a hole in the ice to allow toxic gases to escape and prevent them from poisoning fish. Do not break the ice with a heavy object such as a hammer as fish may be harmed by shock waves traveling through the water. Instead, thaw a hole; fill an old tin can or pot with boiling water and standing it on the ice. It may need refilling several times if the ice is thick. If possible, use a pond heater to stop the pool freezing over again.

# ornamental garden: *general tasks*

*It's a good time to clean up the walls behind deciduous climbers now that the leaves are off the plants; it's surprising how many pests lurk under the tangle of stems. And don't put containers away just because the summer bedding plants have finished—they can be enjoyed through the winter, too.*

### Containers for winter interest

Many gardeners rely heavily on plants in containers to provide color near the house, on the patio, and around the garden during the summer, but far fewer make full use of them through the winter months.

◀ *Make use of evergreens as well as winter-flowering subjects such as pansies and primulas to give containers winter and spring interest.*

There are lots of plants that will give a good display in winter, even in the coldest weather—try dwarf evergreen shrubs (especially variegated varieties), dwarf conifers, winter-flowering viola (pansies) and heathers, ornamental cabbages, and trailing plants such as hedera (ivy).

Tubs, windowboxes, and even hanging baskets in a sheltered position can be used. In very cold areas, insulate the roots of the plants by lining the inside of the container with bubble wrap before filling with soil mix. Bubble wrap can also be used to lag already-planted containers by being tied around the outside. Be careful with terracotta (clay) containers outdoors in the winter. Porous material absorbs water which expands when frozen, and this can shatter the pot; look for brands which are guaranteed frost proof.

### Checking trees for root rock

Recently planted trees (and shrubs) can be disturbed by wind: it catches the branches and rocks the plants backward and forward. This disturbs the roots in the soil and often opens up a hole around the base of the stem; water may channel down and cause rot. Check trees and shrubs regularly; firm them back in the soil with the ball of your foot if necessary.

### PROTECTING YOUNG TREES

Newly-planted trees are often attacked by rabbits in gardens near fields or open spaces. Rabbits (and other small mammals) strip off the bark, weakening the tree and making it vulnerable to disease. If they remove a complete strip of bark from around the whole trunk, the tree will die. They can be thwarted, though, by using a rabbit guard in the form of a spiral plastic strip slipped around the trunk. Being spiral, the guard is able to expand as the trunk swells and does not restrict the tree's growth, even if forgotten.

# wall maintenance under climbing plants

The appearance of an area of blank wall is greatly improved by growing climbing plants over it, but maintenance work on the wall beneath the plants will be necessary occasionally to keep it in good condition. Now that the climbers are not in active growth, this is a good time of year to carry out such work.

## KEEPING HELLEBORE FLOWERS CLEAN

The winter-flowering *Helleborus niger* (Christmas rose) bears its blooms very close to the ground, where they may be spoiled by soil splashes if it rains. When the plants are in bud, tuck some straw or similar material around their base to prevent this.

1 Climbing plants should be grown on a trellis fixed to the wall rather than directly on the wall. It improves the air flow round the plants while making the wall accessible for maintenance. Attach the trellis to battens 2in/5cm thick and fix to the surface of the wall (**right**).

2 Prune back shoots that have outgrown the available space, and thin out the climber's growth if necessary. Unscrew the trellis and carefully lower it, still clothed with the climber's growth, to ground level. Two people are necessary unless the trellis is very small.

3 The wall behind a dense climber is a favorite hiding place for snails, and you will probably find a surprising number clinging to the wall's surface. Remove and dispose of them, and then sweep all the dirt and debris away from the wall with a stiff broom (**right**).

4 Carry out any necessary repairs to brick or plasterwork before reattaching the trellis. If screws are difficult to work with, a hook and screw eye system can be used to attach the trellis instead. Great care is needed to avoid damage to the main stem of the climber while the trellis is being lowered and raised.

◄ *This is the time of year for checking trees and shrubs for root rock; they may well have been disturbed by windy weather.*

# ornamental garden: *plants in season*

*This is the time of year when the bark and branches of both trees and shrubs begin to be appreciated—there are some beautiful and striking shapes, textures, and colors to admire. Plenty of leaves, flowers, such as the beautiful snowdrops, and berries, such as those found in seasonal favorites holly and ivy, can be enjoyed, too.*

▲ *Snowdrops are among the earliest flowers of the year. The double flowers of* Galanthus nivalis *'Flore Pleno' are especially attractive.*

▶ Hamamelis intermedia '*Westerstede*' (witch hazel) bears its fragrant, ragged-petaled flowers on leafless branches.

▼ *The sweet-scented, pale yellow flowers of Mahonia japonica are carried all through the winter, undeterred by the coldest weather.*

## TREES AND SHRUBS

*Acer,* especially *A. capillipes, A. davidii, A. griseum* (maple)

*Arbutus unedo* (strawberry tree)

*Aucuba japonica* 'Crotonifolia' and others (spotted laurel)

*Betula,* especially *B. ermanii, B. nigra* (black birch), *B. papyrifera* (paper birch), *B. utilis* var. *jacquemontii* (Himalayan Birch)

*Chimonanthus praecox* (wintersweet)

*Cornus alba* (red-barked dogwood)

*Corylus avellana* 'Contorta' (Harry Lauder's walking stick)

*Cotoneaster*

*Elaeagnus* x *ebbingei*

*Erica carnea* (alpine heath)

*Euonymus fortunei, E. japonicus* (variegated)

*Fraxinus excelsior* 'Jaspidea' (European ash)

*Hamamelis mollis* (Chinese witch hazel)

*Hedera* (ivy)

*Ilex* (berry-bearing and variegated varieties) (holly)

*Jasminum nudiflorum* (jasmine)

*Lonicera fragrantissima, L. standishii* (winter honeysuckle)

*Mahonia*

*Prunus serrula, P.* x *subhirtella* 'Autumnalis' (autumn cherry)

*Pyracantha* (firethorn)

*Salix alba, S. babylonica* var. *pekinensis* 'Tortuosa' (dragon-claw willow)

*Skimmia japonica*

*Sorbus*

*Tilia platyphylos* 'Rubra' (red-twigged lime)

*Viburnum*

## PERENNIALS

*Helleborus niger* (Christmas rose)

*Iris unguicularis*

*Schizostylis coccinea* (kaffir lily)

## BULBS

*Crocus imperati*

*Cyclamen coum*

*Galanthus* (snowdrop)

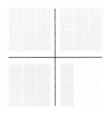

# kitchen garden: *general tasks*

*Continue pruning fruit trees during the dormant season, except when the weather is frosty. Winter digging of the vegetable plot should also be proceeding; it is worth digging the ground as deeply as you can, adding plenty of organic matter to improve the soil.*

### Protecting beans and peas

Pea and bean seeds sown in the vegetable plot earlier in the fall should have germinated and be showing through the soil by now. Although they are hardy, very cold and windy weather will take its toll of the young plants, so it is worth giving them a little extra protection to see them through the worst spells. Plants can be protected by glass barn cloches placed over the rows that will keep off the worst of the cold weather and wind, and protect the plants from excess rain. The glass acts as a mini-greenhouse, trapping the warmth of any sun there may be. Unfortunately glass cloche are very prone to breakage, and can be dangerous, especially where there are children or pets in the garden. Mini-polytunnels are a safer option, although condensation can be a problem, causing fungal rots to affect the seedlings. One of the easiest materials to use is lightweight horticultural blanket that is draped loosely over the crop. The edges must be pegged down or secured to prevent the blanket from blowing away in windy weather.

▲ *Protect fall-sown beans and pea seedlings from the worst of the cold weather and wind with mini-polytunnels.*

### PRUNING LARGE TREES

—

Most modern fruit trees are grown on dwarfing or semidwarfing rootstocks, but older trees can grow very tall and wide spreading, making pruning difficult. If you use a ladder, have someone hold it steady. Long-arm pruners make reaching high branches easier; make sure the blades are sharp and the cutting mechanism works smoothly.

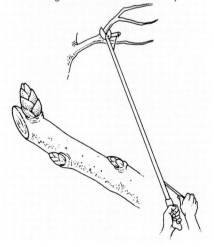

## PRUNING FRUIT TREES

Continue pruning bush trees as described on page 192. Pruning in the dormant season stimulates strong, vigorous growth the following spring, and that is why the major pruning of trees trained as restricted forms takes place in summer. Hard winter pruning of apples and pears grown as cordons or espaliers would result in uncontrolled growth. Winter pruning on trained trees should mainly be restricted to removing dead, dying and diseased wood, and thinning out overcrowded spurs.

Plums should not be pruned in the winter because this invites an invasion by silver leaf disease spores. The disease slowly weakens the trees, and forms bracket fungi on affected branches that release spores mainly during the late fall and winter. The spores enter new wood through fresh wounds. Plums should be pruned in the spring and summer when spores are less likely to be around, and in any case the trees more quickly produce natural resins to seal over pruning cuts. The popular plum variety 'Victoria' is particularly prone to this disease, which also affects almonds, apricots and cherries, although not usually producing such serious effects as it does on plums.

# *start winter digging*

Since digging is satisfying but hard physical work, large plots should be completed in stages to avoid the back problems that trouble so many over-enthusiastic gardeners. Digging is best carried out as early in the winter as possible, leaving the ground rough for the maximum time to allow frosts to break up the clods of soil.

1 Dig a trench one spit (the depth of the spade's blade) deep across the top of the plot (**left**). Throw the soil into a wheelbarrow so that it can be moved to the other end of the plot. Try to keep your spine straight while digging.

2 Fork over or chop the soil at the base of the trench with the spade. Move backward and dig a second trench behind the first (**left, below**). Throw the soil from this to fill the trench in front. Try to turn the soil over as you throw it.

3 Continue in this way until you reach the other end of the plot. If you have any rotted manure or garden compost to incorporate, it should be placed at the base of each trench before it is filled in. Annual weeds can be buried, but perennial weed roots should be removed.

4 Once the last trench has been dug, fill it in with the soil from the first trench that has been barrowed to the end of the plot. Leave the soil surface rough; repeated freezing and thawing of the moisture in the soil over the winter will break down the clods and improve soil structure.

# protecting kitchen garden crops

Cloches and polytunnels are useful in almost every season in the kitchen garden, but never more so than when bad weather is threatening to damage crops. They keep off rain, wind, and a degree of frost; they can also protect plants from attack by a range of pests. In late winter and early spring they give early plants that little extra protection that will bring them on well ahead of the rest. Earlier still, they can be used to cover strips of soil required for early sowing. Keeping the rain off the soil will allow it to warm up and become workable much earlier than uncovered areas.

Tunnels and cloches are most suitable for low-growing plants, though with imagination they can also be pressed into service for taller crops. A pair of barn cloches, stood on end and wired together, are perfect around outdoor tomato plants to ripen the last fruits in the fall.

## Cloches

Cloches are made from glass or rigid plastic. Glass has the advantage of retaining heat better (like a mini-greenhouse) and being more stable in windy weather, but it is very fragile and dangerous when broken, especially in gardens where children play. It is also expensive, and makes cloches heavy and awkward to move about. Plastic cloches are cheap and lightweight,

▲ *The earliest cloches were used for individual plants. Bell-type cloches are still available, but open-ended styles are now more popular.*

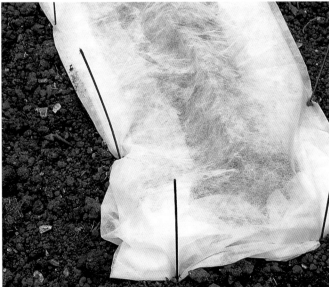

▲ *A lightweight polypropylene blanket provides young plants with surprisingly good protection against adverse weather.*

▶ *The polytunnel is very popular with gardeners because it is cheap to buy and easy to use, though it has a relatively short life.*

## STORING CLOCHES AND TUNNELS

At the end of their season of use, all parts of cloches and tunnels should be cleaned thoroughly before storing. Barn and tent cloches can be stored on edges stacked inside each other to save dismantling and rebuilding them, but take care to store glass cloches safely to avoid breakages and injury. Plastic materials should be stored out of sunlight to extend their life.

and not as easily broken as glass; they do not retain so much warmth and need to be thoroughly secured or they will blow away in even slightly windy weather. Cloches may be made from clear plastic, PVC, twin-walled polycarbonate or polypropylene. All plastic should have been treated with an ultraviolet inhibitor.

Early cloches were bell shaped (*cloche* is French for bell) or lantern shaped, and used to cover individual plants. This individual type of cloche is still available but larger cloches, used end-to-end to cover whole rows of plants, are now more popular. They may be made from two pieces of glass (or plastic) fixed together in an inverted "V" to form a tent shape, or from four pieces of glass to form a barn cloche with its slightly sloping sides topped by a wide tent roof. The barn cloche is useful for taller plants, and can usually be ventilated by raising or removing one side of the roof. Barn cloches are generally made from glass held together by a number of wire clips, and are much more difficult to construct than tent cloches. Another popular cloche shape is an arc, made by bending a flexible, semirigid sheet of plastic, usually corrugated, and securing it with hoops.

To prevent rows of cloches from becoming wind tunnels, they should be fitted with end panels, which sometimes have adjustable ventilators. Cloches with built-in sprinklers are also available for easy watering.

### Polytunnels

These are made from plastic sheeting that is stretched over wire hoops positioned over the crop. They are usually available as packs of hoops with a separate plastic sheet, but brands that have the plastic ready fitted over the hoops and which are folded up concertina fashion make erecting the tunnels easier. They are cheap, and easy to use and store.

### Floating row cover

This is a term applied to lightweight perforated plastic or fiber materials that lie loosely on top of the crop, and are held in place by the edges being buried or staked in the ground. The material is light and flexible enough not to restrict the crop as it grows. Polypropylene fiber blanket is the most popular kind, and insulates the plants against cold and wind while remaining permeable to air and moisture. It tears easily but with care will last for several seasons, especially if it has strengthened edges. It is available cut to measure from a roll, in sheets, or as a "grow tube" 3ft/90cm in diameter that is cut to length and used to fit over individual plants.

# greenhouse: *general tasks*

*Get a head start on some of the crops that like a long growing season by sowing seeds now, with the aid of a heated propagator to supply the extra warmth they need. Remember to keep a regular check on greenhouse temperatures to insure that heating systems are working efficiently.*

## Sowing seeds in a heated propagator

A number of seeds like an early start to give them a long growing season—onions and pelargoniums are two that traditionally are sown in early winter. Seeds need more warmth than growing plants to insure good germination, and the extra warmth can quite conveniently be supplied by using a heated propagator.

Electrically-heated propagators have a heating element sealed into the base that supplies a steady warmth to the soil mix. Plastic seedtray covers help to retain the heat. The warmth leads to a build-up of condensation inside the propagator cover, so adjustable ventilators should be fitted to the covers to prevent the humidity becoming too high.

Various sizes of propagator are available, from models that take a single seed tray to those that can accommodate four trays or more. More sophisticated (and expensive) propagator models have an adjustable thermostat that enables you to vary the temperature according to the requirements of the particular seeds you are sowing—usually from 60–75°F/15–24°C. As an alternative to buying a complete propagator,

▲ *Heated propagators can supply a constant warmth to flats of seeds sown in soil mix and help to encourage good germination.*

it is possible to make up your own propagating bench to the size you require by buying soil-warming cables and an appropriate thermostat.

### GREENHOUSE TEMPERATURES

A maximum/minimum thermometer is invaluable for insuring that greenhouse heating systems are working efficiently, so make a habit of checking and resetting the thermometer every day. It is important that temperatures do not dip too low, but you should also make sure that fuel is not being wasted by maintaining too high a temperature. The best time to check this is on a cold, frosty morning, insuring that the minimum temperature recorded the previous night was not significantly higher than required. If necessary, adjust the heating thermostat up or down, as appropriate, but do be careful to make only small adjustments at a time.

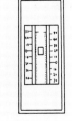

## *easy, early flowering narcissus (daffodils)*

One of the simplest varieties of narcissus for growing in the home during the winter season is the variety 'Paper White.' It needs no special treatment, and quickly produces multi-headed stems of pure white, star-like blooms with a penetrating, sweet fragrance. Planting several batches of bulbs two weeks or so apart will make sure there is a long succession of blooms for the house.

1 'Paper White' bulbs can be grown in bowls or pots of soilless potting mix, or even on pebbles or in a glass jar filled with water. Plant the bulbs in pots or bowls so that their tips are just showing above the soil surface (**right**).

2 Water the mix so that it is just moist. Unlike most forced bulbs, 'Paper White' requires no cold, dark period. Place the planted bulbs on a windowsill in a light but cool position; a frost-free greenhouse is an ideal place.

3 The plants need bright light as the stems grow, and become very tall and spindly if grown in a warm or dull position. Each stem should be supported with a slender split cane, but take care not to spear the bulbs (**below**).

4 The bulbs will usually come into flower six to eight weeks after planting (**below**). Plants growing in the greenhouse should be taken into the home just before the flowers open. Keep them in a cool, bright position for the longest life.

### INDIAN AZALEAS

*Azaleas* make very attractive winter-flowering houseplants, but they do need moist compost and a humid atmosphere. Plants in bud and in flower should be sprayed daily with a fine mist of plain water. When plants are in the home, keep them in a cool position at 50–60°F/10–15°C, away from artificial heat or direct sunlight.

# midwinter

*This is often the most trying season of the year for gardeners. The weather may be at its most miserable and, although the shortest day is just past, there is no real evidence yet of the daylight hours lengthening. Spring might seem a long way off but in reality there is not too long to wait.*

All the dormant-season tasks in the garden continue. Planting bare-root specimens of new trees and shrubs will be possible for some weeks yet; if the weather is freezing or very wet when the plants arrive, heel them in until conditions improve. After heavy frosts, check plantings in case they need firming back into the soil if the frost has lifted them.

The prolonged wet spells show up any badly drained areas. If puddles are still standing on the soil surface hours after the rain has stopped, it is a sign drainage needs to be improved.

This is the most likely time for snow. Snow can make the garden look beautiful, but if you can bring yourself to spoil its unsullied whiteness it's a good idea to take action to prevent it from damaging plants and trees. It's only the physical weight of the snow that does the damage; snow actually helps to insulate plants against the cold.

Some border plants can be increased by root cuttings, and in the vegetable garden the soil can be made ready for early spring sowings. In the greenhouse things are moving ahead rapidly — stock up with the equipment you need for the busy sowing and growing season ahead.

◄ *Midwinter is the most likely time for snow in many regions. It may be beautiful but its weight can cause damage to trees and plants.*

## MIDWINTER TASKS

**General**

- Check and maintain tools before putting them away for the winter
- Improve drainage where necessary

**Ornamental garden**

- Weed and check emerging spring bulbs outdoors
- Take root cuttings of phlox, Papaver (poppy), Verbascum (mullein) and other border plants
- Continue planting bare-root and container-grown trees and shrubs, and refirm newly-planted specimens after frost. Heel in bare-root plants when weather is unsuitable for planting
- Knock snow off evergreens before it breaks their branches
- Order young plants from seed catalogs for delivery in early to mid-spring

▲ Root cuttings are an easy way to propagate many border plants.

**Lawns**

- Keep off the grass in frosty or wet weather
- Watch out for snow mold disease
- Sweep away leaves and debris

**Kitchen garden**

- Continue digging
- Force outdoor rhubarb for an early crop
- Sow sprouting seeds for winter salads
- Order vegetable seeds, seed potatoes, young vegetable plants and onions sets from catalogs as soon as possible
- Sow beans and peas for an early crop
- Continue to check fruit and vegetables in store
- Cover the ground with cloches to dry it out ready for early sowings
- Continue to plant fruit trees, and soft fruit bushes and canes
- Complete pruning of fruit trees
- Deter birds from attacking fruit buds

**Greenhouse**

- Remove dead plant material promptly to avoid disease. Ventilate whenever possible to keep the atmosphere dry
- Buy new seed flats, pots, propagator tops, and labels etc., ready for the main sowing season
- Continue sowing early seeds in a heated propagator
- Start overwintering fuchsias and pelargoniums, chrysanthemums and dahlias into growth to provide cuttings
- Sow Lathyrys ordoratus (sweet peas)
- Sow some stump-rooted carrots and radishes in a growing bag

▼ Grow a quick and early crop of carrots in a growing bag in the greenhouse.

# general garden tasks

*Snow hides all the imperfections of the winter garden and covers it in a pristine whiteness, but it can bring problems for the gardener, especially if it persists for more than a few days. Frost is more common than snow in most areas, and brings its own set of difficulties, particularly for lawns.*

*Preventing snow damage*

A moderate fall of snow can pose a real danger to evergreen trees and shrubs. In just a few hours they can be permanently misshapen, or branches can be broken by the weight of snow.

If the snowfall is heavy enough, knock it from the branches of any tree or shrub that looks as though it may be damaged. It is usually easily dislodged with a broom, but you will need to do this shortly after the snow has fallen—don't wait for it to freeze again or it becomes much more difficult.

The thaw brings more problems because a lot of water is released as the snow melts. On lawns, look out for more or less round patches of dying, yellow grass which gradually enlarge and may show signs of a fluffy white mold. This is snow mold, a fungus disease that is common on lawns that have been covered in snow for some time, especially if they have been walked over regularly. Treat the disease with a lawn fungicide.

▲ *Snow may bring a seasonal beauty to the winter garden, but it can also spell problems for some trees and shrubs.*

## STORING TOOLS

Garden tools need to be kept in good condition if they are to give good service, and the winter is a good time to give them all a thorough overhaul. Hand tools such as spades and forks should be cleaned thoroughly after use, removing all soil, and the metal parts rubbed with an oily rag. Wooden handles can be smoothed down with sandpaper to prevent splinters.

The moving parts of tools such as shears and pruners should be oiled, and blades of all cutting implements can be sharpened with a carborundum stone. Don't forget to sharpen the blades of tools such as hoes and edging irons as well. Any tools that are not being used over the winter should be stored in a dry place, and tools that have reached the end of their useful life should be replaced before the main growing season starts.

# make a cold frame

Cold frames are more useful in the garden than is generally realized. They are invaluable for overwintering slightly tender or young plants, and are ideal for hardening off greenhouse plants destined for outdoors in the spring. While purpose-made aluminum and plastic cold frames can be bought, it is quite easy to make your own, often entirely from waste materials.

1 A typical cold frame has a wooden or brick base about 12–18in/30–45cm high at the back, sloping down toward the front, and is covered with a glass lid called a light. The usual size for a frame is around 4 x 2ft/120 x 60cm but size can be adjusted to suit your needs.

3 If the frame is constructed in a sheltered area it is unnecessary to cement the bricks together. The window frames can be laid on top of the base and held in place by bricks around the edge (**right**). With wooden bases, attach the frames with hinges to make ventilation easier.

2 Demolition yards can often supply glazed window frames very cheaply, and they make excellent lights. Choose those with as large an area of glass as possible because glazing bars cut down the amount of light considerably. Once you have obtained the lights, build the base to fit.

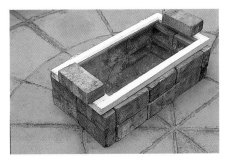

4 On cold days a piece of old carpet or sacking should be laid over the frame for extra protection (**below**); in sunny weather ventilate the frame by removing the light or propping it open with a wooden stay. In windy areas, make sure the open light is secure and cannot be blown away.

◄ *Walking over frosted grass will crush and kill the frozen stems, leaving a pattern of blackened footprints later on. Walking on the lawn in wet weather should also be avoided. Make an extra effort to stick to paths in winter.*

# use of fertilizers

Plants make their energy from the sun by photosynthesis, but in order to carry this out, they need certain minerals that they normally absorb from the soil. These minerals are generally referred to as plant nutrients or plant foods. The three main minerals plants require are nitrogen, phosphorus, and potassium, often referred to by their chemical names of N, P, and K. Along with calcium, magnesium and sulfur, they are the minerals required in the largest amounts.

Other minerals are no less important but are needed in only very small quantities. These micronutrients or trace elements include boron, copper, iron, manganese, molybdenum, and zinc. Some other elements, such as cobalt, aluminum, and silicon, are also required by plants, but are thought to be beneficial rather than essential.

In good, fertile soils, enough essential nutrients are available for the plants' needs. In other soils, however, there may be a shortfall of one or more nutrients. This can be due to the physical makeup of the soil, or to repeated heavy cropping that has used up the mineral reserves; it might also be that the minerals are present but not in a form that is available to plants (for example alkaline soils often "lock up" micronutrients such as iron). Where the nutrients are not available in the soil, they can be supplied as supplements in the form of fertilizers.

## Fertilizers

Fertilizers can either be straight (supplying one nutrient) or compound (supplying a mixture of nutrients). Details of which nutrients they supply are always given on the pack. The three major nutrients (nitrogen, phosphorus, and potassium—always in this order) are the most popular ingredients of compound fertilizers, and the proportions are often expressed as N:P:K 7:7:7, or just 7:7:7. A fertilizer labeled 5:5:9 is high in potassium, while 30:10:10 is high in nitrogen. Straight fertilizers may be labeled in the same way—for example, sulfate of ammonia 21:0:0, or sulfate of potash 0:0:50.

The three major nutrients are the ones most likely to be in short supply in the soil, but other nutrients can be deficient too. Some fertilizers contain a mixture of both major and micronutrients, while others specialize in providing micronutrients only, and are often called trace element fertilizers. Sometimes the micronutrients are formulated to insure that they will not be altered by the

◀ *Liquid fertilizers are fast acting and give a rapid boost to plants. Some types are formulated for absorption by the leaves.*

soil chemistry and made unavailable to plants; they are known as fritted or chelated compounds, and are ideal for alkaline soils. Other trace element fertilizers are formulated so that they can be taken up by the foliage, a further way of avoiding the soil chemistry problem.

## Methods of application

Fertilizers come in the form of powders, granules, and liquids. Always read the application instructions carefully—some powders are applied direct to the soil while others need to be dissolved in water first. The application rate varies according to the product and the type of plant being fed. Wear gloves when handling and applying fertilizers, and keep dry fertilizers off the plants, especially the growth buds because they are likely to be scorched. Liquid fertilizers are less likely to scorch plants and are quick acting; they can be applied through a watering can or a hose-end dilutor for large areas such as lawns. Dry fertilizers can also be obtained as soil sticks or pills for easy application.

Slow-release fertilizers give extended feeding over several weeks. They are normally granules that are gradually broken down to release the fertilizer, and require a combination of moisture and warmth to act.

▲ *Fertilizer granules: it is important to wear gloves when handling and applying any form of fertilizers and keep dry fertilizers off the plants.*

▼ *Fertilizer pills are now available for ease of application to soils where there is a shortfall of important nutrients.*

## NUTRIENT DEFICIENCY SYMPTOMS

| Nutrient | Symptom of deficiency |
| --- | --- |
| Nitrogen | leaves small, pale green or yellow, especially older leaves; growth stunted |
| Phosphorus | leaves small, tinged with purple; older leaves fall early |
| Potassium | leaf tips and margins turn yellow or brown, and look scorched; older leaves affected first. Poor flowering and fruiting |
| Calcium | death of leaf tips and growing points; blossom end rot on tomatoes and peppers, bitter pit on apples |
| Magnesium | leaves yellow between the veins; older leaves affected first, spreading to young leaves |
| Sulfur | yellowing of leaves, first on young leaves then spreading to the whole plant. Not a common deficiency |
| Iron | leaves yellow with dark green veins; young leaves affected first (unlike magnesium deficiency) |
| Manganese | yellowing and dead patches between the veins on young leaves |
| Zinc | yellowing between the veins on young leaves; small leaves; browning of buds |
| Boron | growing points die, leaves deformed with discolored areas |
| Molybdenum | distinctive strap-shaped, "whip tail" leaves on cauliflowers |

223

# ornamental garden: *general tasks*

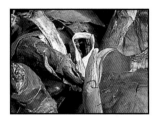

*Even though it is midwinter, there are definite signs of growth from spring-flowering bulbs. Help them on their way by making sure they are not smothered by weeds and debris. Meanwhile, root cuttings are an unusual but easy way of increasing a range of border plants, shrubs, and trees.*

## Bulbs in store

Many plants that develop specialized storage organs, such as bulbs, corms, and tubers, can be stored over winter in a cool, dry, frost-free place such as a garden shed; if left in cold, wet soil in the garden there is often a real risk of them rotting away. However, they are not immune to rotting even when lifted and stored under cover.

There are several fungi and bacteria that are responsible for storage rots. Many of the pathogens are present in the soil while some are airborne, and they usually attack the plants through damaged tissue. Check stored bulbs regularly all through winter, and remove and destroy any that show signs of rotting. Rots may take the form of red, brown, or black lesions that are often soft but may also be hard and dry; mold growth may also be visible. Dust remaining bulbs with a fungicide powder to try to prevent the spread of the problem.

▼ *Boxes of daffodil bulbs can be stored quite safely during the winter months provided their environment is dry and frost-free.*

### EMERGING SPRING BULBS
___

The leafy shoots of spring bulbs are already emerging through the soil. Carefully remove weeds, leaves, and other plant debris from around the shoots, and prick over the soil between them with a hand fork if there is room; this helps to aerate the soil and prevents a soil "cap" from forming. Where bulbs are planted under trees, moss may form on the soil surface; this does not harm the bulbs but you may want to scrape away the moss to improve the general appearance. On poor soils, a balanced fertilizer can be sprinkled around the bulbs once the surface has been cleared.

# take root cuttings

Most gardeners are familiar with the idea of taking cuttings from shoots and encouraging them to form new roots. Less well known is the technique of growing new plants from sections of root which send out new shoots. This is an easy way to propagate plants, and one of the few methods of propagation which can be carried out in midwinter.

1 A number of shrubs and herbaceous plants can be grown from root cuttings taken in the dormant season; among them are anchusa, *Anemone* x *hybrida*, Papaver (poppy), phlox, Primula (primroses), Romneya (tree poppy), daphne, and *Rhus typhina*.

3 Choose firm, healthy roots, removing two or three from each plant by cutting them cleanly with a knife (**below, left**). Replace the soil around the parent plant and firm it in well. Trim off any whiskery side roots from the cuttings and place them in a plastic bag to prevent drying out.

2 The cuttings can be taken at any time in the dormant season when the soil is not waterlogged or frozen. Herbaceous plants can be lifted carefully, or the plants can be left in situ and the soil scraped away to expose some roots if lifting is not practical.

4 Cut the prepared roots into sections about 2in/5cm long, but make sure you know which is the top and bottom of each piece. Insert into pots of moist, sandy cuttings mix so that their tops are level with the soil surface (**below, right**). Keep in a cold frame over winter.

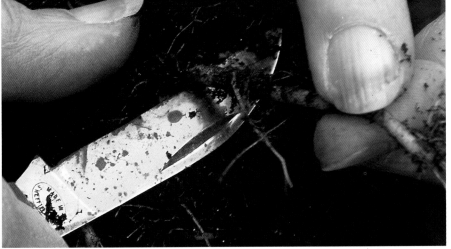

## REFIRM SPECIMENS

A heavy frost can expand the soil and cause it to lift around the roots of newly-planted trees and shrubs, loosening them in the ground. Inspect plants after a frost, and where necessary, firm them back in place by treading around them with the sole of your boot, pushing the soil back against the stems.

# ornamental garden: *plants in season*

*Evergreen plants continue to give good value, especially the variegated varieties that light up the garden in dull weather. Many of the trees and shrubs flowering now have the bonus of an intense fragrance, and more and more bulbs are blooming.*

▼ *Winter-flowering hellebores bring life to the garden. Although they are frost-hardy, low-growing varieties need protection.*

## TREES AND SHRUBS

Acer (bark effects) (maple)
Aucuba japonica (spotted laurel)
Betula (birch)
Camellia
Chimonanthus praecox (wintersweet)
Cornus alba (red-barked dogwood)
Corylus avellana 'Contorta' (Harry Lauder's
   walking stick)
Cotoneaster
Daphne odora
Erica carnea (alpine heath)
Euonymus fortunei, E. japonicus (variegated
   varieties) (spindle tree)
Garrya elliptica
Hamamelis mollis (witch hazel)
Hedera colchica 'Dentata Variegata' and
   others (ivy)
Hippophae rhamnoides (sea buckthorn)
Ilex (berry-bearing and variegated varieties)
   (holly)
Jasminum nudiflorum (jasmine)
Lonicera fragrantissima, L. standishii
   (winter honeysuckle)
Mahonia
Prunus serrula, P. x subhirtella 'Autumnalis'
   autumnn cherry)
Pyracantha (firethorn)
Salix alba (white willow), S. babylonica
   pekinensis 'Tortuosa'
Skimmia japonica
Sorbus
Viburnum

▲ Pyracantha, *with its startling red berries,
will liven up any garden at this time of year.*

## PERENNIALS

Ajuga reptans (bugle)
Bergenia
Helleborus atrorubens, H. foetidus (stinking
   hellebore), H. niger (Christmas rose)
Iris unguicularis
Phormium tenax (New Zealand flax)
Viola (winter-flowering pansies)

## BULBS

Crocus ancyrensis, C. imperati, C. laevigatus,
   C. tomasinianus
Eranthis (winter aconite)
Galanthus (snowdrop)
Iris danfordiae, I. histrioides, I. reticulata

◀ Camellia x williamsii *'Jury's Yellow'
is a winter-flowering delight.*

# kitchen garden: *general tasks*

*Plant canes and bushes to extend your range of soft fruits, and take action against birds that destroy fruit buds before they even start into growth. Cloches help to get the soil ready for early sowings, but if you can't wait that long, grow your own salad in a jelly jar in a matter of days.*

## *Protecting fruit buds from birds*

Various species of small birds can ruin the potential fruit crop of trees and bushes by pecking at the buds on the dormant branches. Every climate zone and local regions have their particular culprits, even including squirrels. Apples, cherries, gooseberries, plums, pears, and currants can all be affected.

The birds usually eat the tender shoots right in the centers of the buds. It is also believed that sometimes the birds are searching for insects sheltering in and around the buds, and that the damage to the buds is incidental. Either way, the effect is the same: long lengths of branches and shoots are left bare and the fruit crop is reduced. Bitter-tasting bird repellents can be sprayed on the trees but may not be very effective, while bird scarers also give mixed results. The surest way to prevent damage is by providing a physical barrier with netting or horticultural blanket.

### BUSHES, CANES AND FRUIT TREES

Fruit and vegetables form an important part of a healthy diet, and having plenty of home-grown fruit to harvest will certainly enable you to increase your consumption. Spells of good weather will allow you to plant fruit trees and soft fruit canes and bushes now.

Extend your range of soft fruits by trying some of the new, improved varieties that find their way into the catalogs every year. Particularly popular are the hybrid berries (mainly raspberry/blackberry crosses) such as boysenberry, silvanberry, tayberry, youngberry, sunberry and veitchberry. They should provide a talking point and a good crop of tasty fruit.

▶ *Netting protects a fruit crop from birds, but earlier in the year it can also help to prevent them from destroying the developing buds.*

## sprouting seeds for winter salads

Winter is a difficult time to produce fresh salad crops, but sprouting seeds couldn't be simpler to grow. They are ready in a matter or days, and have a pleasant crunchy texture and a range of interesting flavors. Many varieties are also thought to be beneficial to health, with particularly high concentrations of cancer-preventing compounds. A good range of suitable seeds for sprouting are available from the mail order catalogs of major seedsmen.

1 Sprouting seeds can be grown in a wide-necked glass jar topped with a piece of muslin or fine mesh net secured with an elastic band. A square cut from an old pair of nylon pantyhose makes a good cover.

2 Put a couple of spoonfuls of seeds into the jar and cover them with water; allow them to soak for a few hours or overnight (**right**). Drain the water off through the top of the jar, fill with fresh water, swirl around the jar and immediately drain the water off again.

3 Place the jar of seeds in a moderately warm position. If they are grown in the dark the sprouts will be white; if they are in the light they will be green and have a slightly different flavor. Every day, fill the jar with fresh water, swirl it round and immediately drain it away.

4 After a few days the sprouts are ready to eat (**below**); they will bulk up to almost fill the jar. Among seeds that can be grown are mung beans, alfalfa, and fenugreek; mixtures are also available. Only buy seeds produced for sprouting as many pulses are poisonous if eaten raw.

### THE VEGETABLE PLOT

In a sheltered place in the vegetable garden, cover an area of ground with cloches to get it ready for seed sowing a little later. Although the cloches might help to trap what heat there is, this is not why they are useful. Their main purpose is to keep the rain off the soil so that it can dry out, enabling it to be broken down to the fine crumbs necessary to form a seedbed.

# greenhouse: *general tasks*

*The spring sowing season will soon be upon us, so make sure you have all the necessary equipment. Meanwhile, make a start by sowing sweet peas, and some carrots or radishes for a tasty early crop. Plants that have been overwintering under cover can be started into growth to provide cuttings.*

## Waking up plants

The roots of plants such as dahlias, chrysanthemums, fuchsias, and pelargoniums have spent the winter in a more or less dormant condition, tucked into almost-dry compost or peat. As long as you can provide a little heat in the greenhouse, it's time to wake them up again, and start them into growth.

Pot up the roots in fresh compost if necessary, and bring them out into the light. Water the compost thoroughly so that it is evenly moist (but not wet) throughout, and maintain a steady temperature of around 45°F/7°C. New shoots will soon be produced, and they can be taken as softwood cuttings to provide sturdy, vigorous new plants for setting out after the risk of frosts is over.

### STOCK UP ON EQUIPMENT

When the main sowing season starts, a surprising number of seedtrays and pots will be necessary for all the seeds you want to try. Large volumes of sowing and cuttings mix will disappear quickly, too. Check the state of existing equipment—seedtrays and flats, various sizes of pot, plastic covers, dibbles, presser boards, watering can rose sprays, labels and markers. Discard broken or damaged equipment, and buy replacements. Also buy one or two large bags of compost and leave them unopened in the greenhouse until you need them.

▲ *It is easy to increase your stock of chrysanthemums by taking softwood cuttings over the next few weeks.*

# sow some early vegetables

In a frost-free greenhouse it is possible to make a sowing of spring vegetables now, and enjoy some extra early young crops. Both radishes and carrots grow well if sown direct into a growing bag. You won't get a very big crop, but it will be particularly welcome because they will be available so early in the year.

## SWEET PEAS

If you didn't sow sweet peas in the fall (or if you want another batch of plants), sow some now in exactly the same way. The seeds germinate best at around 50°F/10°C, and can be placed in a heated propagator. They will flower later than the fall-sown sweet peas, but still give excellent results.

1 Choose the right varieties for a growing bag—they must be short-rooting types. There are lots of suitable round radishes, but carrots need more care. Globe-rooting types such as 'Parmex' are ideal, and stump-rooted varieties like 'Nantes' are also good.

2 Cut out the top of the growing bag, leaving just a border of plastic around the edge. Make short drills in the soil with a cane or dibble, and sow the seeds thinly (**right**). Pull soil back over the top, pat down and water using a fine rose on the watering can.

3 Place the growing bags in the lightest position possible, and keep the soil just moist. When the seedlings emerge, thin them to an appropriate spacing as soon as they are large enough to handle.

4 Keep the soil moist as the plants develop. Start to pull the roots as soon as they are large enough to eat (**below**), taking alternate plants so that the ones that are left have the chance to grow bigger.

# lighting for greenhouse and houseplants

Warmth is not the only requirement for plant growth that is missing during the winter months—in addition, light levels are nowhere near the optimum for most plants. Even though the equivalent of summer temperatures can be provided by heating, the plants will not respond as they would in a real summer, simply because they are not receiving sufficient duration or quality of light.

Of course, supplementary lighting is available in almost every home at the flick of a switch. However, the type of artificial light that peope find useful is not that useful to plants.

### Light quality
Not all visible light is used by plants for photosynthesis, only light of certain wavelengths. The intensity of light is

▲ *Ordinary fluorescent lighting offers the domestic gardener a useful alternative to the high-power lighting used by commercial growers.*

## EFFECTS OF DAY LENGTH
## ON FLOWERING

Day length is a very important factor for controlling flowering times in certain plants. In some species flower buds are initiated only when the daylight hours fall below a specific length; they are called "short-day plants" and include chrysanthemums, poinsettias, kalanchoes, and Rieger begonias. "Long-night" plants would be more appropriate because it is actually the number of hours of uninterrupted darkness that is important.) Commercial growers manipulate flowering times very effectively by the use of supplementary or night-break lighting.

When artificial lighting is used by home gardeners, they can unwittingly prevent the flowering of short day plants by decreasing the hours of continuous darkness to which the plants are exposed. A single, short illumination interrupting the hours of darkness may be sufficient to prevent flowers from forming.

▶ *Chrysanthemums are among those flowers known as "short-day" plants because their buds are initiated only when day lengths are short.*

important, too—most forms of artificial lighting have to be placed relatively close to plants for a useful intensity of light to be absorbed.

Most lamps produce heat as a by-product; this heat is sufficiently intense to damage plants when the lamps are placed close to them. This factor alone rules out the use of ordinary household incandescent bulbs as a light source for plants.

Commercial growers use high-pressure sodium and metal halide lamps which have been specifically designed to promote plant growth, but these are expensive, and not particularly attractive in living rooms. A good alternative is ordinary fluorescent lighting; it remains cool in use and provides light of a useful wavelength. Fluorescent tubes give a good spread of light over a relatively large area. Compact fluorescent bulbs have the advantage of being suitable for a normal screw- or bayonet-type light fitting, but they cast their light over a much smaller area.

### Using artificial light for plants

Artificial light can be used to boost natural daylight during normal daylight hours, or to extend the length of the day by providing light during the hours of darkness. Extending day length has been found to be the most successful approach. If you are using fluorescent lamps they should normally be positioned 9–24in/23–60cm above the tops of the plants.

In the home, a compact fluorescent bulb in a "rise and fall" light fitting that has been positioned over a group of house plants makes an attractive feature. Alternatively, a plant stand incorporating a fluorescent tube can be constructed.

In a greenhouse, a more utilitarian plant lighting kit can be used; this will incorporate waterproof fittings that are an essential safety feature.

Providing 12–18 hours of total light (including natural daylight) has been shown to give good results for the majority of plants.

# late winter

*Although the weather can be terrible, there is no longer any doubt that spring is on its way. The days are lengthening; buds on the branches of trees and shrubs begin to swell, and more and more early bulbs are producing their flowers. Get those dormant season tasks finished as soon as you can.*

If jobs such as winter digging, planting bare-root trees and shrubs, and pruning fruit trees are not yet finished, this is the time to complete them. In most areas roses can safely be pruned now, too.

A few dry, breezy days will help to get the soil in good condition for sowing to take place outdoors shortly. If you do not know what type of soil you have in the garden, this is a good time to carry out tests.

Flower borders should be tidied, removing weeds and debris that shelter slugs and snails. This is particularly important because the tender young shoots of plants newly emerged through the soil are very vulnerable to these pests. Mulching is equally important because it helps prevent further weed growth, keeps some of the moisture in the soil ready for drier weather, and makes the garden look much tidier and more attractive.

In the greenhouse there are increasing numbers of seeds to be sown and cuttings to be taken. It's vital to insure that the greenhouse heater is properly maintained and adjusted. It will still be needed for some time yet—there will soon be dozens of tender young seedlings that need warmth to develop. Seedlings from earlier sowings need pricking out, and space in the greenhouse will soon be at a premium.

In the kitchen garden, winter crops such as leeks and parsnips need to be used up before they start into growth again, and if you have forced rhubarb and kale for early crops you should harvest them now.

◀ *Now is the time to tidy up your flower borders because any slugs and snails sheltering in weeds and debris will attack young shoots.*

## LATE WINTER TASKS

**General**
- Check tools and equipment, and buy new replacements if needed
- Carry out soil tests on various sites around the garden

▲ *Add moisture-retaining compost to the bottom of the pole bean trench.*

**Ornamental garden**
- Weed and clear borders, and mulch with bark
- Prune roses
- Finish planting bare-root trees and shrubs
- Weed overwintered hardy annuals and provide supports as necessary
- Protect vulnerable plants from slugs
- Sow Lathyrus odoratus (sweet peas) outside
- Continue to plant lily bulbs as available
- Prune winter jasmine after flowering
- Prune summer-flowering clematis hybrids
- Feed flowering shrubs with sulfate of potash

**Lawns**
- Mow the grass lightly if necessary. Carry out repairs to edges and aerate compacted areas
- Choose a new lawn mower if one is needed, before the main mowing season starts

**Kitchen garden**
- Use up winter vegetables such as leeks and parsnips from the garden before they regrow
- Complete winter digging and apply lime if necessary
- Prepare seed beds if the weather allows
- Use blanket, cloches etc. to protect pea and bean seedlings, and spring greens
- Set seed potatoes to chit (sprout) in a light place as soon as they are purchased
- Plant shallots and Jerusalem artichokes
- Prepare a pole bean trench with moisture-retaining compost
- Harvest forced kale and rhubarb as soon as the shoots are large enough
- Prune fall-fruiting raspberries
- Feed fruit trees and bushes with high-potash fertilizer

**Greenhouse**
- Clean up the greenhouse to prepare for the new season
- Feed forced bulbs that have finished flowering, ready for planting in the garden later
- Take cuttings from chrysanthemums, dahlias, fuchsias, and pelargoniums
- Begin sowing tomatoes, melons, and cucumbers for greenhouse cropping. Sow half-hardy annuals, and beans in pots for planting out later. Prick out seedlings sown earlier
- Start begonia tubers into growth
- Bring potted strawberries into greenhouse for early crops
- Increase ventilation during the day in suitable weather

▲ *Sow bush or fava beans in pots ready for planting outdoors later.*

# soil testing

There are many different types of soil, varying from county to county and even from one garden to another in the same area. The soil type is of real significance to the way plants grow, and getting to know the soil in your garden is a great aid to successful cultivation.

Soil is derived largely from rock that has been broken down over countless years into tiny particles. The size and type of these particles varies according to the type of rock from which they have been derived, and the way in which they were broken down. The other main ingredient of soil is organic matter. Organic means anything that has once lived—plant or animal remains. These are gradually broken down by a variety of organisms until they form humus, a friable, spongy material whose origins can no longer be identified.

### Identifying soil types

Soil types are classified according to their particle size. The smallest particles are clay; slightly larger particles are silt, and largest are sand. The larger the particles, the larger the air spaces between them, and the more easily water can drain away. Sandy soils are free draining, but clay drains very slowly. Sandy soils also tend to be low in plant foods because the soluble nutrients are easily washed away, whereas clay soils are usually richer in nutrients and more fertile. Humus, because of its spongy texture, absorbs moisture and helps to break up tightly-packed soil particles, making it the ideal soil improver for both light sandy soils and badly drained, heavy clays. In general, most soils are a mixture of clay, silt, and sand in varying proportions.

▲ *Simply squeezing a handful of garden soil or rubbing it between the fingers can supply a surprising amount of information about its type.*

▲ *The varying proportions of the main constituents of soil can be seen at a glance if they are allowed to settle out in a jar of water.*

## ADDING LIME TO SOIL

Most plants grow best in soil that is just the acid side of neutral, but vegetables may benefit from the addition of lime that reduces the soil acidity. This is largely because clubroot disease, which affects brassicas, is less severe in neutral or alkaline conditions. Lime should not be added unless a pH test has shown that it is necessary; if the pH is 6.5 or above, lime is not needed. It is certainly not necessary to lime the vegetable garden every year as was once a traditional practice.

### Carrying out soil tests

Dig up a small handful of soil from just below the surface and moisten it, if necessary, with a little water. Then rub it between your thumb and forefinger; if it feels gritty it is sandy soil, and if it's smooth and slippery or sticky it is silt or clay. Now squeeze the handful of soil tightly then open your hand; sandy soils fall apart while clay soils hold their shape. You can also roll the soil into a ball, then into a long snake, and try to bend the snake into a circle. The more of these steps you can do, the higher the clay content.

Place a further trowel of soil into a clean jelly jar, half-fill the jar with water, put on the lid and shake vigorously. Allow it to settle for several hours. The largest stones and soil particles will settle at the bottom, grading up to the finest clays, while the organic matter will float on the surface of the water. The relative depths of each layer shows the different proportions present in the soil.

Take a number of soil samples from different parts of the garden and use a proprietary soil-testing kit to give a reading (full instructions are on the pack). The most useful test is for soil acidity (pH) because some plants will grow well only in acid soils. Tests for major nutrients (nitrogen, phosphorus, and potassium) can also be carried out, but the results are not always reliable.

▼ *Add lime to the soil only if a pH test shows that it is necessary. It may help to prevent club root disease in the vegetable garden.*

# ornamental garden: *general tasks*

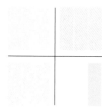

*The new shoots of herbaceous plants will soon be appearing through the soil in milder regions, and hardy annuals that were sown last fall need to be provided with supports. If you want long-flowering plants especially suitable for containers, it's time to start begonia tubers into growth.*

### Border plants and slugs

If the weather is mild, some of the early herbaceous border plants will be growing, and their tender, succulent shoots are an irresistible lure to slugs.

Destroy slug habitats by clearing weeds and debris from the border, and the surrounding areas: remember that it is relatively easy and common for them to travel some distance from the shelter of hedge bottoms and similar hideouts.

Protect individual plants by surrounding them with a barrier; crushed egg shells, sharp sand and grit, garden lime, and clinker are traditional deterrents, but strips of plastic are much more effective.

Simply cut strips that are about 3–4in/7.5–10cm wide from empty plastic bottles and push them firmly into the soil around each plant so that 2–3in/5–8cm remains above the ground. At this time of year it's usually a better method than slug pellets.

If you have to use a slug killer, there are a number of organic controls that are less harmful to the wildlife than methiocarb and metaldehyde, including a biological control using a parasitic nematode.

◀ *Slugs spend the day concealed in weedy areas or hedge bottoms, traveling surprising distances to feed during the night.*

## MULCHING FLOWER BORDERS

Remove weeds from flower borders and mulch the borders with, say, chipped bark or mushroom compost to deter fresh weed growth and improve the look of the bed. The mulch will also help to retain soil moisture throughout the spring and early summer. Be careful not to apply mulch too closely around emerging plants because it can encourage slugs (see opposite). Leave a clear space immediately around the crowns, described, or mulch up to the plastic strip barriers.

## *start begonia tubers*

Tuberous-rooted begonias make excellent plants for pots and hanging baskets, and are not difficult to keep from year to year. Tubers that have been stored over winter can now be started into growth in a warm greenhouse.

## HARDY ANNUALS

Hardy annuals that were sown last fall should be weeded and the plants thinned out if necessary. Provide them with supports to prevent them from flopping over as they grow. The most inconspicuous supports are twiggy sticks (such as peasticks) that can be cut from hedges or garden shrubs and pushed into the soil among the plants. As the annuals grow, they will hide these supports almost entirely. If your fall sowings did not survive the winter, don't worry—another sowing can be made next month.

1 Begonias produce rather odd-looking tubers which means it is not always easy to tell which is the top and which is the bottom (**below**). The top is dished, and shows signs of knobbly growth buds; the underside is rounded and whiskery, covered with fibrous roots.

2 Prepare pots of sandy, soilless cuttings mix and press the bases of the tubers into the surface (**below**). The concave side must face upward, and should not be covered with mix. Keep the pots in a light, warm position, ideally about 57°F/14°C.

3 Keep the soil mix moist, but take care not to splash water into the top of the tuber. If growth buds are slow to appear, lightly mist the tops of the tubers with a fine spray of water once, but otherwise keep the tops dry to avoid rotting.

4 Once strong growth buds appear, the plants can be propagated. Cut the tubers into two or three sections, each with a growth bud, or the buds can be allowed to develop into shoots which are used as softwood cuttings.

# maintaining paths, patios, and steps

Hard surfaces in the garden will stand a good deal of wear, but they do need regular maintenance to keep them in good condition. This is a convenient time to clean off the winter's accumulated dirt and grime, and spruce up surfaces for the spring; cleaning will also enable you to find and repair any damage that has occurred. The correct maintenance of paths, steps, and patios will not only prolong their lives and improve their appearance, but is a necessary safety precaution. Uneven surfaces can easily cause people to trip, and on steps, this could lead to nasty injuries.

### Cleaning

The first step is to brush the whole area with a stiff broom, paying particular attention to corners and under the overhang of steps where litter and soil accumulates. Use a paint scraper or similar tool to loosen compacted dirt in awkward positions, and to scrape out the gaps between paving slabs where weeds often grow. If a pressure washer is available, this is ideal, as it reaches into all the nooks and crannies with a high pressure water jet which has a powerful scouring action. Pressure washers can usually be hired by the day or weekend if you don't want to buy one.

Moss and algae are common where the surface is constantly damp and shady. Remove all traces of their growth; dichlorophen will kill moss and lichens on hard surfaces. Try to correct the conditions that caused their appearance in the first place. As for areas where dirt and soil have lain for a long time, they can appear discolored when first cleaned. These marks can often be removed by a pressure washer or scrubbing. Other stains on paved and concrete areas, such as those caused by oil, can be more difficult to tackle. There are various proprietary products available, or you could try mixing a spirit (such as paint thinner) with sawdust until the sawdust is thoroughly dampened, and apply this in a thick layer over the stain. Sweep it off with a stiff broom and repeat until successful.

Incidentally, concrete will have a longer life if it is coated with a waterproof sealant. Special products are available for applying to old concrete.

◀ *Before any repairs on slabs or concrete are attempted, all loose material must be removed by using a wire brush.*

▲ *Sometimes it is necessary to use a hammer and chisel along the sides of the crack to open it out before it can be repaired.*

## Repairs

Paving slabs may have settled unevenly to create protruding edges which can trip people up. Where necessary the uneven slabs should be removed, the base leveled and the slabs relaid.

Isolated cracks in concrete or slabs can be repaired. Use a hammer and chisel to chip along each side of the crack to neaten it, then wire brush the crack thoroughly to remove all the loose material. Coat the sides with a proprietary bonding agent before filling the crack with mortar or a patching compound.

Concrete pigments can be mixed with the mortar to help match the surface color, and make the repair less obvious.

Concrete areas may look unsightly because poor workmanship when they were laid has caused the surface to wear badly, so it is pockmarked with shallow holes. As long as the base is sound, the top can be resurfaced, but the new layer must be at least 2in/5cm thick to prevent it from flaking away. The worn surface must be cleaned thoroughly and coated with a bonding agent before a sand and cement mix is applied. Resurfacing is often only a temporary solution; complete replacement of the concrete may eventually be needed.

◀ *Fill in the prepared crack with mortar or a patching compound, smoothing it out carefully to keep the surface level.*

### SAFETY PRECAUTIONS

- Wear eye protection when using a chisel and hammer to work on hard surfaces, or to break up slabs.
- Take care to avoid back strain when trying to prise up or lift slabs—two people make the job much easier than one.
- Wear a mask when working with dry cement to prevent breathing in the dust.
- Protect your skin when handling concrete and mortar; always wear gloves to prevent irritation.

# ornamental garden: *plants in season*

*The number of flowers blooming in the garden increases rapidly during this time as the winter slowly but surely moves toward spring. Catkins on bare branches elongate and become more prominent, and some of the earliest flowering cherries give a foretaste of the pleasures to come in the months ahead as the days begin to lengthen and the light returns.*

▲ Prunus subhirtella *'Pendula Rubra'*
*offers a stunning display during late winter.*

▲ Hamamelis intermedia *'Westerstede'*, with its delicate yellow blooms, adds color to winter.

▶ Mahonia aquifolium *'Smaragd'* supplies rich shapes and textures to the garden.

## TREES AND SHRUBS

*Acacia dealbata* (acacia)
*Camellia*
*Chaenomeles japonica* (Japanese quince)
*Chimonanthus praecox* (wintersweet)
*Cornus alba* (red-barked dogwood), *C. mas* (cornelian cherry)
*Daphne odora*, *D. mezereum*
*Erica carnea*
*Garrya elliptica*
*Hamamelis* (witch hazel)
*Hedera colchica* 'Dentata Variegata' and others
*Jasminum nudiflorum* (winter jasmine)
*Lonicera fragrantissima*, *L. standishii* (winter honeysuckle)
*Magnolia campbellii*
*Mahonia* x *media* 'Charity' and others
*Prunus incisa* 'February Pink' (Fuji cherry), *P. mume* (Japanese apricot) and others
*Pyracantha* (firethorn)
*Salix alba* (white willow), *S. babylonica* var. *pekinensis* 'Tortuosa'
*Sarcococca hookeriana*, *S. humilis* (Christmas box)
*Skimmia*
*Sorbus*
*Stachyurus praecox*
*Viburnum*

## PERENNIALS

*Bergenia*
*Helleborus niger* (Christmas rose), *H. orientalis* (Lenten rose)
*Phormium tenax* (New Zealand flax)
*Primula* (primrose)
*Pulmonaria* (lungwort)
*Viola odorata* (English violet)

## BULBS

*Anemone blanda*
*Chionodoxa* (glory of the snow)
*Crocus*
*Cyclamen coum*
*Eranthis hyemalis* (winter aconite)
*Galanthus* (snowdrop)
*Iris danfordiae*, *I. histrioides*, *I. reticulata*
*Narcissus* (daffodil)

◀ Daphne mezereum *'Rubra'* is a delight in the garden at this time of year.

# kitchen garden: *general tasks*

*Dry, breezy days at this time of year will dry out the soil and allow seedbeds to be prepared shortly, but if the weather should turn windy and cold, young crops may need some protection. Jerusalem artichokes are a very easy crop to grow, and the tubers can be planted now.*

## Protecting seedlings

This is still an unpredictable time of year as far as the weather goes—it can produce some of the coldest conditions of the winter, often after a mild spell has already started plants into growth. The young plants of beans and peas that were sown in the fall can be given a severe set-back by poor weather now, but they can be protected from the worst of it with cloches or lengths of lightweight horticultural blanket.

Spring cabbage plants not planted out in the fall can be set out in their cropping positions when the weather is suitable. Like the pea and bean seedlings, they can be protected with cloches or blanket if conditions deteriorate after planting.

▼ *At this time of year it may be a good idea to use a fleece (or cloche) used to protect pea and bean seedlings against harsh weather.*

### PLANTING JERUSALEM ARTICHOKES

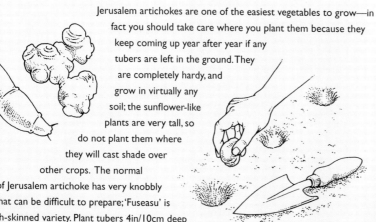

Jerusalem artichokes are one of the easiest vegetables to grow—in fact you should take care where you plant them because they keep coming up year after year if any tubers are left in the ground. They are completely hardy, and grow in virtually any soil; the sunflower-like plants are very tall, so do not plant them where they will cast shade over other crops. The normal variety of Jerusalem artichoke has very knobbly tubers that can be difficult to prepare; 'Fuseasu' is a smooth-skinned variety. Plant tubers 4in/10cm deep and 12in/30cm apart, with 3ft/90cm between the rows.

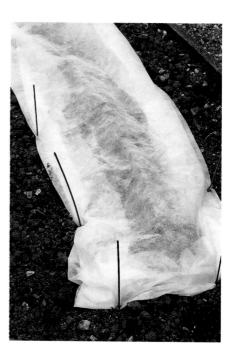

# prepare for pole beans

Pole beans are one of the most worthwhile crops for gardeners. They produce a very large crop in relation to the space they occupy, and have an extended season throughout the summer, right up until the first frosts. Although it is a little too early to think about raising the plants yet, it is not too soon to start preparing the soil where they are to grow.

### KALE AND RHUBARB

Stems of kale (pictured below) and rhubarb that have been forced into early growth in a frost-free greenhouse should be ready for cutting now. The shoots should have been kept completely dark by covering them with a black bucket or container— this gives the most tender results and prevents kale from becoming bitter. Kale is an unusual luxury vegetable (not to be confused with kale beet, which is quite different). It is often compared to asparagus, but the creamy white stems have a flavor all of their own.

1 Choose a warm, sheltered site for pole beans, preferably moving them to a new position each year to avoid root-rotting fungi building up in the soil. Dig a trench at least one spit deep—more if you can manage it—and 60cm/2ft or so wide. Fork over the soil in the bottom of the trench to break it up (**right**).

2 Beans need fertile, and above all moisture-retentive soil. Adequate levels of soil moisture are necessary to insure reliable setting of the flowers (flowers often drop off unfertilized in dry conditions, leading to poor crops), and rapid development of tender, juicy pods.

3 Add a layer of moisture-retentive material to the base of the trench. Ideally this should be well-rotted manure containing plenty of straw (**below**), but a mix of materials such as grass clippings, spent hops, spent mushroom compost, and even old newspapers can be used.

4 Leave the trench open to the rain until it is time for sowing or planting the beans after the last frosts in the spring. Then make sure the base of the trench is thoroughly soaked, by watering if necessary, before returning the topsoil and treading it thoroughly to firm.

# crop rotation

It is not good practice to grow the same crops in the same places in the vegetable garden year after year. There are several reasons for this.

Different crops have slightly different nutrient requirements. Brassicas, for instance, are known as greedy crops (or gross feeders) because they take a high level of nutrients, particularly nitrogen, from the soil. If brassicas are grown on the same piece of ground year in, year out, the nutrients in the soil could soon be exhausted, particularly if no organic matter or fertilizers are added to replace them. Brassicas are also prone to certain specific pests and diseases, such as clubroot; they can persist in the soil, or on crop remains, ready to infect the new crop the following year.

If a different crop is grown in the brassica's plot next year, however, it is likely to take different types of nutrients from the soil. It will also be immune to brassica-specific pests and diseases, so that the cycle of infection can be broken. This practice of insuring that different types of crop are grown in succeeding years on the same piece of ground is known as crop rotation. Deciding exactly which crop should be grown where obviously needs careful planning. There are various crop rotation schemes, but a common one is to divide the types of crops that are grown into three main groups.

## Dividing the crops

The first group is the brassicas—cabbages of all types, Brussels sprouts, kale, broccoli, cauliflower, and so on. They have a high nitrogen requirement, and are prone to clubroot disease. The second group is root crops—potatoes, parsnips, carrots, beets, Jerusalem artichokes, salsify, and scorzonera, and so on. They have a slightly lower nitrogen requirement, and are likely to be misshapen if fresh manure has been added to the soil recently. Finally there are peas and beans—these are unusual because they obtain nitrogen from the air rather than the soil, because of nitrogen-fixing bacteria that live

▲ Cauliflowers fall into the brassicas group of vegetables. This group is known as "greedy crops" because they need a high level of soil nutrients.

▲ Peas tend to be placed in a group that includes lettuces and leeks, simply because they are neither root crops nor brassicas.

▲ Carrots belong to the root crop group,
alongside potatoes, parsnips, beets,
and Jerusalem artichokes.

## CROP ROTATION

|        | Bed A          | Bed B          | Bed C          |
|--------|----------------|----------------|----------------|
| **Year 1** | Brassicas      | Roots          | Peas and beans |
| **Year 2** | Peas and beans | Brassicas      | Roots          |
| **Year 3** | Roots          | Peas and beans | Brassicas      |
| **Year 4** | Brassicas      | Roots          | Peas and beans |

## SIZE MATTERS

There is one major difficulty with a rotation, and that is the need for
each of the three groups to occupy exactly the same amount of space.
The imaginative use of miscellaneous crops (such as lettuce, squash,
spinach, and so on) can help here because they can be placed in any of
the three groups, as necessary, to balance things out. However, the
rotation does not have to be followed slavishly—it will have to be
adjusted for practical purposes.

on their roots. This means they will actually add to the
amount of nitrogen in the soil.

Of course, not all crops fall neatly into one of
these three groups. Crops such as rutabaga and turnips
are both brassicas and root crops, so which group would
they go in? And what about spinach, or squash and
zucchini, or onions? Rutabaga, turnips, and kohlrabi are
included in the brassica group, mainly because they can
be infected by clubroot disease. Since spinach is a hungry
crop with a high nitrogen requirement it also fits well
into the brassicas. Most other crops such as lettuces,
tomatoes, squash, leeks, onions and so on are generally
included with the peas and beans, simply because they
are neither brassicas nor true root crops. However,
there are no hard and fast rules about these
miscellaneous crops, and onions are sometimes included
with the root crops, while spinach joins the peas and
beans, for example.

### Establishing the rotation

The vegetable plot is divided into three and each of
these three main groups of crops is grown in their own
section—for example, brassicas in bed A, root crops in
bed B and peas and beans in bed C. Next year, peas and
beans move into bed A, brassicas into bed B, and roots
into bed C. The following year they all move round one
place again, and the year after that they are back where
they started.

This means that the bed with roots can be
manured at the end of the season ready for the
brassicas, and the roots follow the peas and beans
that have added nitrogen to the soil to make up for the
absence of manure.

Four or five bed rotations are also possible by
splitting the groups up further, but they become
increasingly complicated. The three-bed scheme is the
most practical for the majority of gardens.

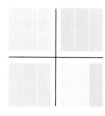

# greenhouse: *general tasks*

*Sowing starts in earnest now, and there should be plenty of material for cuttings from overwintered plants. Don't be in too much of a hurry to forge ahead if you cannot provide reliable heating, though; better to be a little later than take unnecessary risks, because the weather is still cold.*

▲ *Take cuttings of plants such as pelargoniums and fuchsias to provide strong young plants for setting out in containers later on.*

### Sowing greenhouse crops

Vegetable crops to be grown in the greenhouse through the summer should be sown now, preferably in a heated propagator to keep them at a constant temperature.

Tomatoes, cucumbers, melons, peppers, and eggplant are among those to try; a germination temperature of 65–70°F/18–21°C suits most of them. Don't forget to label each variety individually.

It is easy to sow too many seeds and have to give away dozens of seedlings later on. Most greenhouses have limited space for crops, and no more than six or so plants of each type can usually be fitted in.

Sow the seeds in pots rather than in seedtrays, and save the seeds that are left over for another year. You should be able to store them quite satisfactorily in a dry, screw-top jar for at least one season.

### TAKING CUTTINGS

Plants such as dahlias, chrysanthemums, pelargoniums, and fuchsias that have recently been started into growth should be producing shoots suitable for use as softwood cuttings.

Let the shoots grow to 3–4in/7.5–10cm long before snapping them or cutting them off with a sharp blade. Trim the base to just below a leaf joint and remove the lower leaves; dip the base of the cutting in hormone rooting powder and insert in sandy seed and cuttings mix. Cover trays, flats or pots with a clear plastic propagator cover to maintain humidity while the cuttings root.

## CLEANING UP THE GREENHOUSE

Good hygiene is particularly important when seeds and cuttings are being raised, otherwise plant diseases can lead to excessive losses. Clear out all dead and dying plant material that remains in the greenhouse, and treat any pests and diseases that are seen with an appropriate remedy. Tidy up pots and trays, and sweep down the staging and potting benches. At the same time, check through your stock of garden chemicals and dispose of any that are past their sell-by date, or that have illegible labels or instructions.

# beans in pots

If you didn't get round to sowing beans in the vegetable plot last fall, it's still not too late to make sure of an early crop. Sowing seeds in pots in a cool greenhouse or cold frame now should give you pods to pick in early summer. This method is often more successful than fall sowing in areas that have very cold or wet winters.

1 Beans are often one of the first of the new season's crops for picking in the garden. Any variety can be sown successfully in pots now, but for the earliest harvest, choose one of the faster maturing varieties.

2 Fill individual 3½ in/8cm pots with sowing mix, and push the bean seeds below the compost surface (**right**). Water with a fine rose until the compost is just moist; label the pots with the variety and date.

3 Beans are very hardy, and do not need high temperatures to germinate. A frost-free or unheated greenhouse or cold frame are good places in which to keep the pots.

4 Once the seeds have germinated, keep the seedlings moist and in a good light to insure sturdy young plants for planting out. Those grown in individual pots will suffer less root disturbance on transplanting, and should produce a slightly earlier crop than those in trays (**left**).

# glossary

**acid**

referring to soil having a pH of less than 7, suitable for lime-hating plants

**adventitious roots**

roots springing directly from the plant stem

**alkaline**

referring to soil having a pH greater than 7, unsuitable for lime-hating plants

**alpine**

plants that naturally occur in mountainous regions above the tree line. Generally also means low-growing rock garden plants

**annuals**

plants that germinate, flower, produce seed, and die in one season

**anther**

male part of a flower that produces pollen

**aquatic**

plants that grow in water

**bare-root**

plants that are lifted from the open ground for transplanting in the dormant season

**bedding**

plants that are set out in beds or containers to give a temporary, seasonal display of flowers or foliage

**biological control**

the deliberate use of a natural organism to control a pest or disease

**blanching**

excluding light from leaves and stems, usually to make certain vegetables more tender and prevent bitterness (for example, with Belgian endive and kale)

**blossom end rot**

a disorder where tomatoes and related plants bear fruit with a sunken, dark brown patch at the base. It is caused by lack of calcium in the tissues as the fruit is developing, generally because of water shortage

**blown**

loosely formed or over-mature, e.g. Brussels sprouts that fail to form dense, tight buttons, or flowers such as roses that have passed their best

**brassica**

a member of the cabbage family, including vegetables such as Brussels sprout, cauliflower, turnip and so on

**bulb**

storage organ formed from a modified stem and leaf bases

**cloche**

low protective structure made from glass or plastic, used to protect individual plants or rows of plants from adverse weather. A floating row cover is a lightweight film of perforated plastic or fiber lying loosely on top of the crop

**cold frame**

an unheated, protective structure, usually with solid sides and a removable glass or plastic lid

**compaction**

the process whereby the air is squeezed from between soil particles by heavy loads on the surface (such as repeated treading). This destroys the soil structure, impedes drainage and makes the soil unsuitable for root growth

**compost**

the organic substance produced by rotting down vegetative matter that is used as a soil improver or top-dressing. Can be bought commercially as well as homemade

**containers**

pots, tubs, hanging baskets, window boxes etc which are used for growing plants

**cordon**

plant trained usually as a single stem with pruning to remove side-shoots (e.g. greenhouse tomatoes and apples)

**corm**

a plant storage organ consisting of a swollen stem base. Unlike a bulb, a corm replaces itself each year

**crown**

the part of a plant where a collection of stems is produced. Herbaceous plants have a crown at soil level where the roots and stems join. The crown of a tree is where the head forms on top of the trunk

**cuttings**

portions of plants that are detached and encouraged to grow new roots or shoots (or both) in order to make new plants. Cuttings may be taken from stems, leaves or roots

**deciduous**

a plant which loses its leaves at the end of the growing season

**deficiency**

a shortage of one of the essential nutritional elements, causing specific symptoms that need to be quickly diagnosed and rectified

**division**

a method of propagation; the process of splitting a plant into a number of smaller pieces, each capable of leading an independent existence

**dormant**

plants, seeds and so on, that are temporarily not in active growth

**drill**

a shallow trench in the soil where seeds are sown; usually made with a draw hoe

**dwarfing**

rootstocks that control the growth of varieties which are grafted on to them, making them smaller and more compact than they would be if they were growing on their own roots. Semidwarfing rootstocks have a less pronounced dwarfing effect

**earthing up**

drawing soil up around the stems of plants. This may be blanch them (e.g. leeks and celery), encourage the growth of tubers (e.g. potatoes) or simply to help support them in the ground (e.g. tall brassicas)

**espalier**

a trained form of fruit tree with horizontal tiers of branches

**evergreen**

a plant that keeps its leaves the whole year round (*see* deciduous)

**force**

to encourage a plant into early growth, usually by providing extra warmth. Light is often also excluded from plants being forced

**frost pocket**

an area where cold air collects—usually at the bottom of a valley, in a hollow in the ground, or against an obstruction such as a solid wall. Temperatures in frost pockets remain lower than in surrounding areas, and plants in such an area are more liable to cold damage

**frost**

frost occurs when the temperature falls to 32°F/0°C or below. When this occurs only at ground level it is called a ground frost; when the freezing temperatures extend upward it is known as an air frost, which is more damaging to plants

**fungicide**

a chemical used to control fungus diseases

**hardening off**

the process of gradually acclimatizing plants which have been raised under protection to outside conditions

**hardy**

able to survive the natural climate, including frosts, without protection. Half-hardy means able to survive outdoors for part of the year, but unable to withstand frost

**heeling in**

temporarily covering the roots of a plant with soil to prevent it from deteriorating until it can be planted

**herbaceous**

a plant whose non-woody top-growth dies down to a root-stock in the dormant season

**herbicide**

a chemical to kill plant growth; weedkiller

**humus**

the organic remains of rotted-down vegetable matter that improves soil structure

**hybrid**

a cross between two distinct parents. Crosses are often between plant varieties; they may also be between species (interspecific hybrids) or less often between genera (intergeneric or bigeneric hybrids). F1 hybrids are a first generation cross between two selected, pure-breeding parents and have the advantage of uniformity and, often, of hybrid vigor

**insecticides**

chemicals used to kill insects

**laterals**

a side-shoot growing from the main stem of a plant. A sublateral is a side-shoot growing from a lateral

**leader**

the terminal shoot of a plant or stem

**leaf axil**

the area where the leaf stem joins the plant stem, from which growth buds often arise

**leaf mold**

rotted-down leaves used as a soil additive

**macronutrients**

the minerals required by plants in relatively large quantities, including nitrogen, phosphorus, potassium, calcium, magnesium, and sulfur

**micronutrients**

minerals required by plants in very small quantities, such as iron, molybdenum, manganese. Also known as trace elements

# glossary

**mulch**

material applied in a layer to the soil surface. It may be organic (e.g. compost, shredded bark) or non-organic (e.g. gravel, plastic sheeting). Mulch retains soil moisture and inhibits weed growth

**organic**

derived from material that has once lived (i.e. plant or animal remains)

**oxygenators**

submerged pond plants which produce oxygen to keep the water clear and healthy

**pathogen**

disease-causing organism

**perennial**

surviving for a number of years

**pesticide**

chemical used to control pests including insects, slugs and snails, mites, and so on

**photosynthesis**

the process by which plants manufacture energy from light

**pollination**

transfer of pollen from the male to female parts of a flower

**potting on**

moving a plant into a larger container

**pricking off**

moving a seedling from the tray or pot in which it germinated to a container where it is given more room to develop

**racemes**

a flower head containing a number of individual flowers that are carried on an unbranched stem

**repotting**

moving a container-grown plant to a fresh pot which may or may not be larger than the one in which it is currently growing

**reversion**

the tendency of a plant to return to its original state, for example, when a variegated-leafed plant that originally occurred as a mutation from a plain-leafed variety begins to produce plain-leaved shoots again. Many mutations are unstable

**rootstock**

a plant used to provide the root system of a plant that is grafted on to it because for some reason the grafted variety is not suitable for growing on its own roots (*see* dwarfing)

**rotation**

the moving of vegetable crops to different areas of soil each year to prevent the build up of pests and diseases

**runner**

a long stem which bears young plants at the end, or at intervals along its length

**semiripe**

shoots that have just begun to harden at their base but are not completely woody

**softwood**

shoots that are still soft and flexible, and show no signs of woodiness

**soilless mix**

growing mix that contains no loam. Most once based on peat, but composts made from peat substitutes such as coir are now common

**soil mix**

the medium used for growing plants in containers instead of garden soil. Various mixes are available for seeds, cuttings, and mature plants

**stopping**

pinching out a terminal bud to encourage branching of the stem

**sucker**

an unwanted shoot arising from a rootstock

**tender**

vulnerable to damage by cold temperatures, especially frost

**tilth**

soil which has been broken down to small, even crumbs, suitable for seed sowing

**top-dressing**

fertilizer or organic matter applied to the soil surface; also mulches such as gravel around alpine plants

**trace elements**

minerals required by plants in very small quantities (*see* micronutrients)

**triploid**

having three sets of chromosomes. Triploid apples need to be pollinated by two other varieties rather than one

**tuber**

a storage organ which consists of a swollen stem or root

**variegated**

marked with two or more colors. Usually applied to leaves, but can also describe stems and flowers

# index

# index

# index

# Acknowledgments

The publishers would like to thank Roger Benjamin, Georgina Steeds, and Smith's Nurseries, New Denham, Middlesex, UK, for their help with properties, and the following for their help with images: **Liz Eddison/Designers**: Aughton Green Landscapes—Tatton Park 2001, 131b; James Basson—Hampton Court 2000, 126bl; David Brun—Hampton Park 2000, 62b; Bill Cartlidge—Tatton Park 2000; 9r & 56; Paul Dyer—Chelsea 2001, 130br; Sarah Eberle—Hampton Court 2001, 22; Guy Farthing—Hampton Court 2000, 8 & 6, 19bl; Sally Fell—Hampton Court 2001, 18b, 146br; David Gibson—Tatton Park 2001, 39b; Carol Klein, 92; Douglas G. Knight—Tatton Park 2001, 60, 61; Colin Luckett—Tatton Park 2001, 124; Angela Mainwaring—Hampton Park 2001, 82; Tom Stuart-Smith—Chelsea 2000, 12b; Ian Taylor—Chelsea 2001, 105br; Geoffrey Whiten—Chelsea 2001, 97bl. **Neil Holmes:** 162bl; 173t, b; 186, 187t, b; 189t; 220; 234. **Hozelock**: 76bl; 158b,r; 159. **Parasene**: 199tr, bl. **Harry Smith Collection**: 27t; 51; 74; 75bl; 84r; 96b; 132; 138; 144; 153bl; 178br; 192; 193bl; 199tl, br; 204; 205tr; 207b; 221bl; 228; 232; 245bl.